PRINCESS GRACE

PRINCESS GRACE

SARAH BRADFORD

STEIN AND DAY/*Publishers*/**New York**

First published in the United States of America in 1984.

Copyright © 1984 by Sarah Bradford

All rights reserved, Stein and Day, Incorporated

Printed in the United States of America

STEIN AND DAY / *Publishers*
Scarborough House
Briarcliff Manor, N.Y. 10510

Library of Congress Cataloging in Publication Data

Bradford, Sarah.
  Princess Grace.

  Bibliography: p.
  Includes index.
  1. Grace, Princess of Monaco, 1929–
2. Monaco—Princes and princesses—Biography.
I. Title.
DC943.G7B73   1984   944′.949′00994   [B]   83-40360
ISBN 0-8128-2958-1

For William

Contents

Illustrations

Acknowledgements

The writing of this book would have been impossible without the co-operation of His Serene Highness Prince Rainier III of Monaco who kindly granted me an interview and facilitated my access to the family, friends and staff of Her Serene Highness the late Princess Grace of Monaco.

I am also grateful to Prince Rainier's niece, Baronne Elisabeth de Massy, and to his cousin, Prince Louis de Polignac, for their reminiscences. Nadia Lacoste, chief Press Officer of Monaco, provided me with the most kind and efficient assistance, as did, with unfailing courtesy, Vane Ivanović, Consul-General of Monaco in London.

I should like to express my gratitude to the Princess's family in Philadelphia, to her brother, John Brendan Kelly Jr, who kindly provided me with a copy of his father's unpublished autobiography and of his original will, and to her sisters, Margaret ("Peggy") Kelly Conlan and Elizabeth Anne ("Lizanne") Kelly LeVine. Marie Magee, close friend and bridesmaid to Princess Grace's mother, was most generous with her time and also provided me with photographs for the book. Alice Godfrey Waters, a childhood friend, gave me useful information on Princess Grace's early life, and Francis James Dallett, archivist of the University of Pennsylvania, kindly provided me with valuable material on the Majer family.

The co-operation of the Princess's close friends has been invaluable to an understanding of her life and personality. I am particularly grateful to Maree Rambo of Philadelphia, her schoolfriend and bridesmaid, to Rita Gam, Bettina Thompson Gray, Sally Parrish Richardson and Judy Balaban Quine, who were also her bridesmaids, and to Rupert Allan, her press adviser and friend over many years, who gave me hours of his time. I would also like to thank Brian and Elinor Aherne; Sam Spiegel; Vera Maxwell; Lynn Wyatt; Ann Levy Siegel; George Stacey; Fleur Cowles Meyer; Phyllis Earl, the Princess's former secretary; Virginia Gallico and Jacqueline Ardant, her former ladies-in-waiting; Maureen King Wood, formerly nanny to

Prince Albert and Princess Caroline; Oleg Cassini; Jean-Pierre Aumont; Alexandre de Paris; and Marc Bohan of Dior.

I owe a debt of gratitude to artistic colleagues of the former Grace Kelly: to Sir Alec Guinness, Donald Sinden and Stewart Granger, her co-stars in *The Swan, Mogambo* and *Green Fire*; Fred Zinneman, who directed her in *High Noon*; Andrew Marton, director of *Green Fire*; the late Raymond Massey, who directed her first Broadway appearance; Gene Reynolds; Francisco Day and Arthur Jacobson who worked with her on *The Bridges at Toko-Ri* and *The Country Girl*; William and Sandra Allyn; Jay Kanter, her former agent; Douglas Fairbanks Jr; Joshua Logan; Natalie Core O'Hare; Whitfield Connor for his reminiscences of Grace's season at the Elitch Gardens Theater, Denver; Virginia Darcy, chief hairdresser at MGM, who accompanied her to Monaco for the wedding; and Radie Harris and Milton Goldman for their kind help and advice.

For Princess Grace's later artistic career I am particularly grateful to John Carroll, who devised and directed her public poetry-readings; to Jean Dalrymple, Oleg Briansky and Robert Dornhelm, who worked with her on *The Children of Theatre Street*; to Kevin Billington, who directed her in William and Sandra Allyn's television biography, *Princess Grace ... Once upon a Time is Now*, and Lee Grant who acted as interlocutor; and to Jacqueline de Monsigny and Edward Meeks, who collaborated with her on *Rearranged*. I am much indebted to Dirk Bogarde and Anthony Burgess for their perceptive accounts of her cultural activities in Monaco.

In Monaco Rosine Sanmori, who worked with the Princess in the Red Cross, the Garden Club and the La Lèche League, gave generously of her time, as did the Princess's *chef de cabinet*, Paul Choisit, and her private secretary, Louisette Levy-Sousann, André Saint-Mleux, *administrateur délégué* (managing director) of the SBM, Patrick Hourdequin, administrator of the Théâtre Princesse Grace, Christine Plaistow, formerly housekeeper at the Palace, and André Levasseur, designer of the Red Cross Galas in Monte Carlo.

I am grateful to Professor Charles Louis Chatelin, Professor at the Faculty of the Hôpitaux de Paris and Head Surgeon of the Centre Hospitalier Princesse Grace in Monaco and to Professor François Lhermitte, Head of the Department of Neurology of the Faculty of Paris, for medical details, and to Dr Fred Plum, chairman of the New York Hospital–Cornell Medical Center, for advice on the subject.

I am much indebted for their kind help to the following (in alphabetical order): Professor Digby E. Baltzell; François Bessemoulin; Eugene-Clarence Braun-Munk; Sister Bridget, I B V M; State Senator Peter J. Camiel; Pierre Cattalano; Helen Chaplin; Contessa Donnina Cicogna; Alexander H. Cohen; Doris Snyder Coleman; Stephen Cristea; Madame Katherine Dorfman; Senator Patrick J.M. Durcan; Sister Elizabeth Mary of the Order of the Assumption; Charles Fish Jr; Wendy Foulke; Gwendoline de Flandres; Philip French; Pierre Galante; Morton Gottlieb; Nancy Grace; Caroline Graham; Ralph Graves; the Honorable William D. Green Jr; Florence Grinda; Thomas Guinzburg; George Hauptfuhrer Jr; Dr Samuel Hazo; Kenneth A. Hecken; Addie Herder; Celeste Holm; Mary Keats; Bernard Kelly; Tessa Kennedy; Archer King; Marcel Kroenlein; the office of Irving Lazar; Ben Lightman; the Hon. Lady Lindsay; Matthias Lukens Jr; Moss Mabry; Katherine MacLean; Roderick Mann; Josiane Merino; Ivan Moffat; Sir Iain Moncreiffe of that Ilk; Francis Mumford-Smith; James D. Murnan; Father Murphy of St Bridget's, Falls of Schuylkill; Terry Nation; Lady Packer; Samuel Peabody; Antoine Pialoux; Madame Arpad Plesch; Homer L. Poupart; Patrick Quinn; Françoise Ratyé; Audrey Russell; Nabil Saidi; Eva Marie Saint; Pierre Salinger; Edgar and Hope Scott; Rose Tobias Shaw; Jill Spalding; Ginette Spanier; Barry and Dorothy Spikings; Mrs Robert Surtees; William Tuttle; Hugo Vickers; Alexander Walker; Sam Wanamaker; John F. Warren; Sam White, O B E; Thomas M. Whitehead; Albert Whitley; Henry C. Williams.

I should also like to acknowledge my debt to: Gwen Robyns, author of *Princess Grace*, first published in 1976 and updated in 1982; to Peter Hawkins, for his authorized biography, *Prince Rainier of Monaco* (1966); and to Arthur H. Lewis, author of *Those Philadelphia Kellys* (1977), who kindly allowed me to use material from his book and from his files deposited in the Special Collections at Temple University. I am much indebted to Donald Spoto and to his publishers, Little Brown & Co., Boston, and William Collins & Co., London, for permission to use an interview which Donald Spoto had with Princess Grace and for much invaluable information gleaned from his authoritative *The Dark Side of Genius: The Life of Alfred Hitchcock* (1983). I am grateful, too, to Paddy Calistro for permission to quote from *Edith Head's Hollywood* (1983).

George Cuttingham, director of the American Academy of Dramatic Arts, has been most kind in providing me with documentation and pictures relating to Grace's time at the Academy. I have

ACKNOWLEDGEMENTS

been permitted access to the files of the *New York Times*, thanks to the kindness of the vice-chairman, Sydney Gruson, and to his archive staff, and to those of *The Philadelphia Inquirer & Daily News* for which I am indebted to the president, Sam S. McKeel, and to Gail McLaughlin of the Library, while I have been helped by other members of the *Inquirer* staff to whom I express my gratitude – Ruth Seltzer, Larry Eichler and Howard Shapiro. Herbert S. Nusbaum was most courteous in his hospitality to me at MGM and in allowing me access to Grace Kelly's contract files, for which I am most grateful. I am immensely grateful, too, for the opportunity to consult and use material at the Margaret Herrick Library of the Academy of Motion Picture Arts and Sciences and to the staff there for their kindness, and I am also greatly indebted to Ron Simon and the staff of the Museum of Broadcasting in New York for allowing me to use their excellent facilities for viewing Grace Kelly's early television films. I should like to thank Gillian Hartnoll at the British Film Institute Library in London and Douglas Matthews and the staff of the London Library for their kind help. I also made use of the BBC Data Enquiry Service.

I owe an enormous personal debt of gratitude to Marietta Tree in New York, to Sylvia Kaye in Beverly Hills, to James Biddle, Maree Rambo and Jane Krumrine in Philadelphia, and to Sylvie Avizou in Paris. Without their unfailing kindness, help and generous hospitality, researching this book would have been much more arduous.

I should like to thank Edwin L. Knetzger Jr and the staff of Johnson Higgins, Inc. of Philadelphia and New York for their kindness in smoothing my paths through the United States, and my brother-in-law, Anthony Messenger, for his introduction to them. Carol Epstein has done a superb job as my researcher in Los Angeles and her help has been invaluable. I should like to thank my publishers, Stein and Day of New York, and Weidenfeld & Nicolson of London, my editors, Patricia Day and Alex MacCormick, my picture researchers, Lynda Poley and Carol Epstein, and also Margaret Godson, who helped collect pictures in New York and Philadelphia. I am more than grateful to Mary Killen, who typed the manuscript with great skill under pressure of time and coped with a considerable volume of correspondence, and to my sister, Constance Messenger, who kindly helped with the typing of letters. Lastly, I should like to thank my husband for his unfailing encouragement and support.

Sarah Bradford

PRINCESS GRACE

Introduction

Small bunches of faded flowers still mark the spot 800 feet above the Mediterranean where, on 13 September 1982, a brown Rover 3500 saloon plunged off Departmental Road 37, fatally injuring Grace Patricia Kelly Grimaldi. Thirty-six hours later her family switched off the life-support machine. Princess Grace of Monaco was dead.

Grace's death stunned the world, evoking headlines normally reserved for leaders – a Pope, a President of the United States or of the Soviet Union – and a general sense of grief and loss which leaders call forth. The reaction was indeed far greater than might have been expected at the passing of a Hollywood star long since retired to become the wife of the ruler of a small Mediterranean principality.

Her career was the ultimate fulfilment of the American dream: the beautiful daughter of two second-generation immigrants, Irish and German, first makes it to the top in Hollywood, joining an instant American aristocracy, and then becomes a princess with a string of titles and a castle on the Riviera. She was the golden girl of Hollywood, the international celebrity whose regal image imprinted itself on the public mind through countless newspaper photographs and magazine covers.

All this would have been enough to explain the sensation created by her death, but not perhaps the genuine sadness experienced by people all over the world, people who did not know her, had never even seen her in the flesh, people as diverse as the New York taxi driver who could only repeat how beautiful she was and how "a lot of people over here hurt when she died", or the wife of an English landowner explaining her own reaction: "Grace never tried to reach out and grab your attention, but somehow you felt terribly sad that she was gone."

For her close friends, members of a concentric web of relationships stretching from Monaco to Los Angeles, Philadelphia, New York, London and Paris, and from her days as a teenager in Germantown,

Philadelphia, to her middle age as Princess of Monaco, the loss was irreparable. Six months after her death, many of them could not hold back their tears as they talked of Grace, finding it hard to adjust to the reality that they would never see her again. Cary Grant, interviewed in Hollywood on the first anniversary of her death, when asked what he most missed about her, replied simply "her presence".

The answer must lie with Grace herself – who she was, what she was and why she was the way she was. Grace never understood the reasons for her own celebrity, for the intense interest which strangers took in her life. Skilfully defending her own private persona from the prying questions of the press, she projected a coolly regal image which was only half the truth but was nonetheless a perfect shield for the real self which lay behind it. To understand Grace it is necessary to go back to the roots which were so important to her, to her family and to Philadelphia, the city where she was born, and even beyond – to Ireland, the home of her ancestors; for the Kelly story in its beginnings is a great Irish-American saga.

PART ONE

The Curtain Rises

I

The Kelly Clan

Grace Patricia Kelly was born on 12 November 1929 in Philadelphia, a city where the social distinctions are sharper than in any other city in the United States with the possible exception of Boston, home town of that other Irish clan, the Kennedys. Home for Grace was a colonial-style house built by her father, John B. Kelly, a newly rich brick contractor, on the edge of the Philadelphia suburb of German-town, overlooking the Falls of Schuylkill, where Kelly himself had been born.

John B. Kelly was the son of an Irish immigrant, a fact which disqualified the Kellys from being part of white Anglo-Saxon Society with a capital "S". A tangible symbol of the Kelly background, which set them poles apart from what was known as "Main Line" society, still stands not half a mile from the Kelly home on Henry Avenue – a grim row of stone buildings down by the Schuylkill River: the textile mills where John B. Kelly, his father and his brothers and sisters worked in the closing years of the nineteenth century and the opening decade of the twentieth. Built in the mid-nineteenth century and now forgotten in the shadow of the modern bridge across the Schuylkill, the mills of Scott's Lane are deserted monuments to Philadelphia's booming industrial past, when the textile industry drew impoverished immigrants from the other side of the Atlantic – and Grace's grandparents from Ireland and from Germany. The story of the rise of the Kelly family from the wild shores of County Mayo in the west of Ireland through the portals of those desolate mills to national and international fame is as remarkable an achieve-ment in its way as that of the Kennedys in Boston. And, as in the case of the Kennedys, the Kelly family destiny became charged with dynamism on reaching America, the land of opportunity.

A few miles from the Atlantic coast of Ireland, just outside Newport, County Mayo, a green hollow shelters a still, reflecting lake from the bare moorland which surrounds it. The horizon is enclosed by the edge of the moorland; above it the smoke-blue shape of Mount Nephin stands out against the soft grey sky. Fifty yards from the reed-fringed edge of the lake three rough stone buildings huddle against the hillside. Today they are roofless, their walls bare to the weather; one hundred years ago, when Grace's grandfather lived there, the roofs were thatched with reeds from the lake and the bogs, the walls thick with layers of white lime renewed over the generations. This is Drumirla, a small farm like hundreds of others in the west of Ireland; it is where the Kelly story begins.

The Kelly farm at Drumirla consists today, as it probably did over a century ago when Grace's grandfather was born there, of a small dwelling house and two almost indistinguishable outbuildings. The house still has the smoke-blackened fireplace of the room where the family lived and ate, and where some of them slept. There is a niche beside the fireplace for a bed, and the end of the room would have been curtained off to make another sleeping-place for the children, while through the door behind the fireplace is a small, dark room where the parents slept. The two outhouses sheltered the family's livestock and provided a rudimentary dairy, while the family's few acres surrounded the house, with grazing land on the hillside behind and vegetable plots perhaps on the richer soil between the house and the lake.

Drumirla provided subsistence farming, a living just above the poverty line dependent upon weather, hard work and the health of the crops, the livestock and the family themselves. It was a hard, claustrophobic life with no amenities and practically no schooling, for Mayo is on the western fringe of Ireland, part of the province of Connaught, which is cut off, physically and economically, from the rest of the country by the River Shannon. It is far removed from the lush green fields and parkland of the counties round Dublin, then ruled by the English from Dublin Castle. Indeed Mayo had a reputation for uprisings against the British, and local tradition has it that John Henry Kelly, Grace's grandfather, had to leave Ireland in a hurry to escape reprisals for his part in one such incident. Hatred of the British was part of family tradition: Grace's father recorded in his autobiography that his grandfather "really hated the English", and Walter Costello, Grace's paternal great-grandfather, never forgot having been evicted from the family farm when his father died by an English landlord. Government persecution may have been one reason why John Henry Kelly left his native country; it may equally well have been because of crop failures, since the 1850s and the 1860s, following on the Great Hunger of the potato famine, were disastrous years for Irish agriculture, and in those thirty years Mayo lost almost a third of its population. All that is certain is that some time towards the end of the 1860s, John Henry Kelly, fourth of five sons, a strong, handsome farm boy not yet twenty, turned his back on Drumirla for ever and left, probably from nearby Westport, to make a new life in America.

In Rutland, Vermont, in 1869 he met and married Mary Ann Costello, a seventeen-year-old Mayo girl who, since she had arrived in America at the age of thirteen, had been living with her paternal grandmother and a spinster aunt in Vermont. John Henry Kelly was a tall, attractive man with the rugged features and magnificent moustache of a frontiersman but, beyond taking the vital decision to emigrate from Drumirla, his ambitions were not high and he was dominated by his strong-willed, self-educated wife. In about 1872 the couple moved to Mineville in Upper New York State, where John Henry worked as a labourer on a railroad gang. He lost his job and when Mary Ann's cousin, John Costello, a foreman at Dobson's Mills in the Falls of Schuylkill in Philadelphia, arranged a job for him at the mills, the family moved there in about 1875 with their two young sons, Patrick Henry, born in Rutland in 1872, and Walter Costello, born in Mineville in 1873.

The Falls of Schuylkill in north-east Philadelphia on the banks of the Schuylkill River was, and is, a small working-class community with a strong sense of identity – after fifty years' residence you earn the right to be called a "Fallser". St Bridget's Catholic Church dominates the streets of neat two-storey nineteenth-century brick and frame houses running from the banks of the river up to the brow of the hill where the smarter suburbs begin. St Bridget's is the Kelly family church, and the present large Gothic-style stone edifice, which replaced the simpler building which was there when Grace's grand-parents arrived, was constructed in 1925 by Grace's uncle, Patrick Henry Kelly. St Bridget's is in the East Falls, airier and sunnier than the gloomy precincts of Scott's Lane down by the river, where John Henry Kelly and his children went to work.

Ironically, Kelly and the other Irish immigrants escaped from English-dominated Ireland only to work for Englishmen in Philadelphia. The grim grey mills in the Falls of Schuylkill were owned by

Englishmen from Yorkshire, John and James Dobson, who emigrated to Philadelphia in 1848 and set up textile mills there in 1851. The Dobsons made their fortunes selling blankets to the Union Army during the Civil War and by the 1870s, when Kelly and his young family arrived in the Falls, the Dobson brothers' companies grossed more than $20 million annually and James Dobson had a twenty-eight-acre estate on the brow of the hill, where John Henry's son would later build the seventeen-room house in which Grace was born.

Dobson's Mills formed the sombre background to the Kellys' lives. Patrick and Walter, the two eldest children, went to work in the Dye House at the mills when they were ten years old and their younger brothers and sisters, with the exception of the three youngest – George, Grace and John Brendan – started work in the mills before they were thirteen. Curiously, Grace's maternal uncles, Bruno and Carl Majer, also worked at the mills; but they were designers, at a more exalted level than the manual-labouring Kellys. The Dobson brothers, as owners of the mills, were kings of the Falls. "Even if you hated them", a Fallser remembers, "you did what they said, never crossed them, and followed their orders to a tee. It was that or else. ..." Except, of course, if you were Mary Ann Costello Kelly from County Mayo.

It had become a Dobson tradition that whenever a Dobson daughter married, Mrs James Dobson would give the Catholic Irish children from the Falls a penny or two to line the path outside the Anglican church of St James the Less to cheer the bridal pair. For the Irish nothing could have been more symbolic of the hated English domination which they had fled Ireland to escape, and on one famous occasion Mary Kelly took her stand against Dobson pretensions. In accordance with local tradition the Falls Irish children, including four of the youngest Kellys, were already lined up under Mrs Dobson's orders when Mary Kelly heard what was going on. She ran down the street to the church, grabbed her children, some by the ears and some by the arms, and, within earshot of the bridal party, shouted, "To hell with your pennies! No Kelly's going to stand up in front of a Protestant church and cheer the Dobsons, now or *ever*!"

Mary Ann Kelly was the archetype of the American immigrant mother upon whose indomitable will, hard work and unrelenting drive the success story of the second generation rests. Indeed in 1925, by which time three of her sons had reached national prominence, *American Magazine* ran an article entitled "Oh, For A Million Mothers Like Mary Kelly". As she told the writer, William A. McGarry: "In all the years of my life I've never been sick a single day, except when my children were born. I had neither the time nor the heart to be sick." Indeed she had not; eight more children were born after the Kellys moved to the Falls, where they first occupied the rear of a house in the gloomy Scott's Lane by the mills and then, as the children kept coming, a house on Summer Road, now Clearfield Street, where Grace's father, John Brendan Kelly (usually known as "Jack"), was born on 4 October 1889. He was the last but one of the Kelly children and the youngest son, preceded by Patrick H., Walter C., Ann, another John who died of sunstroke before Jack was born, Charles, Mary, Elizabeth and George. After Jack came Grace, the last child, who became an actress and who died when she was only about twenty-two.

"I had to be cook, baker, laundress, scrubwoman, dressmaker, milliner, valet, lady's maid, waitress, chambermaid," Mary Kelly told McGarry.

I've been a lawyer, for I laid down the code of justice in the family; and I was the policeman that kept order, and the jury that decided the cases, and the judge that handed out the punishment. Yes, and I've been the banker that received the money, the accountant that kept the books – in my head – the cashier, and the paymaster. I had to know groceries and dry goods, fuel and light, plastering and papering and carpentering. That is what it means to be the wife of a poor man and the mother of ten children.

Two qualities distinguished Mary Kelly from the other hard-working immigrant wives of the Falls of Schuylkill: her intellectual curiosity and her passion for books and self-education. "I tried to grow in knowledge," she told McGarry.

From the time I was a child I had a hunger for books. I couldn't buy them, but I begged and borrowed them at every turn. All my life, I have kept up my reading.... I was up at five o'clock in the morning and often it was midnight before I went to bed. But I never stopped reading and studying. I've stood by the stove hundreds of times, a baby under my left arm and a book in my left hand, while I made pancakes with my right one.

Her grand-daughter, the late Marion Kelly Cruice Smith, remembered her grandmother's interest in history and above all her know-

9

ledge of Shakespeare, a love inherited by her son George and her grand-daughter Grace. She was altogether a formidable woman, and a tough, hard one, dominating her family and ruling them with her iron will. If her husband displeased her she would send him to Coventry, often refusing to talk to him for days on end. She would laugh, but she would not cry, and the keynote of her household was discipline, organization and hard work. The children queued for the one bathroom in order of seniority and, while the girls helped their mother with the chores and cared for their younger brothers, the boys were expected to do odd jobs to increase the family income. "Everyone had a task assigned to him," her son Jack was to write later. "All money that was earned, whether in a regular job or just running errands, picking strawberries, milking cows, caddying at the golf club, had to be turned over intact to Mother." Her son remembered her as being "very fair in our allowances" and that she always tried to set aside a fund for a summer trip to Atlantic City "even if it were only a day excursion". Mary Kelly was careful, but she did not believe in cutting corners on the family food bills. "I will never economize on the table, because that is a false economy," she used to say. "You only have to pay later to the doctor what you save."

The Kelly family values were honesty, discipline and decency. Jack Kelly remembered his mother as "forever pointing out to us horrible examples of people cheating honest traders and forbearing to pay their debts". He remembered, too, the time his father quit his job at Dobson's to save the late-night horse-drawn streetcar from Center City to outlying Manayunk. The streetcar company threatened to withdraw this service because drunken Irishmen from the Falls and equally drunken Poles from Manayunk habitually beat up the driver and the conductor when the latter attempted to collect the fares. John H. Kelly, over six feet tall and proud of his great physical strength, applied for the job of conductor on the last run of the night. To quote his son: "After several hectic months, during which time many heads were broken, peace and quiet was restored." It was this strain in the Kelly upbringing which was to lead Jack Kelly into politics as a "white knight" fighting corruption.

Together with honesty and decency, Mary Kelly instilled into her children the fierce patriotism characteristic of Irish-Americans, which her grand-daughter Grace would share. "She always told us", her son wrote, "that 'your first duty is to your country - you can be a Republican or a Democrat later', and she made us proud of our neighbourhood and our state."

So the Kellys grew up a healthy, vibrant household; Jack later recalled that there was a great deal of sparkling conversation at table in the Kelly home and that any child who wanted to be heard "had to be very fast with his words". John Henry Kelly had had no formal education, but, according to his son, he was highly intelligent, with a gift for mathematics, and later in life he succeeded in setting up a small insurance business. He had a remarkable memory and to the day of his death could recite a 300-page book, *Perry at the Gate*, which he had read many times as a boy tending sheep at Drumirla. Mary Kelly was a fount of stories, which she told to her own children as well as to the neighbours', while of her sons, Walter, with his quick wit and talent for mimicry, became one of the great vaudeville stars of his time, and George, who was given to striking Shakespearean attitudes around the house, was to become a Pulitzer Prize-winning playwright.

If the Kellys and their cousins, the Costellos, were a clan in themselves, they were also part of a close-knit Irish community, which in the Falls centred on St Bridget's Church with its school and upon the famous Gun Boat saloon on Midvale Avenue, not far from the house at 3365 in which the Kellys finally settled. Religion and a common background united the Irish in defence against the prejudice of the older-established Protestant communities, which in Philadelphia, as elsewhere, looked down upon the Irish newcomers as dirty, drunken, lazy and violent. Yet it was all very far removed from the hopelessness and claustrophobic atmosphere of County Mayo and, despite the prejudice, for a family with the wit, energy and drive of the Kellys America was indeed the land of opportunity. Philadelphia was a booming industrial city and there was plenty of work available in the mills and in the burgeoning, Irish-orientated construction industry.

While the Kelly girls went to night school and qualified for jobs in offices as stenographers and book-keepers, the boys – with the exception of Walter, who became a machinist on a steamship, and George, who worked briefly as a draughtsman – took jobs in the construction industry. Jack Kelly's first job after leaving Grammar School at the age of fourteen was on a building site where Wanamaker's department store was under construction: he worked as a telephone boy for $6 a week. His duty was to answer the site telephone and then go after the foremen and steeplejacks high up on the girders to bring them down to take the call. After a while, he was promoted to timekeeper at double the salary, a job which still involved climbing the framework and riding the derricks and material elevators on the multi-storey project. Jack Kelly liked to take risks: "No one would follow me around over the steel frames in those days," he later told a reporter, and on one occasion he fell four storeys to land safely but bruisingly on a pile of cinders. Then, because his father wanted him to learn a trade, he, like his brothers Patrick and Charles before him, became an apprentice bricklayer, rising to foreman after three years' training, and working on big construction sites all over the city.

At seventeen the young bricklayer was an exceptionally handsome man. Tall and strong like his father, he was beautifully built, with a physical magnetism which is compelling even in an old photograph. He had classical features, with a straight nose, blue eyes, dark blond hair, fine teeth and the firm, distinctive Kelly jaw which all his children, including Grace, would inherit. Like his father, he was proud of his physical strength and, ahead of his time in his belief in the importance of physical fitness, he filled all his leisure hours with sport. At first he thought of taking up boxing; his earliest sporting memories were of Tissot's Inn on Stanton Street near the Kelly house where all the Irish fighters trained – Terry McGovern, Tom Sharkey, Bat Nelson among them – and the neighbourhood kids would watch them work out in the ring and on the road. Boxing suited the battling Irish temperament and Jack Kelly, with the experience of taking part in bouts organized by the professionals for the boys at Tissot's, became an expert boxer; but the great Philadelphia sport, which was to become his passion, was rowing.

The Schuylkill River, a tributary of the Delaware, runs from the centre of the city through Fairmount Park to the Falls of Schuylkill and beyond; on its banks stands an eccentric collection of brightly coloured balconied brick and timber buildings known as Boat House Row. Even in the bitterest weather there are rowing shells on the river. "As a kid", Jack Kelly reminisced, "I was always on the banks, and if I could catch the oar or hold the sweater of one of the great oarsmen of the day, my day was complete." The seventeen-year-old Jack went into rowing with that determination to win which was to be a Kelly hallmark. He had the build of an athlete, but he also had the intelligence and discipline necessary to make a champion. Between bricklaying and night school he kept himself fit through the winter; then, as soon as the rowing season began, he would rise at six in the morning to practise on the river, get to his job at seven, work till five and then row until 8.30 pm. On Sundays he would row all day. The First World War intervened; Jack Kelly, turned down as an aviator because of his poor eyesight, volunteered and went to France in the Ambulance Corps. Even there he kept himself fit, and prepared for the future by boxing twelve rounds a day, not smoking or drinking, and spending his nights planning how to win the National Single Sculls title.

Lying awake at night Jack Kelly would remember his mother's dictum: "Thoughts are things, but they won't be things if you just think about them. You must put forth whatever effort or intelligence is required to bring them into being."

"I didn't let it go at just thinking," Jack Kelly wrote later. "I made great sacrifices as a soldier to condition myself for the goal I was seeking. I studied every trick of timing. I planned races against men I thought I would have to beat." He won the National title in the season of 1919 after his return from France, but his eyes were set on another goal, the Diamond Sculls at Henley, England. Assured that his entry would be accepted, Kelly bought himself a new shell and booked his passage. Three days before he was to sail the blow fell. He received a cable from Henley: "Entry rejected. Letter follows." "I remember", Jack Kelly was to write years later, "reading that cable over and over, and seeing the tears drop on the paper, and realizing that all my castles were tumbling down about my ears ... The letter never did follow, so I assumed the old rule that a man who worked with his hands could not compete [was responsible] ... As I looked through the tears, I felt that my grandfather, who really hated the English, was right and all the disappointment that I felt was turned into bitterness towards the English."

Bitterness – and the sweets of revenge: Jack Kelly beat Jack Beresford, winner of the Diamond Sculls at Henley in the year his entry was refused, in the Singles of the Olympic Games at Antwerp in 1920, topping the feat by winning the Doubles title with his cousin Paul Costello on the afternoon of the same day. Sixteen years later Kelly admitted to a reporter that his entry had been rejected because of a feud between the Henley stewards and his club, the Vesper, but the story that he had been rejected because he worked with his hands and was "not a gentleman" became part of the Kelly myth, a myth which he did not take much trouble to counter, perhaps because in his heart of hearts he believed that social prejudice had really been at the bottom of it. He was to revenge himself through his son, whom he pledged on the day of his birth to win the Diamond Sculls; "Kell" would reward him by doing so not once but three times. The myth is important, too, because Jack Kelly's daughter Grace certainly believed it or liked to pretend to do so, although she must have known of the official explanation. Years later, when as Princess of Monaco she visited the old Kelly home in Mayo, she would often repeat the story of how her father had been turned down by the Henley stewards "because he worked with his hands". For her it was not only an affirmation of her father's character and exploits but also of her own roots in the people beneath the glittering outward image of herself as princess.

Jack Kelly returned from his Olympic triumphs to a hero's welcome in his native town. At the dock in New York a large delegation from the Falls of Schuylkill was waiting to escort him and his partner Costello back to Philadelphia on a special train, and at North Philadelphia station they were greeted by the mayor and officials, the policemen's and firemen's bands, one hundred mounted police and thousands of Irishmen wearing the Kelly green rowing cap which Jack always used. After riding with his mother and Costello in an open car through the crowded, decorated streets of the Falls, Jack attended a banquet in his honour at the old Tissot's Inn, now renamed the Fairmount, where he was moved almost to tears by the pride and affection shown him by his "own people" of the Falls. Among the shower of congratulatory letters and messages which the returning hero received was one "particular" letter: it was from Margaret Majer, a beautiful blonde girl of German descent, who hitherto had been keeping him at arm's length.

Margaret Katherine Majer was nine years younger than Jack Kelly. Born in Philadelphia of German parents who were, like Jack Kelly's, first-generation immigrants, she was an exquisitely beautiful girl with fine features, blonde hair and an athletic figure. She was just sixteen when Jack first set eyes on her at what he described as "a kids' swimming meet" at the Philadelphia Turngemeinde in 1914; it would be ten years before he succeeded in persuading her to marry him, for Margaret Majer was an independent girl, intent on gaining her degree in physical education at Temple University, pursuing a career as swimming instructor and posing for the covers of respectable magazines. The fine features that she bequeathed to her daughter Grace could be seen on the covers of such publications as *The Country Gentleman*, where, clad in sporting beret and scarf, and kneeling beside a gun-dog, she presented an image of healthy, gentlewomanly beauty.

Margaret Majer had every right to pose as a gentlewoman, since her family line could be traced back to the sixteenth century in the German state of Württemberg. While the Kellys might claim, as most Irish families do, kinship with the High Kings of Ireland, and, in the words of a genealogical expert, "Grace Kelly's forefathers may well have been Kings of Ui Maine centuries before the Grimaldis became Princes of Monaco," the fact remains that the mists of Irish history obscure the Kelly ancestry beyond their undoubted existence at Drumirla in the mid-nineteenth century. By contrast, Margaret Majer's father, Carl Majer, was born in 1863 in a castle, Schloss Helmsdorf, near Immenstadt am Bodensee (Lake Constance), where his father was a landowner, proprietor of the castle with its farms and estate; and the Majer forebears included a judge, a professor of law, a pastor and an architect, one of whom had been granted the right to the rank of nobility and the use of "von" for his lifetime. A genealogist has also linked Margaret Majer with the philosopher Hegel and with the de Monpezats, the family of the husband of the Queen of Denmark.

All this, however, did not save Margaret's grandfather, the squire, Johann Christian Carl Majer, from an obscure financial disaster as a result of which he sold his estate and, apparently, emigrated with Carl, his son by his marriage to the daughter of a factory manager in Tübingen. The family arrived in Philadelphia some time in the last decades of the nineteenth century, for Carl Majer married Margaretha Berg there in 1896. Margaretha, a round, laughing, bouncy little woman always known as "Grossmutter" to her Kelly grandchildren, was the daughter of a saddle and harness maker of Erbach, near Eppenheim, and her ancestors were Catholic farmers and millers of considerably lower social standing than the Majers. She and Carl were married in St Paul's Independent Lutheran Church and her family of two sons, Carl and Bruno, and daughter Margaret were brought up as Lutherans.

The Majers lived in North Philadelphia in a solidly middle-class, respectable area. Carl, according to his daughter Margaret, was a textile designer and taught at the Philadelphia Textile Institute, while his sons, Carl and Bruno, were also textile designers, designing carpets for the mills. Grace's artistic sense, her feeling for colour and design, evidently came from her Majer relations; years later she, too, was to design textiles. The family all spoke German and in 1914 Margaret's mother, who always called her by her German name Margaretha, took her back to Germany to show her where the family came from. The First World War broke out while they were there and they were forced to hurry back to America in steerage.

It must have been shortly after their return that Jack Kelly first met Margaret Majer, and when he returned from the war he pursued her, although perhaps with less vigour than he devoted to rowing titles. The romance did not prosper and at the end of the 1919 rowing season, when Jack had won the National Singles title, Margaret, in her future husband's words, "asked for waivers on me, as she couldn't compete with my boat". For the handsome Jack, his mother's pride and joy, Margaret's rejection came as a shock to his ego and, although he saw her several times that winter skating on Gustine Lake, "she treated me as if I had B.O." A year later came the Olympic titles and Jack's triumphant return to Philadelphia as the conquering hero. Margaret wrote to congratulate him, but Jack, unsure of her intentions and afraid that his pride would again be wounded if he precipitately asked her for a date and was turned down, did not dare do so. For several weeks he went to places where he thought he might see her, then his hopes were dashed by seeing her at a dance "with a fellow who stuck to her like glue". For over a year both Margaret and Jack played hard to get, aware of each other but ostensibly ignoring each other until, on a chance meeting in the street, he finally asked her for a date. Even then he was, he says, fifth on the list, and it was not until 30 January 1924, almost ten years after they had first met, that they were married at St Bridget's in the Falls, Margaret having converted to Catholicism to marry Jack.

By the time Jack and Margaret Kelly got married, Jack was not only a sporting hero but also well on the way to becoming a millionaire. For this, as for so much in her son's early life, his mother was partly responsible. He had never forgotten what she said to him when, as an apprentice bricklayer aged seventeen, he used to get up at dawn to go to work. "Here you are at six in the morning going out into the snow," she told him. "All the smart ones are still abed. You get smart, John. The harder you work, the less money you get. Work with your hands, John, but at the same time work with your head."

Jack used his head; on his return from France he borrowed $2,000 from his brother George, who was by now a successful vaudeville actor and well on the way to becoming a playwright, and $5,000 from Walter, who was at the height of his fame as a vaudeville star. With this money he started his own brick contracting business. By the end of 1924 he had landed several big, profitable contracts, the first of which was for the same company he had once worked for as telephone boy. Now Jack Kelly had money and he wanted a home of his own.

He looked, literally, upwards from East Falls, where he was born and where he and Margaret had rented a small apartment on the site of the old Gun Boat Saloon, to the land on the ridge where his former boss, James Dobson, had his estate. On the corner of Henry and Coulter Avenues in Germantown there was an old orchard, where as a boy he had climbed the trees for apples and pears. He had always had a feeling for the land; now he could afford it. He bought the site and hired an architect, an old rowing friend named Ed Hoffman. The scale of the house showed the size of Jack Kelly's dreams: built of Kelly bricks in the colonial style, it had a white porticoed entrance, shutters, dormer windows, a green slate roof and seventeen rooms to accommodate a new Kelly clan.

Work on the house began in April 1925; in June, Jack and Margaret's first child, Margaret (known as "Peggy"), was born, and on 15 September 1925 the family moved into their Germantown home. With the precise organization for which Margaret Kelly was to be famous, three more children arrived at regular intervals. John B. Jr, the only son, always called "Kell" by his family, was born on 24 May 1927; his father's wish at his christening was characteristic and would have an enormous influence on young Kelly's life: "I hoped he would like to row and one day win the Diamond Sculls, the only major rowing trophy that didn't have the name of John B. Kelly on it." Grace came next, born on 12 November 1929, and, three years and seven months later, on 25 June 1933, the last child, the baby of the family, Elizabeth Anne ("Lizanne"). The new Kelly clan was complete.

2

Philadelphia Story

Though she was named after her father's younger sister, who had been an actress, the strongest immediate influence on Grace's young life was that of her parents, with their exceptional good looks and commanding personalities, and their strict code of honour and discipline. Years later, when they were growing old, Grace would say to friends, "You should have seen my parents when they were young, they were *so* beautiful." Roosevelt once called Jack Kelly "the handsomest man in America" and, when Kelly ran for mayor of Philadelphia in 1935, hostile newspapers used to sneer at him as "the Manayunk Adonis". Indeed Jack Kelly's one weakness was a harmless vanity; as his hair thinned, he always wore a hat to conceal it, and although he was, like Grace, extremely short-sighted, he would never be seen wearing spectacles. Even the children who came to play at the Kelly house never saw him without a jacket on; he was always "Gentleman Jack". He had dignity and presence, both of which qualities he bequeathed to his daughter. "He commanded attention wherever he went," Matt Lukens, a childhood friend of the Kelly children, remembers. "You could like him or not like him, but you had to know he was somebody."

Jack Kelly was, his son-in-law Prince Rainier recalls, very far from being the stock image of an Irishman. Although he was witty and good company, loved public speaking and was outgoing among friends or when he knew it was expected of him, Prince Rainier found him personally surprisingly shy and reserved, two qualities which Grace inherited from him. Grace, the Prince said, had "the same poise as her father" and the "quality of not giving out too much straight away to people she didn't know". Like him, she was reserved and observant of people, the Prince said. Jack Kelly, unlike many Irishmen, drank little and never went too far, always conscious of his image and of the proprieties. He was fond of jokes and generous in his hospitality, especially on the annual all-male excursion to the

Kentucky Derby, when he would hire a coach with lavish food and drink for his friends, or on trips to the Atlantic City race-track, of which he was a director. On such expeditions there would always be a singing Irishman, Prince Rainier remembers, and Jack Kelly would join in, but if it went too far he would quickly tone it down. "He would think two or three songs all right, but in a restaurant other people might not like it and he was very observant of that," the Prince said.

"My father was a leader of men," Grace was to say of him after his death, and in the early 1930s, while she was still very young, he proved it by plunging as "a white knight" (his own words) into the turbulent and murky world of Philadelphia politics. Philadelphia and indeed Pennsylvania politicians were a byword for corruption; it was a Philadelphia politician who coined the succinct phrase "shaking the plum tree", which meant milking the system for everything you could get, and a Pennsylvania political boss who was author of the equally memorable "An honest politician is one who, when bought, stays bought". Philadelphia was a Republican fief under the notoriously corrupt Vare brothers, and the city's few Democratic leaders were also paid and run by the Vares. Despite warnings that "the gang would ruin my business and break me in short order", Kelly and his friends formed a new, honest Democratic machine to challenge the system, and in 1935 Kelly ran for mayor against an unscrupulous politician named S. Davis Wilson.

Roosevelt, watching from Washington the outcome of the vicious pitched battle in Philadelphia, described Kelly to Harry Hopkins as "a square and honest young man", and Kelly's honesty helped lose him the election. The old Republican machine functioned much better than the new Democratic organization, even, Kelly claimed, to the extent of dumping 30,000 of his votes in the river. Wilson, an abrasive, wily politician, proved to be the better demagogue – "as a gentleman that was not Kelly's way", an observer commented. Jack Kelly fought the campaign like a gentleman and took his defeat like the champion sportsman he was, quoting in his concession speech verses which his daughter Grace would remember and recite forty years later:

> The harder you're thrown, the higher you bounce;
> Be proud of your blackened eye.

It's not the fact that you're licked that counts,
But how did you fight and why.

Kelly had gone into politics, as he himself put it, "buckling my armor on to go out and fight this entrenched machine". The machine unhorsed him, but the manner in which he took his defeat became part of the Kelly legend.

There was one other major reason why Jack Kelly lost: he was an Irish Catholic in a city which was still predominantly Protestant. It would be twenty years before Philadelphia was to elect a Catholic mayor, and nearly thirty before John Fitzgerald Kennedy would become President of the United States. For the Irish Catholic minority, their religion and their roots were things to be proud of and to be fiercely defended, something too which Grace would never forget. Jack Kelly abandoned politics in 1940, but Grace always remembered the toll they had taken upon the family, her father's frequent absences and the mud-slinging and dirty tactics of party politics. "My father was in politics and I grew up hating it," she told Pierre Salinger in a television interview shortly before her death.

Politics and business meant that Jack Kelly was rarely at home. He was an authoritative but kindly father, teasing with his daughters, stricter with Kell, his only son. He never disciplined the children and often acted as mediator between them and Margaret, whom they somewhat unkindly called "our Prussian General Mother". Margaret Kelly was the real authority in the household. "All the kids called her 'The Boss'," Matt Lukens remembers. "If she said two and three was four it was all right by us." Nonetheless, he recalls her as having "class, charm and beauty", while Prince Rainier describes her as more outgoing than her husband with a German *gemütlich* side to her. "She was very giggly," he said, "and she loved to play a good joke on people."

The children saw less of this side of their mother while they were growing up than of the stern disciplinarian who would use the hairbrush on them if they were naughty or the back of her hand if the hairbrush was not readily available. Rules were strict. The house must be kept tidy and there was to be no dropping of schoolbooks in the hall as the children came in. They were not allowed to put their elbows on the table at meals and were made to eat everything that was put in front of them. They could never wangle anything out of their mother; if the girls overspent their allowance, they would go to their father. "Ma" Kelly, as they all called her, was frugal in comparison with her husband's open-handedness. "Pop Kelly's got money to burn," the family manservant and friend "Fordie" used to say, "and Ma Kelly don't like to smell the smoke."

Margaret Kelly was economical as far as what she regarded as unnecessary expenditure was concerned, and Grace, too, inherited this from her, but privately and anonymously, as her friend Marie Magee recorded, she was generous with help to people in need. She saved money on the children's clothes, making many of the girls' dresses herself; Grace, being the second daughter, often had to wear Peggy's hand-me-down clothes. Ma Kelly never stinted on food and entertainment, however; all the Kellys' friends remember that "they lived well and entertained well".

Like a good German *hausfrau*, Ma Kelly was a capable cook. Although Fordie's wife came in with him from Philadelphia to do the cooking, Ma Kelly would cook the breakfast and often other dishes as well. She had help – a succession of girls were imported to look after the children, most of them from Germany – but she herself knew all the domestic skills and she was determined that her daughters should do so too. From the age of eight they were taught to knit, crochet, sew and cook, and Ma Kelly used to say to Peggy, "If you get married, how are you going to have a maid if you don't know what to do yourself?" Grace learned embroidery and needlepoint from Grossmutter; throughout her life her friends remarked that whenever Grace had a free moment she would be knitting or doing needlepoint.

Grossmutter, described by "Aunt" Marie Magee as a "little five by five with the biggest, most beautiful eyes I have ever seen ... which smiled and sparkled all the time", Grace's only surviving grandparent, was very much part of the family circle, as was her son Carl, nicknamed "Midge" because he, like his mother, was tiny and cheerful. Nonetheless, the German side of the family was quite swamped by the huge Irish Kelly clan, and indeed Grace, whose Irish roots were to be of such importance to her, never showed any interest in her German origins. While the Kelly Irishness seemed something to be proud of, the children grew up as teenagers during the Second World War, when being German was not something you broadcast. Peggy Kelly remembers her mother taking out the German books in the evening, hoping that the children would take an interest in the language, but "Kell used to get Lizanne to hide them, because then

21

Hitler was getting such a bad press and we didn't want to know about it." Their mother understood and did not insist.

Margaret Kelly was frugal, too, with her affection and not given to demonstrations of love either to her children or to her husband. She worried about them, cared for them, ran their lives, but she did not shower them with love. When Grace was a teenager, a friend remembers, her mother was "not nice" to her. Grace, in contrast, had an enormous capacity for loving; as her father told a newspaperman when she won the Oscar, "She was one of the most affectionate persons I've ever known," and she would lavish on her own children all the love which her mother had withheld from her. Grace found caring affection in other members of the household, in Fordie, the valet, butler-cum-chauffeur and gardener who was "everything" to the Kellys, and in Florence Merckel, her mother's spinster friend who lived with them while they were growing up.

George Godfrey Ford, known as Fordie, was the central character in the Henry Avenue household. Short and black, with a great sense of humour, he had worked with the young Jack Kelly on a construction site and when Kelly went into business on his own he hired Fordie to be, as Peggy put it, his "man's man, his chauffeur, his butler, his everything". Ma Kelly taught him to wait at table, but he regarded the garden and the outside of the house as his absolute preserve. One day Grace came home from school and traced her initials "GPK" and her birth date on a new cement path. Fordie, Marie Magee said, "nearly hit the ceiling, because Fordie kept that place, he knew every blade of grass in the place". Fordie was a privileged member of the Kelly household; when his rheumatism struck, Ma Kelly would put him to bed in whichever room he fancied, and Jack Kelly remembered him fondly in the will he dictated in 1953: "I want him to be kept in employment as long as he behaves himself well, making due allowances for minor errors of the flesh, if being slightly on the Casanova side is an error. I want my survivors to feel an obligation regarding his comfort and enjoyment and ... overlook his pipe as I have felt the need of a gas mask on many occasions."

"Fordie", Grace's greatest friend, Maree Rambo, said, "practically brought Grace up." On Thursday nights, when the girls who looked after the children were off duty, Fordie put the children to bed. "Before bedtime Gracie used to ask my opinions," he told an interviewer in 1954. "I'd tell her what I thought, and she'd usually follow my advice. She still consults me on a lot of things." Fordie taught Grace to drive and, although she managed to get her licence despite her poor eyesight and lack of skill, Fordie had it on record that "she was never any good at parking". Fordie died peacefully in bed in 1968 and among the many wreaths at his funeral was one from "Grace and Rainier de Monaco".

The other person of consequence in Grace's childhood was "Aunt Flossie" Merckel. A close friend and bridesmaid of Margaret Kelly, she was, in Peggy's words, "just the girl who came to dinner and never left". When Ma Kelly found that her husband's political activities involved her too much outside the house, Flossie Merckel became her right-hand woman, her social secretary and book-keeper, taking the girls to dancing classes and acting as surrogate mother to Grace and Lizanne.

Jack Kelly, like his children, needed love and admiration and did not get it from his undemonstrative wife. Women naturally adored him; when Philadelphia women remember Jack Kelly it is as "such a *beautiful* man ... honest, humorous, charming ... a lovely Irishman". With his domestic life run on oiled wheels by his wife and his business and political life under the control of his severely protective secretary, Mrs Lucy Du Val, Jack Kelly found time for many flirtations in Philadelphia society and a long, serious affair with a society woman, Ellen Frazer. Kelly took great pains to conceal this affair from his family and it appears his children never knew about it. Margaret Kelly certainly must have suspected that her husband had affairs, but, dignified as she was, she made no scenes. For her, the matriarch, the important thing was to keep the family together; she was, one of her old friends said, "always the pilot of the whole family".

Apart from her family, Margaret Kelly had one abiding interest, the Women's Medical College, which at that time was situated in Germantown, not far from their house on Henry Avenue. The only medical school in America for women doctors, it was in financial straits when Margaret Kelly took it under her wing in the late 1930s. According to Margaret's closest friend, Marie Magee, who was, like her, of German descent married to an Irishman, Margaret Kelly "went out on her own and raised $10 million" for the college. Marie Magee recalls how, when they went on a trip to the West Coast, "there wasn't a morning we got up that Mrs Kelly didn't call the Medical College ... how was this going, how was that? Because if anything happened, she would have dropped our trip immediately and gone right back."

"She was very, very strong," Marie Magee continued, "and she would never let things drift by. If she started to do something, she finished it. Gracie was exactly the same way ... she was very, very persistent. If she was going to do something, she did it."

Grace, both in looks and in character, was a blend of both her parents, a highly successful mingling of Irish and German stock. She had her mother's exquisite features, her father's strong Kelly jaw, the myopic blue Kelly eyes and teeth which a friend said "were so good you thought they were false". She inherited her height and figure from the Kellys, but from both parents she inherited the self-discipline which shaped her life, and from her father the determination to "go out and win". She had her mother's executive capacity in her domestic and charitable activities, and her quality of carrying things through, of keeping everything under control. From them both she inherited the physical stamina which enabled her to stay up for a party well into the early hours of the morning and then to get up a few hours later and set to work. The blending of Irish and German characteristics meant that Grace had two completely different sides to her character. There was the outward aspect of her, which was organized, disciplined, executive and ambitious, and the inner Grace, which was romantic, emotional, soft-hearted, vulnerable, sensitive, instinctive and feeding on fantasies. "She was a dreamer and so it was natural she should end up in movies," a close friend said.

In the competitive Kelly household Grace learned that you have to be tough to preserve your identity. As a child she did not have an easy time. "At home we were always competing," Grace recalled in a film biography in 1976, "competing for everything, competing for love." And in that competition Grace started with several built-in disadvantages: she was the middle child, skinny and sickly, suffering badly from colds and sinus trouble. Her father, whom she worshipped, doted on Peggy, whom he called "Baba", a lovely, bright, athletic extrovert with a wild sense of humour. Once, years later, when his son Kell reported regretfully to his father that his first child was not a boy but a girl, Jack Kelly, with considerable insensitivity, replied, "Don't worry, son. My greatest joy in life has been Peggy."

Jack Kelly never really understood Grace, although, paradoxically, of all the four children she turned out to be the most like him.

She was the most feminine of his daughters and yet she would prove to have his qualities of leadership, determination, judgment and self-discipline and, not least, his supreme desire to succeed. He never seems to have perceived how much his second daughter's yearning for his approval was a factor in her determination to make a career for herself and, when she did succeed, he remained puzzled by her universal appeal. "I don't get that girl," he once told a Philadelphia friend. "We're an athletic family, very good athletes and she can barely walk. She wants to act and when she gets up on stage I get a kick, but otherwise. ..." He shrugged his shoulders. Even when she won the Oscar, he publicly remarked that of all his children he had thought that Grace would be "the least likely to support me".

Grace felt this conflict – "Grace and her father were contestants," a childhood friend remembered – and that she could never succeed by his standards, expressing it when she said of him years later: "People were compelled to follow him. It would have been easier for me had I been a boy. That's why I didn't want to be a girl." As a girl she could not compete with Peggy in her father's affections. She was well co-ordinated, good enough at sports like hockey and basketball, but by the high Kelly standards of sporting achievement her capacity and her commitment were just not enough.

For Kell life was not easy either, but at least as the only boy he did not have to compete with his siblings. His father was stricter with him than with his daughters; in Marie Magee's words, "Kell was right under his father's nose, every minute!" Tall, strong and a great athlete like his father, he was constantly aware of his father's ambitions for him. At the age of seven his father had made for him, down on "the shore" at Ocean City, a small replica of a lifeguard boat, which was kept in a miniature boathouse on the beach in front of their house, "and Kell was taught to row that tiny little boat over those enormous waves and he was seven years old ...". Kell's young life was shaped by his father's ambition that he should win the Diamond Sculls at Henley and, when other boys would be out drinking and chasing girls, Kell would be training. His athletic career would be a brilliant reward for such dedication: eight times U.S. Single Sculls Champion, twice the winner of the Diamond Sculls and Olympic Singles bronze medallist in 1956 among many other major titles; but it would take its toll later in life when Kell decided to have his fun in middle age.

Lizanne (known as "Lizzie", because in the Kelly family everybody had an "ie" added to their name), "Gracie's" younger sister, was her mother's favourite, the baby of the family and indulged as such. She was a spoiled brat and behaved like one, fiercely rejecting her older sister's attempts to dominate her. Grace was Peggy's slave, sometimes an ill-treated one – neighbours remember seeing Peggy dragging Grace along by her hair – but, when she in turn attempted to impose the same pattern on her younger sister, she met with no success. "Lizzie," she would plead, "why can't you be nice to me like I am to Peggy?" and their relationship was epitomized in a home movie taken by Jack Kelly, known as the "tea-party scene", in which a ladylike Grace reaches graciously for the teapot only to have it snatched away by a scowling Lizanne.

Grace, unlike her sisters, was timid and shy with strangers. When they went to downtown Philadelphia, Grace was so frightened by the crowds of people that she would cling to her mother's hand and, because she was so retiring, she was often forgotten. She used to tell friends later, with a wry smile, of her humiliation when, walking in Ocean City with her mother and two sisters, they would meet somebody and her mother would say to this acquaintance, "You know Peggy? And, of course, you know Lizanne?", completely forgetting that Grace was there.

In the circumstances it is hardly surprising that Grace should have retreated into her own private fantasy world. "Grace was always very good at being alone," her friend Maree Rambo said, and Lizanne remembers that Grace would spend hours by herself happily playing with her dolls. Perhaps even then her fantasy games included playing the role of Princess, a role which she always demanded when they acted their childhood plays. Indeed her childhood nickname was "Princess"; Mary Keats, who came to know Grace well in Hollywood when she did her hair at MGM, remembers her as a child in Philadelphia, where Mary used to stay with the Wolfs, neighbours of the Kellys: "She was called the Princess as a little girl." "Grace was born a princess," Frank Sinatra was to say many years later in his grief at his friend's death, a glib-sounding statement which was nonetheless, in its way, true. At the Convent of the Assumption, housed in a grey Gothic mansion called Ravenhill, only a few blocks from where she lived, and to which Grace was sent at the age of five, the English-born nun who taught her remembers her as being "always neat and dainty". Grace with her self-containment, her quiet poise and her air of refinement was different from her athletic, extrovert brother and

26

sisters. When asked if this ladylike quality in Grace was something which she had deliberately cultivated, Maree Rambo, who had known her since her teens, replied, "No, she was always like that." Grace was different from her siblings and sensed that she was different, an experience which gave her an early awareness of self which was to be one of her strengths.

Sibling rivalry apart, Grace's childhood was happy, protected and far from lonely. The Kelly clan beyond the nucleus of Henry Avenue was a force to be reckoned with in East Falls. Of the eight surviving children of John Henry and Mary Ann Kelly, six were married and living in the area with their numerous children. Patrick Henry, the eldest, known as "P.H.", was also a building contractor and had a stone mansion which was "the showplace of the Falls", complete with ballroom and miniature golf course. Lavish in his expenditure, P.H., who had feuded with the rest of the family, died broke, leaving nine children, one of whom, George, became National Pocket Billiard Champion but died an alcoholic on Philadelphia's Skid Row. It was P.H. who built the new St Bridget's Church which dominates the Falls.

Charles, Jack Kelly's favourite brother, worked for him as his right-hand man in the brick company. Short for a Kelly, dynamic, fiery and with scant education, he kept the Kelly employees up to the mark, saving his generous brother's money, hiring men and sacking them if he thought they were not needed. He also, according to his daughter Mary, "did all of Uncle Jack's dirty political work and he wasn't afraid of anybody". Ann and Mary, both married with daughters, lived in the Falls a few blocks from Henry Avenue and every Sunday, after Mass at St Bridget's, the John B. Kellys and their children would stop in to see Mary Cruice and her children. The Cruice children and Charles Kelly's son and daughter were often at the house on Henry Avenue, although their parents did not come to the Kellys' big parties. "The John B. Kellys had their friends and they had the family, another whole social life," said a friend.

"Their house was a hub of activity," recalls Alice Godfrey Waters, whose parents were such close neighbours and friends of the Kellys as to be known as "Uncle Bill" and "Aunt Babe". Inside, the staircase rose out of the entrance hall, which ran through to the back of the house. To the left was the dining-room, where Jack and Margaret Kelly ate on the rare occasions when he was home for dinner, and on the right-hand side was the formal living-room, where no one ever went except perhaps on the occasion of Grace's engagement to Prince Rainier. The children ate in the breakfast-room beyond the kitchen and the family sat either in the sun porch, which ran along the outside of the living-room, or in the basement room, where all the Kellys' parties were held. The basement room walls were of Pennsylvania fieldstone and the room featured what Alice Waters described as a "*ratskeller* bar with swinging doors"; at the other end of the room, opposite the bar, the Kellys' big model train set would be laid out over Christmas and New Year.

Above the dining-room was Ma Kelly's bedroom with a bathroom connecting with her husband's bedroom. Kell had his room with bunkbed next to his father's room and his own bathroom, and Flossie Merckel slept in the room opposite Margaret Kelly's. Upstairs, on the "attic" floor, Peggy had her own room, while Grace and Lizanne shared a room with white-panelled walls, white-painted Early American furniture and a large bookshelf on which was ranged a collection of dolls brought back by their parents from their travels. Here, Lizanne remembers, "We had great arguments, but no actual fist fights – Mother would shout warningly, 'If I have to come up those stairs ...' Then Grace would say, 'Let's play tickle-backs,' and then we would go to sleep."

Outside, at the back of the house, there was a large garden with a cement tennis court which was flooded in winter for ice-hockey games, and in summer Jack Kelly filled a huge cement-mixing skip with water as a swimming-pool. The girls had their own small house in the garden called the Doll House, used by Peggy and Grace and their friends – "we didn't let Lizzie in there too much" – and Kell had his own Club House for himself and his gang, called the Tomato Men because the house was next to the tomato bed. Peggy and her friends were graciously allowed into the Club House because they were older than Kell and his friends, but Grace and Lizanne, according to ex-Tomato Man Matt Lukens, "were told to get the hell out of here". One Saturday morning, when Kell was thirteen and Grace eleven, Grace, egged on by Peggy, attempted to storm this bastion of male chauvinism on the pretext that Kell had invited two girls whom he thought were "pretty special". Kell refused to allow Grace inside, whereupon she dealt her brother "a roundhouse right to my nose which knocked me down, stunned me momentarily and caused my nose to bleed". Nevertheless, although they had little in common

("Grace never appreciated many of my athletic friends," said Kell), Grace adored her brother, whom she used to call "Kell-Bel".

Each summer there was Ma Kelly's Labor Day party and an open-air barbecue at Ocean City. Parents, children, everybody was invited and "there were games and we had water-melon spitting contests and we had hide-and-go-seek, and we sang and ate toasted marshmallows", Alice Waters recalls. "It was something I grew up with and loved." The Kellys spent summer holidays and weekends on the New Jersey shore at Ocean City, "America's Greatest Family Resort". In front of their Spanish-style house on Wesley Avenue with its central tower and red-tiled roof the big Atlantic rollers coasted in to the long beach where the Kelly children spent their days. Physical courage was a Kelly characteristic; Marie Magee described how Grace loved swimming and how "little as she was she would go out in that ocean and swim" through the huge waves. Ocean City was an important part of Grace's life; she would bring her own Grimaldi children to "the shore" every year, as if to remind them that this solid Middle America resort with its healthy pleasures was as much a part of their heritage as the glittering life of the Côte d'Azur.

In winter, the family often spent Saturday mornings at the Penn Athletic Club in Rittenhouse Square, where the children had swimming lessons and the girls were taught ballet. After lunch Jack and Margaret Kelly would take them to a movie or to a show; once, Grace was taken to a performance of the Ballets Russes, an experience which fired her imagination and inspired her lifelong interest in ballet. Each spring the children put on a show for their parents: Kell boxed and the girls danced, or there would be a fashion show in the ballroom with catwalk, orchestra and master of ceremonies with the girls as models. Since Marie Magee remembers Lizanne modelling at "exactly eighteen months old", Grace must have made her public début at a very early age at the Penn Athletic Club in Rittenhouse Square.

29

3
The Princess from Germantown

For a shy person like Grace who is also a dreamer acting is a natural outlet, a means of communicating, of impressing oneself on other people in a way which would normally be hard, if not impossible. For Grace acting was to be both a means of self-expression and also of personal achievement in a success-orientated family.

She took acting seriously at an early age. Sister Elizabeth, a teacher at her first school, the Convent of the Assumption, Ravenhill, remembers her as the Virgin Mary in the annual nativity play: "She understood the drama of the thing – she was reverent and serious ... she came in majestically and sweetly, laid down Baby Jesus and made a deep genuflection." Alice Godfrey Waters recalls Grace's first performance before a paying public. It took place in the basement of the Godfrey house, where oil-executive Bill Godfrey had set up a stage with a curtain, footlights and two dressing-rooms. The two Godfrey girls, Alice and her older sister Edie, who was Peggy's best friend, and the three Kelly girls – Peggy aged about ten, Grace about six and Lizanne about four – were the stars in front of an audience of neighbourhood children. "Grace did like a ballet dance and Lizanne was supposed to come out of a box, but she wouldn't come out of the box and the curtain closed and Peggy said, 'If you don't get out of that box I am going to beat you up.' Of course everyone in the audience heard." It was hardly an illustrious beginning, but Grace had other opportunities to perform; every year Ma Kelly gave a fête with a mock circus performance in aid of the Women's Medical College and Grace would have the chance to play a tightrope-walker dressed in a white tutu carefully stepping along a line marked on the grass or, in a joint role with Alice Godfrey, a Siamese twin. At seven she met her first real movie star, Douglas Fairbanks Jr, who visited her father at Henry Avenue. Dazzled, she fell instantly in love. "He kissed me goodnight," she remembered. "And I knew I should never wash off that spot on my face again."

The real source of inspiration for Grace as an actress was the Old Academy Players, a small amateur theatre group in East Falls of which her uncle "Midge" Majer and his wife were members. Grace, aged eleven, was taken to see a production, after which, her mind made up, she rushed home to tell her father she wanted to be an actress. Jack Kelly clearly did not think much of the idea. "He just looked up at me from his desk for a long time," she remembered, "then he said: 'All right, Grace, if that's what you want to do – go ahead.'" Grace did so: the next year, at the age of twelve, she made her stage début with the Academy Players in *Don't Feed the Animals*, showing a precocious professionalism in rescuing another actress when she fluffed her lines. On another occasion, she played in her Uncle George's play about Philadelphia, *The Torch-Bearers*, and received a good review. "From where I sat", the critic wrote, "it appeared as if Grace Kelly should become the theatrical torch-bearer for her family."

The theatre was in Grace's blood, or at least in that of the Kelly side of her ancestry. Her two bachelor Kelly uncles, Walter and George, had found fame in the world of the theatre outside Philadelphia. Walter, who began his career in vaudeville because his father locked him out of the house when he came home late one night at the age of twenty-one, was a top vaudeville star for some thirty years and the first Kelly to appear in movies. A portly, gregarious man with a ready Irish wit, a big cigar and a diamond tiepin, he toured America and England with his celebrated act, the "Virginia Judge", making friends as disparate as Louis Armstrong and Sir Thomas Lipton. According to his obituary in the Philadelphia *Bulletin*, Walter "knew personally all the Presidents of the United States from Theodore Roosevelt to Herbert Hoover, and always dropped in to the White House for a chat when he played Washington. Woodrow Wilson was a particular fan of the Virginia Judge." As a small girl Grace would often have seen her fat, red-faced, jovial uncle when he called in with a joke and a present for the children. He returned home to die after an accident in California when she was nine.

George Kelly, Grace's godfather, was to become her favourite uncle as she grew up; they had a great deal in common: above all, a passion for the theatre. George was exceptionally good-looking, tall like his father and his brother Jack, but dark where they were blond. "He was really black Irish," Marie Magee said. "His eyes and his hair

31

were coal black." He was slender where Jack was robust; hating sport, he had a passion for Shakespeare, which he shared with his niece Grace, and claimed that he had taught himself every line and every part in the plays. He worked briefly as a draughtsman for a bridge-building firm before escaping from Philadelphia on to the vaudeville stage and wrote his first play, a comedy sketch, in 1916. After a short, unhappy spell as a soldier in France, he returned to New York and began writing plays – in 1922 he had his first Broadway hit with *The Torch-Bearers*, followed by another, *The Show-Off*, in 1924 and *Craig's Wife*, for which he won the Pulitzer Prize in 1925. George's plays dealt with the rich middle class, to which he liked to pretend he belonged. He preferred to conceal the reality of his impoverished Irish immigrant background and in interviews would claim to have been "privately tutored as a young boy". Despite his affection for his mother and indeed his female relations, his plays tended to depict women as terrifying harridans; George was a homosexual with a lifelong partner, William Weagly, a former bookkeeper, who acted as his devoted valet-companion. The Falls Kellys, who either would not admit or naively did not suspect George's tendencies, treated Weagly as a servant and even at George's funeral in St Bridget's he was left weeping alone in a back pew.

George Kelly had talent; he also had wit, taste and an innate sense of quality, and earned the right to sit at the famous Round Table at the Algonquin Hotel in New York with Dorothy Parker and the wits. He was also a snob in the most refined sense of the word, detesting paper napkins, napkin rings and teabags as vulgar and decadent, and making a ritual of having an English tea. He was always correcting his niece Jeanne Shirley Turner's Philadelphia accent, which he regarded as provincial and common, and he disliked ugly people, nudity and swearing, although as far as profanity was concerned he made an exception for Tallulah Bankhead, whom he loved and who adored him in return. Uncle George was an original, he had style, and the magic of his name would help Grace take her first steps in the theatre.

Germantown was the centre of Grace's young existence, it was "her" neighbourhood, just as the Falls had been her father's. Germantown was the oldest real suburb in Philadelphia, founded in 1683 by Francis Pastorius for Dutch and German settlers. In the 1940s, when Grace was growing up, it was no longer such a fashionable place to live as were nearby Chestnut Hill and the exclusive suburbs of the Main Line. It was a comfortable, affluent, middle-class area where the newly rich Irish and Jewish families were not looked down upon and snubbed as they would have been in "smarter" places. Not only Grace's home, but both of her schools, her brother's school, Penn Charter, and most of her social life centred on Germantown.

The Convent of the Assumption, known as Ravenhill, was Grace's first experience of foreigners and foreign ways. The order had been founded by a Frenchwoman, most of the nuns were Europeans and the teaching was by the Montessori method; in the afternoon the nuns would serve a *goûté* of fruit and cookies, which seemed to their American pupils an exotic custom. Sister Elizabeth, the English-born nun, remembers Grace as "a good girl . . . she used to work hard and do everything you gave her to do and ask intelligent questions about it". She recalls that in catechism classes Grace would bother her so with her questions that she told her to write the questions in a little black book so that when she got to heaven she could ask God. A few years ago Grace wrote in her annual Christmas letter, "You know, Sister, I still have that little black book."

The story of the little black book is typical of Grace in more ways than one. She was fanatically attached to her possessions, almost as though they were an extension of herself, an affirmation of the reality of her existence. She kept all her dolls; Lizanne remembers that when they were very small Uncle Walter appeared at the Kellys' front door one day with two large baby dolls, one pink and one blue, which he presented to her and Grace. Years later Lizanne opened a cupboard in the palace in Monaco and there, sitting on a shelf, was Uncle Walter's baby doll. Grace kept all her clothes; cupboards in the palace would be filled with dresses from her film roles and from her early years as Princess to the day of her death, while in a room which Uncle George Kelly nicknamed the "sling-a-ling room" decades of magazines and newspapers were piled high to the ceiling. This may partly have been due to an inherited frugality, but it was also partly due to Grace's romantic attachment to the past.

Grace maintained relationships over the years with the same care with which she preserved her possessions, a characteristic which she first showed at Ravenhill, when the sister of one of her classmates had a nervous breakdown at a very young age. Grace was so moved and upset by this that she never forgot the girl and always sent her a Christmas card. After leaving Ravenhill she wrote to Sister

Elizabeth every Christmas, visited her often when she came to Philadelphia and on the nun's jubilee, the fiftieth anniversary of her joining the order, she remembered it and wrote Sister Elizabeth a "beautiful letter" saying that what Sister Elizabeth had taught her as a child she had taught her own children. Gradually over the years Grace was to build up a web of personal contacts, relationships and friendships with numerous people, men and women, young and old, intimate friends and people who served her. Each friendship reflected some facet of Grace's life and each person was made to feel that they shared in some part of her life and that they were important to her. She was not, however, indiscriminate with her friendships; as her great friend Rupert Allan said, "She had a way of turning out people she didn't have anything to do with or didn't like. [But] she never said anything wrong, or hurtful." Once you were a friend you were a friend for ever, until you proved beyond all possible doubt that you were not. All her friends remarked on her fierce loyalty to her family, and to her friends "she was loyal to a fault".

By the time Grace left Ravenhill for Stevens School in Germantown, the thin, sickly child had blossomed into a lovely teenager. Grace never went through an awkward stage, according to a school-friend; nor did she have spots, although she did have a tendency to fat on her hips and behind. A nutritionist had succeeded in curing her of her skinniness and general weakness, although nothing would ever cure her troubled sinuses and susceptibility to allergies and hay-fever, which were to be a particular problem in the smog of Los Angeles. Tall and long-legged with silky blonde hair and a dazzling complexion, she was always being taken as older than she was; an early date, Charlie Fish, who was seventeen at the time, was shocked when by chance he discovered her birth date scrawled on the path at Henry Avenue and found out that she was only fourteen.

At Stevens Grace discovered that she had a power to attract people which, as the disregarded middle child, she had not realized before. It was a power she exercised quite deliberately throughout her life; she would take immense trouble to acquire and to keep lifelong friends, gaining as much reassurance and strength from her friends as they did from her – perhaps more.

With her looks and her bubbling sense of humour it was hardly surprising that people were attracted to her. Ann Levy Siegel, who was four years younger than Grace, and was the daughter of Jack Kelly's friend Isaac D. Levy, recollects her as a Stevens schoolgirl:

"You never saw such a beauty. . . . The minute anyone met her they wanted to know her more ... In those days she was even more beautiful than in her pictures. The texture of her skin was something else [and she was] always smiling, frisky and vivacious." Marie Magee's strongest memory of Gracie as a child was that "she laughed all the time ... when she was at home she was just giggling and bouncing all over the place."

In contrast, people who did not know her well would describe her as "wooden" in comparison with Peggy's radiant vitality. Grace Kelly would never change: reserved, shy, appearing cold and distant with people she did not know; with her old friends she would revert to being the bubbly Gracie from Henry Avenue, Germantown. And after her death this was how her small circle of close friends from the Henry Avenue days remembered her even in middle age: "She loved being around the people she cared about, trusted and could relax with. At parties she'd be chatting and having fun with them ... she loved to kick off her shoes and just laugh with her old friends." Another close friend from her New York days, Judy Quine, said of her: "She was very serious about life and yet the best giggler I ever knew."

Pictures of Grace in her school yearbook show her as a member of sorority Beta Sigma O. Dressed in sweater, pleated skirt, white socks and loafers, her blonde hair turned under in a page-boy style just above the shoulder, she is certainly the prettiest of the girls, and in all the school photographs she is one of the few whom the local photographer has not succeeded in rendering hideous. In the yearbook for 1947, the year of her graduation, the description beside her photograph reads: "Kell* is one of the beauties of our class. Full of fun and always ready for a good laugh, she has no trouble making friends. A born mimic, Kell is well known for her acting ability, which reached its peak this year in her portrayal of Peter Pan in our Spring Play."

Elsewhere in the book, "Stevens Prophecy" ran: "Miss Grace P. Kelly ... now a famous star of screen and radio." Showing an early sense of style, Grace was noted for her three-quarter-length racoon coat, known as "the mink", but she was still plagued with sinus trouble – her "Favourite Haunt" is listed as "Her Doctor's" and her "Needs" as "Kleenex". She was generally popular – a composite of the "Perfect Senior" included "Popularity – Grace Kelly" – and she

---

* Evidently a school nickname, although all her friends called her Grace.

already knew what she wanted. Her "Ambition" was "Broadway" while, somewhat unkindly perhaps, her "Destiny" was "Soap Opera".

Grace entered Stevens School in September 1943, when she was not quite fourteen, and graduated in the summer of 1947, some four months before her eighteenth birthday. Stevens was a small private inter-denominational girls' school housed in a rambling mansion of brick, stone and timber on Walnut Lane, Germantown, between Green and Germantown Avenues. The girls came from the Germantown area and Stevens, perhaps because of this, was imbued with solid middle-class values and a strong school spirit. The school song, written by a graduate of the class of 1917, included such lines as "Hail, all hail, our Alma Mater, hail" and "Love we yield unto thee, Stevens, thy proud name revere ...". Grace was a member of the Glee Club, took part in the Senior Play in 1945, 1946 and 1947, was on the basketball squad in 1944 and a regular member of the Varsity hockey team from 1944-7, playing hockey, her friend Maree Rambo remembers, with a "gazelle-like run". Her tastes as listed in her graduation yearbook were a microcosm of her era: favourite orchestra – Benny Goodman; favourite female vocalist – Jo Stafford; radio programme – *Dawn Patrol*; movie actor – Joseph Cotten; movie actress – Ingrid Bergman; summer resort (the only one she knew) – Ocean City; drink – a "black and white" (chocolate and vanilla) milk shake, while her favourite food then and always was – hamburgers. Her favourite mood was "sentimental" and her taste in classical music romantic, Grieg's "Piano Concerto" and Debussy's *Clair de Lune*, which her classmate, Doris Snyder, used to play for her on the piano at lunchtime in the barn where they liked to put on records, jitterbug and giggle.

Grace, Doris Snyder recalls, had the most exciting social life of the class and on Mondays the less fortunate girls would be agog to hear what she had been up to over the weekend. At Stevens, Grace had met a girl who would be one of her closest friends throughout her life, Maree Frisby, known as "Friz", who was a year ahead of Grace at school. Described in the Stevens Yearbook as "sophisticated and well-dressed" and "always envied for her striking appearance", Maree shared many of Grace's characteristics – her sense of fun, her kindness, her capability and also her reserve. She and Grace would spend weekends together, frequently double-dating. Penn Charter was the centre of their social life, an old-established school where

Kell went, as did many of their Germantown friends and dates – Charlie Fish, son of a local real estate agent, and Matt Lukens, son of a bedding manufacturer. "Maree and Grace went to Penn Charter with Charlie," Matt Lukens joked: there were football matches, fraternity parties, and dances – Junior Proms, Senior Proms, Varsity Club. The boys would invite the girls and order corsages of flowers from the florist, which had to be carefully preserved in the fridge so that they would not wilt before being pinned to the evening dress that night.

Grace's first love, who dated her when she was only fourteen, was Harper Davis, also a Penn Charter boy. Grace's relationship with Harper was recorded in the Penn Charter Class Diary as early as 20 March 1944 in an entry which reads: "Rumours of a rift between a Buick salesman's son [Harper Davis] and a brickmaker's daughter. The buzzards gather ..." Harper Davis was not only Grace's first love but he also provided her first experience of the illness and death of someone close to her. He joined the Navy after leaving Penn Charter and in 1946 contracted multiple sclerosis, from which he died just over six years later. Matt Lukens, who drove Grace down to see Harper in the Veterans' Hospital at Wilmington, thought that Grace and Harper had been very serious about each other and that their relationship "could have led to something". "There was great fondness on both sides and it was always very strong," he said. No one could be sure; even then Grace did not talk about her private feelings. When Harper Davis died in April 1953 Grace, then on the verge of stardom, returned to Philadelphia for his memorial service.

This tragic experience apart, Grace's teenage years were lived in a happy, innocent world before James Dean and Elvis Presley projected the image of the teenage rebel. The main street of Germantown today bears the tell-tale signs of the ghetto: shops boarded up or protected by metal grills, walls scrawled with graffiti from an aerosol can. Then it was a quiet, safe, middle-class place, where Grace and Maree would go to Darrow's drugstore, with its marble-top counter and soda fountain, brown bar-stools and booths, or else to the Dairymaid on Saturdays for hot roast beef sandwiches followed by shopping in Rowell's department store – all long since vanished. Sometimes they would go downtown to Center City Philadelphia by train to try on hats and shoes, to the distraction of the salesgirls. They would go to the Germantown cinemas – the Bandbox, the Orpheum or the Colonial – to see their favourite films such as *The*

Song of Bernadette, Casablanca, Going My Way, The Lost Weekend, and, if the film was a sad one, Grace would cry her eyes out. Once, with her sister Lizanne and Lizanne's future husband, Donald Le Vine, she went to that outstanding weepie *The White Cliffs of Dover* in the Moorlyn Cinema at Ocean City. As the two girls soaked their Kleenex into sodden shreds, Don Le Vine unbuttoned his shirt and offered them each a side to cry into. As he emerged afterwards with a soaked shirt-front he told them, "I'm never going to take you two to a movie again unless it's Walt Disney." Years later, when Maree with her husband Bud Rambo were at the palace in Monaco watching a screening of *The Country Girl*, the film for which Grace won an Oscar, they heard a quiet sobbing in the darkness: it was Grace.

At Ocean City there would be nights on the boardwalk above the long beach, lined now as then with one-storey frame buildings, restaurants selling salt-water taffy, fudge, pork roll and frozen custard, interspersed with miniature amusement parks and bath houses with lockers and showers for bathers, and Morrow's Nut House with its gleaming antique peanut-roasting machines. The Moorlyn Cinema, where Grace often used to go, is still there, a period piece with a façade designed like the nose of a 1950s automobile. There were no bars, because Ocean City was, and is, dry, and Grace and her friends would go to Matt's to have hamburgers and coke after the movies and dance to the jukebox barefoot on the boardwalk so that they got splinters in their feet. On 9th Street the Chatterbox restaurant is still there, a pink-painted Spanish-style building where Grace and Maree once worked as waitresses until Maree's mother found out they intended to work nights and took them away.

It was a happy, carefree world, but also an enclosed one. Philadelphia, the historic city on the Delaware founded by the Quaker William Penn, was, despite the elegance of its architecture, a byword for dullness. That famous Philadelphian W.C. Fields remarked of his native city, "I went there once, but it was closed," a reference to the absolute dearth of entertainment in Center City on Sundays or even Saturday nights. The story that Fields had inscribed on his headstone "On the whole I'd rather be in Philadelphia ..." is apocryphal but, to non-Philadelphians, apt. In Grace's day Center City was a run-down place: everyone who could afford it had fled to the suburbs.

Philadelphia Society lived in a series of rich, élite suburbs with names like Ardmore, Bryn Mawr and Radnor along the main commuter railway line to the west of Philadelphia. This was the "Main

Line", synonymous with "Society" and the aristocratic origins which Hollywood columnists would inevitably attribute to Grace because she came from Philadelphia, but of which she was emphatically never a part. Proper Philadelphia Society meant old blood and old money; *nouveaux riches* were cold-shouldered; for generations the Irish and the Jews were quite beyond the pale. It was a society with hallowed rituals, the débutante Assembly and subscription balls such as the Piccadilly, and exclusive clubs and associations, the Fish House (The Fishing Company of the State in Schuylkill, founded in 1732) and the Rabbit, the Rittenhouse and the Racquet. The Kellys and their friends lived in a different world from the aristocrats of the Main Line, the Biddles and the Montgomerys with their estates and their family traditions stretching back two hundred years or so. Grace's contemporaries in Main Line Society knew nothing of her until she became famous and even then she did not enter their circle. Once she was invited to the exclusive Piccadilly subscription ball, but as an "out-of-town guest" although she was a native Philadelphian. Grace's father, a power in the city, rich, charming and popular, was well known and well liked in Society, but his wife and daughters were not invited to Society parties. The Kellys were not in the *Social Register*.

The Kellys appear not to have cared about this social exclusion. "I don't think she minded that at all," Prince Rainier said. "She was eager to go to New York and do her drama school ... eager to work and to get on." The Kellys had their own social circle, which was not limited to Irish contractors and politicians or to the Kellys' Germantown neighbours, but which went beyond the confines of Philadelphia to the entertainment worlds of New York and Hollywood.

Jack Kelly's great friend was Isaac D. Levy, one of the founders of CBS with his brother Leon Levy, who was married to William S. Paley's sister. The Levys lived nearby at 3333 Schoolhouse Lane and their house would always be full of show-business people from New York or California – Sam Goldwyn, Dinah Shore, Doris Day, Sammy Cahn, Bill and Babe Paley and the big agents like Mike Nidorf, who later married Louis B. Mayer's widow Marina, and Manie Sachs, then of Columbia Records, later of RCA Victor, discoverer and friend of Frank Sinatra. Sinatra married Ava Gardner in Manie's brother's house in Philadelphia, and when Ann Levy married Herbert Siegel in 1949 Sinatra sang at their wedding. This may well have been the first occasion on which Grace met her future friend and co-star, for a family photograph shows them both at the wedding reception. Manie Sachs was close enough to the Kelly family to be honoured with the title "Uncle"; immensely liked and respected in the entertainment world, his advice and contacts would be of considerable help to Grace in her future career.

For a girl like Grace, born into an affluent middle-class family, a career was not considered essential or even necessarily desirable. College and/or marriage were expected to follow on graduation and Grace's mother had been exceptional in her desire for a career. By the time Grace graduated from Stevens in the summer of 1947, her sister Peggy had already been married for three years to George ("Gabby") Davis and had had her first child. Grace's contemporaries in Philadelphia Society would be buying long white kid gloves for their début at the Assembly Ball. Grace, principally to please her parents and to do as the other girls did, tried for Bennington College in Vermont. According to one tradition, she flunked because of her poor marks in mathematics, but Marie Magee, Ma Kelly's friend, who was in a position to know, says that Mrs Kelly had neglected to make sure that Grace applied in time. According to Marie, Mrs Kelly and Grace made a fruitless tour of several New England women's colleges before ringing her up and coming over to her apartment off Broadway on West 55th Street.

"We can't get into any college. What are we going to do?" asked Mrs Kelly.

"Well," Marie replied, "what do you want to do, Gracie?"

"Aunt Marie," she said, "I wonder if I could get in the American Academy of Dramatic Arts?"

Grace must have been thinking of trying for the Academy as soon as she left Stevens. She was, in a neighbour's words, "determined to be an important figure in an important family", to prove herself in her own way. In this achievement-orientated family Kell was now the star. That summer of 1947 Jack and Margaret Kelly, with Grace and Lizanne, had flown to England to watch Kell realize his father's dream by winning the Diamond Sculls. "At last," John B. Kelly Senior wrote in his autobiography, "after twenty-seven years of waiting and hoping, the name of John B. Kelly was on the Diamond Sculls." For Grace, acting was to be her own way to achievement.

As Grace well knew, if she wanted to get into the American Academy, "Aunt" Marie, an actress herself, would help her. Marie's daughter, also called Marie, had been a student there, and the Academy was then at Carnegie Hall, only two blocks away from the Magee apartment. Marie took Grace to see Emil E. Diestel, Secretary and Treasurer of the Board of Trustees of the Academy. Diestel's response on being introduced to Grace was discouraging: "Mrs Magee, I can't take her. Our registration's closed'.'

"Mr Diestel, you have to hear her read."

"I can't," Diestel told her. "We don't have one spot in the school for her."

Grace was then sent to wait outside. "Look, Mr Diestel," Marie said, "this child's father and George Kelly are brothers, and she is coming by this naturally."

George Kelly's name and Marie Magee's forcefulness were enough to make Emil Diestel weaken. "I'll see what I can do," he said before calling Grace in and giving her her "sides", thirty pages of her Uncle George's play *The Torch-Bearers*, which she was to learn for audition the following afternoon.

Grace spent a sleepless night in the bed next to Aunt Marie's before the audition in front of Emil Diestel at three o'clock on the afternoon of 20 August 1947. Diestel's report, annotated "niece of George Kelly", is worth recording. Grace, aged seventeen, was 5'6½" in height and weighed 126 lbs, her colouring is described as "blonde" and her physical condition and personality as "good", her stage presence "very good". Her voice, in contrast, came in for criticism – "not placed", "improperly placed", "very nasal". Her reading of the parts was considered "intelligent", while for spontaneity, versatility, characterization, distinction and pantomime Diestel gave her "good youthful symptoms". "Dramatic instinct" was awarded a "yes", "intelligence" was "good", and "imagination" was "positive". "Lovely child", Diestel noted, "should develop well".

Grace was registered for the Academy as an October Junior for 1947-8. Her father's not very encouraging comment was, reported Alice Waters, "Let her go. She'll be back in a week." As usual he underestimated his second daughter's capabilities and her determination. Grace would not be back in a week; in real terms she would never go back. Four months before her death she wrote to Marie Magee, "You have seen it all from the beginning – when I spent the night (rather a sleepless one) with you before my audition with the Academy." It was indeed the beginning – of a spectacular career.

PART TWO
On Stage

4
New York Beginning

Grace arrived in New York a shy teenager in a twinset with two major ambitions: to discover and shape her own life and personality, and to succeed as an actress. "I had to find out who I was," she observed of her decision to leave home for New York. "She was seeking to create a life away from the Kelly environment," her friend Bill Allyn said, "to evolve her own style, manner of speech, manner of demeanour, and sense of herself ... she made her choices, she learned ...." New York with its pressures plunged the girl from Germantown into an adult world. "Even before I was twenty", she said, "I sometimes used to feel very old. That was always when I learned the truth about people or things. It used to make me feel very frightened." In New York the Kellys could no longer protect her from life.

Indeed, she did not want their protection; she wanted to learn. She was, as Bill Allyn said, "like a giant sponge" in her desire to absorb everything she could and to learn her craft. She wanted, above all, to succeed, and it was her Kelly heritage which gave her the confidence that she could do it. "She once said to me, 'I am going to be the greatest film star that Hollywood ever saw'," Bill Allyn remembered. "And it wasn't out of ego. She said, 'My father was an Olympic oarsman, my brother too, my uncle was a Pulitzer Prize playwright: whatever the Kellys do, they have to do well.' It wasn't done in a braggadocio way, but that's why she studied, that's why she worked, that's why she did television shows, she did everything she could do to learn her craft."

The American Academy of Dramatic Arts was housed on various floors in the Carnegie Hall building on 57th Street and Seventh Avenue, a run-down survivor from a previous era with high-ceilinged, cream-painted corridors, festooned with unconcealed pipes, which then, as now, were a rabbit warren of dance studios. Vice-President and dictator of the Academy was Charles Jehlinger, familiarly known as "Jelly". A student in the first class of the Academy in 1884, he had been Director of Instruction there since 1900 and only retired in 1952. He was a brilliant director, a little white-haired man who called everybody, whether high or low, "Boy", and everybody, as former student Homer Poupart recalls, was afraid of him because he was "fierce, severe and his standards were very high". Jehlinger was a friend of Grace's Uncle George and, says Homer Poupart, took a great deal of trouble with Grace on her uncle's account. Like Uncle George, he was a stickler for manners and decorum, and laid stress on behaving like a gentleman or a lady. "In the theatre it was always Mr and Mrs," Poupart said. "Students had to be properly dressed, no dungarees, no lounging about, everything done with proper decorum. In fact, once he was directing Colleen Dewhurst and he said, "Do it like a lady." Dewhurst asked, "So, what's a lady?" Jehlinger replied, "A lady is a woman who would do anything, but only as a lady would do it."

Jehlinger and the Academy put the development of character and personality first. "The study and practice of the means and modes of expression are important," runs the General Statement in the Academy's prospectus for 1947–8, "but the discovery and development of the powers of human nature itself are more so." The Academy was not cheap at $500 a term, a considerable sum in the late 1940s; this did not include play-books, make-up materials and what the prospectus described as "exercise rompers and sandals", which cost about $20. The course was a rigorous one, intended, the prospectus declared, completely to occupy the student's time for at least six days a week. Classes were devoted to all forms of pantomimic expression, vocal expression and stage expression; there were corrective and formative classes for the body, fencing and dancing classes; there was the life class in which, Bettina Thompson Gray, fellow student and friend of Grace, remembers, "we learned exercises and body and lunging and walking around ... with our tails tucked under, our shoulders down, not back, my dear, but down". Life classes tended to be hysterical affairs. "I mean you're supposed to be blind, or you're a baby or an amoeba and you're just beginning to come into action and to reach out, feel and all this kind of thing. You have to keep your eyes closed and I opened mine and I got hysterical laughing watching these other people crawl around the floor."

Aristide d'Angelo taught vocal and speech training, which included what was known as "English diction". "It takes a trained ear to detect all errors of pronunciation, accent and emphasis, but by careful and persistent criticism the dialects of Pennsylvania or New England, of Canada or the South, are at last dethroned and the speech which accords best with the best standards is substituted," the prospectus announced. Grace had received bad reports on the quality and sound of her voice at her audition; Mr d'Angelo succeeded admirably in "dethroning" her Philadelphia accent and smoothing her tones, so that three years later her voice sounded so mellow that it was described as "cream of tomato soup" and by the time she reached Hollywood, hard-bitten journalists were bowled over by it – "Her voice was a knock out," one commented.

Grace was not only well aware that her nasal Philadelphia accent would not do for the stage, but she was also conscious of the weaknesses of her voice and later took voice production lessons from a friend of Marie Magee's called Mario Fiorella. The Academy was content to "smooth out your accent so that you would have an American one that could not be placed", Grace's friend and fellow student Sally Parrish Richardson said. Grace went further and invented her own accent. "She was always very aware of what she needed to do. She was a perfectionist absolutely in whatever she did." Her accent became a soft transatlantic one, a sound that Americans would call "British". When asked how she achieved this transformation from her native Philadelphian, Sally Richardson answered, "Just common sense and a good ear, she had a wonderful ear for accents, she was great at mimicry." Not for nothing was Grace the niece of two uncles who had excelled in vaudeville.

In addition to transforming her voice, she also learned how to make up and dress herself to effect, skills that would be of great use to her both as a star and as a princess. The Academy prided itself on the thoroughness of its make-up course, even commissioning specially designed kits from Elizabeth Arden for its pupils. Grace, as her sister Lizanne affirmed, became "very clever at make-up" as a result of her Academy lessons. She learned how to match her make-up to her light colouring in a style that was all her own and owed nothing to fashion. She realized early that her colouring and delicate features would not stand dramatic make-up. She did not follow the 1950s fashion for heavily mascaraed eyes, startling lips and darkly defined eyebrows, and, later in life, she avoided the trap that older

47

women often fall into of piling on more make-up as the years go by. The result was that Grace's looks remained natural throughout her life and therefore never went out of style.

"The actor and actress should know how to dress with fitness, good taste and sincerity," the Academy prospectus declared, "as well as with a knowledge of harmony and contrast in color and of suitability to one's own figure and physical characteristics." In Hollywood, Edith Head at Paramount and Helen Rose at MGM would both be impressed by Grace's knowledge of clothes and her sense of what was right for a scene or an occasion, as years later would be Marc Bohan at Dior when she was Princess of Monaco.

During the two years she studied at the Academy Grace lived at the Barbizon Hotel at 140 East 63rd Street. The Barbizon, a magnificent building of the late 1920s, was a legend in New York; its inestimable advantage in the eyes of wealthy, respectable, out-of-town parents like the Kellys with daughters in New York was, in the words of writer Sylvia Plath, who portrayed it as "the Amazon" in *The Bell Jar*, that it was a place "for women only ... mostly girls my age with wealthy parents who wanted to be sure their daughters would be living where men couldn't get at them and deceive them".

Men were not allowed in the hotel after 10 pm and never in the girls' living quarters. Although there were male elevator operators during the day, in the evening they would be replaced by heavily-built ladies in prim dresses who sat sternly, arms crossed, in the lobby to deter any predatory male. According to a former inmate, there were further checks to make the male exclusion system fail-safe: "At about 7 am very quietly someone would look in and see you were there – and by yourself – and shut the door, and when asked about this curious practice they would say, 'Oh, just seeing who's here.'"

Girls needed three good references to be admitted as guests of the hotel and their rooms were far from luxurious: they were small, painted pink, green or blue, and equipped with bed, desk, armchair and a chest of drawers. Few had bathrooms; for most girls these facilities would be down the hall. The architecture of the public rooms was, however, splendid. In Grace's day the entrance lobby resembled a Hollywood set of a Tudor mansion with beams and a pillared gallery, and on an upper floor there was an oak-panelled recital room with an organ, a grand piano, a stage and a bay window with stained-glass panes. According to the hotel brochure for 1941, organ recitals were presented there every afternoon "while complimentary tea is served to residents and their friends". The hotel was run as a cross between a boarding-school and a ladies' club; there was a swimming-pool, a gym and a library, as well as a dining-room and a "cozy Veranda Room – a balcony with lacy ironwork and flower gardens painted against azure sky" – and a bar at which, the brochure admitted, "no attempt is made to push the sale of alcoholic drinks"; as a result it barely broke even. Tea parties, bridge, concerts, and recitals were organized; and all this was for a room price of some $12 a week.

The Barbizon, according to an article in *Time*, "harbored the greatest concentration of beauty east of Hollywood", its residents being largely aspiring models and actresses like Grace. Among former inmates when Grace arrived were Joan Crawford, Gene Tierney, Lauren Bacall, Barbara Bel Geddes and Dorothy McGuire. Photographs of the Barbizon taken in the 1940s show girls with long page-boy hair-styles, carefully crossed legs and wooden expressions, in a time capsule of cocooned safety.

Grace and two other girls from the Academy lived in this protective cocoon. Grace shared a room with Jean Drouillard of Cleveland, while Bettina Thompson, being congenitally untidy, was relegated to a tiny room on her own. She can recall very little of their life at the Barbizon beyond dancing in their slips in the corridor to old Fred Astaire records. The manager at that time, Mr Hugh Connors, remembers Grace as very shy and keeping herself to herself: "I used to see her in the dining-room most nights sitting alone with her glasses on and reading a book through her dinner."

Grace's days were spent either at the Academy classes or working as a fashion and photographic model to help pay her way. Her parents, beyond providing her keep at the Barbizon, were not generous in their allowance to her, perhaps because they secretly hoped she would give up the big city and return to Philadelphia. But Grace, in her father's words, "had always been hipped on the subject of independence" and she was determined to make it on her own. Despite her looks, finding work was not easy; there were many pretty girls around and the competition was fierce. Grace worked hard, pounding the streets, going to all the "go-sees", as auditions for models were called, and by her second year at the Academy she was earning enough to keep herself without her parents' assistance.

49

She worked as a fashion model for between $7.50 and $25 an hour, as a photographic model, doing fashion shorts for newsreels, and in television commercials for cigarettes, skin cream, beer and vacuum cleaners. Her clean, girl-next-door looks brought her cover assignments for *Cosmopolitan* and *Redbook*, but she was not dramatic enough for high fashion and not sexy enough for commercial photographers. Richard Leeds, president of Manhattan's Thomson-Leeds advertising agency, remembers that "she wasn't any good". "We hired Grace Kelly as the 'Convention Girl' for Old Gold [cigarettes]," he recalled. "We paid her $2,000 – an astronomical sum in those days. We photographed her in a short skirt, but she refused to let us use those pictures because she thought it was beneath her. She'd only allow us to use a photo of her in a long skirt. She was supposed to stand next to a full-length photo of herself in the long skirt and be flirtatious with the men who came over to her. That was her job. But she seemed to be saying, 'It's okay to look, but don't come near me.'" Grace herself later admitted she was "terrible" in the Old Gold commercials, and a still of her at the time shows her dressed in a strapless New Look dress and long black gloves proffering a tray of Old Gold with a strained grin and an unhappy look in her eyes. She refused to do lingerie advertisements; she might need the money but there were limits beyond which she would not go. As William Disesa, who gave her her first commercial modelling job in 1948, spraying a room with insecticide for the Bridgeport Brass Company, said, "From the moment you looked at her and heard her speak you realized she didn't have to be posing with a spray can for a living."

Meanwhile Grace's career at the Academy was going well; at the end of April 1948 she was judged good enough to go on to the Senior Course from 15 September until 15 March 1949. The Senior Course was organized as the Academy stock company and the students rehearsed a new act or play each week, to be performed on Friday afternoons either in the Lyceum Theater at Carnegie Hall or in another Broadway theatre. The climax of the Senior Year was a series of performances in Carnegie Hall. Grace played the lead in *The Philadelphia Story* in the role of the spoiled golden girl from the Main Line, Tracy Lord, the same part in which she was to star in MGM's musical *High Society* six years later. She appeared in her favourite play, George Kelly's *The Torch-Bearers*, although the role she always hoped to play, Mrs Pampinelli, was given to another girl. She was also seen in *Stage Door* by George S. Kaufman and Edna Ferber, and *My Sister Eileen* by Joseph Fields and Jerome Chodorov.

Grace was beginning to attract attention as an actress and as a person. "Grace was very popular," Sally Parrish Richardson recollects. "She was popular because she was very responsive, she wasn't 'ra-ra', but she would do what she had to do and was very faithful in her assignments and very conscientious and very much as she went at everything in her life, to do the best that she could." She had, said Sally, an eye for detail and an amazing memory for the lines of plays she had done – "All you would have to do was mention it and she was off and running." She attracted the particular attention of Frances Fuller, who taught her Shakespeare, and would later, through her husband, Worthington Miner, introduce Grace to live television drama. She also attracted the attention of one of her directors, Peter Richardson, who telephoned a well-known agent, Edith van Cleve of MCA, who was to guide Grace's early career and that of another star, Marlon Brando. Richardson, Edith van Cleve recalled, "telephoned me that he had a lovely looking girl whom he thought had great potential for pictures and he thought that I ought to see her. She was going to play that afternoon in *The Philadelphia Story*. I went to see her and I agreed with him one hundred percent. She was lovely looking, dressed beautifully, moved well, spoke well and had everything that I thought would eventually be right for pictures."

Peter Richardson had more than one reason for bringing Edie van Cleve to see Grace; no doubt he was impressed by her acting potential, but he was also in love with her. He was to be the first in a long line of men to meet with the Kelly family's disapproval. The treatment meted out was icy: "They got the message after the first hello," said Lizanne.

Richardson directed Grace in her Senior Year; he was older than she, sophisticated and with a great knowledge of the theatre, all qualities calculated to appeal to the unsophisticated Grace, eager to learn about her profession and about life. Richardson was a prototype; there was often to be a strong element of Pygmalion-Eliza in Grace's relationships with men. Mrs Kelly did not like him, neither did the Kelly men; a New York theatre type, uninterested in athletics and with designs upon Grace, was bound to be in for a rough time in Henry Avenue. Grace invited Richardson for the weekend in Philadelphia. A story related by Kell to biographer Gwen Robyns almost certainly relates to that particular time. Mrs Kelly, quite ruthless, where in matters she thought her children's interests were concerned, told Kell to bring over on Friday night "three of my bigger and better-looking friends ... One was the Olympic Butterfly Champion and looked a bit like Kirk Douglas and the other was a big-looking guy, a weightlifting type,who was my partner in rowing races and was also a lifeguard at Ocean City. There was another guy, also, a big, tall, swimming type ... I gave them the word that this fellow was a bit of a creep, which I had deduced from my mother's description. When they came into the room they gave Grace's guy the grip and in a second had him on the floor."

Grace punished her brother for this ill-mannered stunt by refusing to speak to him. She was living at home at this period, having been summoned back from a Richardson-haunted New York, which meant leaving Philadelphia by the 7 am train and returning home at about 7 pm. Often she and Kell found themselves having dinner alone together; for a month, according to Kell, they ate in silence: "It took a long time before she forgave the rest of my family too." But Grace, despite her resentment, was not strong enough, or fond enough of Richardson, to withstand her family's disapproval, and dropped him.

One episode, above all, highlighted what Prince Rainier was to call Mrs Kelly's "mother-hen" protective instincts, the saga of the Shah of Iran. Grace was the Shah's escort for a week during his visit to New York, a delightful duty arranged, it appears, by family friend Manie Sachs. She went to the opera with him, enjoying playing the role of princess when everybody stood up for them as they entered. "It was her first taste of it," a friend recalled. Grace and the Shah were indefatigable as far as New York night-life was concerned; Grace told a friend that the Secret Service men who accompanied them were so worn out by the hours they kept that one evening they pleaded, "Miss Kelly, could you please stay home tonight, we're exhausted." The Shah gave Grace an enormous silver-framed portrait photograph of himself, which dominated her small room at the Barbizon, and he also sent her some jewellery via Van Cleef & Arpels. His generosity to Grace was reported in the morning newspapers and all the alarm bells rang in Henry Avenue. By 10.30 am, according to Marie Magee, an outraged Mrs Kelly was in Mrs Magee's apartment.

"Get Grace on the telephone. That jewellery – did you see about that jewellery? Get her on the telephone, tell her I want to see her right away."

Marie telephoned Grace. "Gracie, your mother's here."

"Oh, Aunt Marie, what happened?"

"I don't know, she wants to see you, come over."

Grace got in a cab, went over and walked in.

"Gracie! Where are those jewels?"

"Mother, they're in the bureau drawer."

"The bureau drawer. What are they?"

"Oh, they're three pieces of jewellery."

"You mean you took pieces of jewellery?"

("Well," Marie commented later, "Mrs Kelly, she was raised as I was. You took a book, flowers or you took a box of candy. Nothing more.")

"You go get them!" said Mrs Kelly.

"Oh," Gracie said, "Mother . . ."

"I said, go get them and I'm sitting right here till you return. Get in a cab and come back and bring them, I want to see them. Your father says they have to go back."

Grace returned with the jewellery – a solid gold vanity case eight inches long with thirty-two large diamonds in the clasp, a gold bracelet watch with a dome of pearls and diamonds covering the watch-face, and a pin in the form of a gold bird-cage containing a bird "with a diamond body that was at least as large as my finger-nail", remembered Marie.

"You've got to give them back," Mrs Kelly said.

"Mother, I can't give those back."

"Well, you've got to. I'm going to sit here till those jewels go back to that Shah. Your father says they've got to go back. I say they've got to go back."

"Mother," Grace replied. "One does not refuse a king. . . ."

Grace won, and kept the jewellery until her engagement to Prince Rainier. Gradually she was asserting her independence, drawing away from Philadelphia, becoming a part of New York, making a new circle of friends. "Grace fell in love with New York," Lizanne said, describing her friends there as "a good group". The group included two girls from her year at the Academy, Bettina Thompson and Sally Parrish, the darkly beautiful Carolyn Scott, who was a model and roomed at the Barbizon, and a young actor Donald Buka, who, like the others, was to remain a friend for life. Prudence Wise, a cheerful Southern girl whom Grace also met at the Barbizon, later acted as her secretary-companion. After classes they would get together in the Russian Tea Room, then a less sophisticated rendezvous, next door to Carnegie Hall.

Grace left the Barbizon and, after a spell commuting from Philadelphia, she moved into a small apartment in Manhattan House at East 66th and 3rd Avenue, a new apartment building built with Kelly bricks. The building was still being completed when Grace moved in. Mrs Kelly and Marie Magee, on their first visit to inspect and advise on the apartment, found the lobby floor covered with planks and Grace, with a scarf round her hair, up a stepladder in the kitchen polishing. Mrs Kelly and Marie helped buy furniture for the apartment, which had a living-room with large windows and a terrace facing south, one bedroom, kitchen and bath. Sally Parrish moved in to share with Grace, because "her mother had wanted her to have some French companion or someone to give this aura of respectability". Grace and Sally shared the bedroom and there were times when Mrs Kelly would arrive and despair at the disarray. "I remember one time", Sally recalls, "when Mrs Kelly said, 'Oh, Gracie, I hope when you get married you have someone to pick up after you!' – and Grace said, 'I hope so, Mother.'"

"We had wonderful times," said Sally, remembering the stratagems to which Grace resorted in getting rid of unwanted beaux. There was an older man who was very keen on Grace, and "she just wasn't interested at all", so the two girls put their heads together to work out "how in the world we could put a squelch on this". The plan was to have a party at which Grace would pretend suddenly to have become engaged to Richard Aherne, an Irish actor friend of theirs. Grace was wearing Sally's mother's engagement ring and "acting very lovey-dovey with Richard". Everyone at the party was in on the joke except Grace's victim, who was enraged and grabbed her over the drinks. "How could you throw away your life on this Irish actor?" "I just love him. I just have to do it," Grace apparently replied.

Another time there was a "rather stiff, stodgy, very conservative type who was very boring and very persistent", and so the party to get rid of him was organized as a fake seance: "Everyone arrived, the lights were out, and everything was pitch black. The furniture had been pushed on one side and she had asked her friends to come and lie on the floor, covered with sheets, and a candle was burning, and this man walked in and she pretended that this was all very serious and all very much part of her life. Well, that got rid of him."

Initially, Grace's career prospects seemed bright. She won a part straight out of the Academy in the early summer of 1949, hired by the Bucks County Playhouse producer, Theron Bamberger, to appear in stock (repertory) at the theatre in New Hope, Pennsylvania, not far from Philadelphia. Here she met an actress who was to become a great friend, Natalie Core O'Hare, who had been invited to Bucks County to play in *Accent on Youth*. "There", said Natalie, "was this beautiful creature and she was shy as a mouse and scared to death of the leading man, who was this beast who had star ideas about himself." The actor apparently resented the fact that Grace was George Kelly's niece and assumed that it was because of this that Grace had been given the part, "so he actually intimidated her so that she couldn't learn her lines". Natalie coached Grace on the side, cueing her lines and giving her confidence. "Don't let him make you nervous," she told Grace. "You're good in this and you're lovely to look at, and you know what you're doing, so just ignore it." On opening night, Natalie records, "Grace walked on the stage and nobody looked at the leading man."

Grace spent the summer at New Hope, playing once again in *The Torch-Bearers* and *The Heiress*, and that winter she had her first Broadway chance in Strindberg's *The Father*, a grim play in which a Swedish captain of cavalry is driven to madness and eventual death by his iron-willed wife, who, in order to control the upbringing of their daughter, insinuates in his mind the belief that their daughter is not his own. Raymond Massey, who not only directed but was to play the role of the father, had the task of auditioning twenty-one girls for the part of his stage daughter. Grace, he said, "was number two and by the time she left she had the part". Apart from being "just about the most beautiful youngster I ever saw", she was "a lady", which was very important in the role. Moreover, when he talked to her, he discovered she had done her homework. "I thought that she was extremely knowledgeable about the character and talked very intelligently about it." The play tried out in Boston, where Grace celebrated her twentieth birthday, and opened at the Cort Theater in New York on 16 November. Grace received a favourable mention from Brooks Atkinson, the *New York Times* critic: "Grace Kelly gives a charming, pliable performance as the bewildered, broken-hearted daughter," and George Jean Nathan went even further, damning everyone but Grace: "Only the novice Grace Kelly, convincing as the daughter, relieves the stage from the air of a minor hinterland stock company on one of its off-days." *The Father* staggered through the Christmas season dependent on benefits but closed after two months, a bitter disappointment for Grace.

It was to be over two years before she succeeded in winning another part on the Broadway stage, a long, hard road paved with many disappointments. "I read for so many plays I lost count of them," she later told an interviewer. "People were confused about my type, but they agreed on one thing: I was in the 'too' category – 'too tall', 'too leggy', 'too chinny'." Her first brief film appearance seemed to do nothing to help her. In the summer of 1950 she had a small part in *Fourteen Hours*, directed by Henry Hathaway for Twentieth Century-Fox, a film based on a real life drama of 1938 when a young man jumped to his death from a ledge of the Gotham Hotel. Grace appeared briefly as "Mrs Fuller", a neatly dressed young woman in black suit, pearls and pillbox hat with a veil who is seen discussing divorce plans with her lawyer as the suicide drama takes place opposite. It was also her first brief taste of Hollywood, where she stayed in the Beverly Hills Hotel chaperoned by Lizanne and the Isaac Levys, and met her future leading man, Gary Cooper, on the set at the Fox lot. *Fourteen Hours* received favourable reviews, but Grace was not mentioned and her only tangible reward from the film was a mink stole which she bought from her earnings. MGM offered her a stock contract, as did other studios. "I wasn't interested," Grace said. "I could earn more modelling. I wanted to try my luck on Broadway."

Grace was single-minded, unimpressed by the empty glamour of being a minor slave in a Hollywood studio stable; she was determined to make her way as an actress and to make it on her own. She refused to ask Uncle George Kelly for help, nor would she allow her father to contact any of his many show business friends on her behalf. One story is typical of Grace's determined independence of her parents; it happened on the occasion of the Boston try-out for *The Father*, when her father and mother were there. "We had called Grace," Mrs Kelly recalled, "and told her to invite the cast over to our hotel for supper after the show. When Raymond Massey arrived he was delighted to see Jack – Massey used to row for Toronto and all old oarsmen know each other. But he didn't understand why Jack was there. It took him several minutes to realize that he was Grace's father, for Grace hadn't said a word."

The result of such determined independence was a catalogue of disappointments for Grace, at least as far as Broadway appearances were concerned. Jean Dalrymple, who ran the large City Center Theater, remembers wanting Grace to play Roxane in their production of *Cyrano de Bergerac*: "I loved her gentleness and her lovely cultivated voice and speech, and thought she was ideal for the Lady Roxane." But when she told the leading man, José Ferrer, that she planned to use Grace he was very much against it: "Oh, my dear, she's an amateur. I don't think she can play the City Center. She's pretty enough, but she's an amateur." Undeterred, Jean Dalrymple persisted, and asked Mel Ferrer to coach Grace so that by the time José arrived from California Grace would be ready. Both of them worked hard for the great day when the star arrived to audition her. Disastrously, Grace had a cold. "We were in the fourth row and we couldn't hear a word," Jean remembers. "Joe yelled, 'Speak up!' She started coughing and that made her worse." Jean tried to smooth things over, saying what bad luck it all was for Grace. "That's not bad luck," Ferrer said grimly, "that's an amateur." Of course he was right; Grace was lovely and dedicated, but she was still not a good actress.

Milton Goldman of MCA remembers an even earlier disappointment when he tried to persuade Gilbert Miller to cast Grace for the *ingénue* role in the Broadway version of *Ring Round the Moon*. Having met Grace through the recommendation of Arnold Hoskwith, talent spotter for Warner Brothers films, Milton was impressed with her and thought she would be ideal for the part, so he took her over to see Gilbert Miller. Asking Grace to wait outside, Miller told Goldman politely but firmly, "I like your ideas, but I don't think she's had enough experience for this role." Later, Miller turned her down again, this time for *Gigi* and Audrey Hepburn got the part. Many years afterwards Grace told Morton Gottlieb, once Miller's General Manager, that she wondered if her life would have been different had she played in those two shows on Broadway. Joshua Logan auditioned her for a part in *The Wisteria Trees*, and his reaction was the same as Miller's – gloriously beautiful, but not experienced enough. It was not until January 1951 that Grace managed to land a role in a play that was destined for Broadway, Lexford Richard's *Alexander*. The play opened in Albany, New York, but Grace was not a success in the role and was replaced by Betsy von Furstenberg when the production moved to Broadway.

Like most young actors and actresses at the time, Grace was forced to use live television drama as a vehicle for her talents. Fred Coe, an important television producer, saw her in *The Father* and cast her in her first television role in *Beth Meriday*. From her début until she became the hardest-working actress in Hollywood, Grace acted in some one hundred television plays. She acted in CBS's drama series *The Web* in 1950, as did names like Paul Newman, Jack Palance and Eva Marie Saint; in *Treasury Men in Action*, a crime series featuring such names as Lee Marvin, Jason Robards Jr and Charles Bronson; and in *Suspense*, another CBS series. She also played in the *Prudential Family Playhouse* and the *Nash Airflyte Theater* series, which were relatively shortlived, and worked for the big two, *Philco Playhouse* and *Kraft Television Theater*, whose productions featured actors like Rod Steiger, Lee Remick, James Dean and Anthony Perkins.

In those days television was an exciting and demanding medium for actors: scripts would be changed at the last minute and the programmes were broadcast live. Rita Gam, who first met Grace when she was playing Dulcinea in Sidney Lumet's television production of *Don Quixote*, described it as "like shooting the rapids – you only had one chance and if you didn't make it you might end up at the bottom". As an actress, Grace could still be rather wooden; Sidney Lumet is reported to have complained of her lack of warmth – "she has no stove in her belly". But even then the camera loved her and personally she had what Fred Coe described as "style": "She wasn't just another beautiful girl, she was the essence of freshness – the kind of girl every man dreams of marrying." Rose Tobias Shaw, who joined CBS in 1950 and worked with Grace on *Danger*, remembers how impressed they all were by her beauty, poise and manners. "We treated her differently than the run of the mill," she said. "We knew she didn't need the money, and she was so sweet." Grace's ladylike behaviour contrasted strongly with that of other potential stars:

> We used to throw James Dean out of the office, he took a paper cup and we thought he was being a dunce standing in the corner with it but he was urinating into it. Marlon Brando wasn't much better. . . . We all envied her because she was rich and she dressed

exquisitely – she was our inspiration and the girls who were fair like she was copied her. She used to wear full skirts with cinched waistlines and her hair parted in the middle with a ribbon bow at the back.

It was Rose who described Grace's voice as "soft, a mellifluous, cream-of-tomato-soup voice".

But for Grace it was not enough just to get work because she was rich, beautiful, a lady and photogenic. She believed, because of her passionate interest in astrology, that as a "double Scorpio", born with Scorpio rising, she would achieve great fortune, but only through hard work. Her shyness and personal inhibitions made acting hard for her, but she was determined to learn and to succeed as an actress. If she could not find work on Broadway, then she would find it out of town. In May 1951 she landed the role of the *ingénue* Isabelle in *Ring Round the Moon*, for which Gilbert Miller had previously rejected her, at the Ann Arbor Drama Festival. Donald Buka played the leading man and among the young actors was William Allyn, destined to become one of her most constant friends. He was impressed by her dedication and her sense of destiny: "She very much longed to be an actress, she knew she was going to be a star, and everybody knew that ... you didn't have to be a seer to know that, because she was incredibly beautiful and worked hard."

Grace moved on to join the resident repertory company at the oldest and one of the most prestigious of America's summer stock theatres, Elitch Gardens in Denver, Colorado. The theatre, founded in 1890 and situated in a large amusement park in Denver, was owned then, as it is now, by the Gurtler family, who had interviewed and signed Grace in New York that spring. Grace, who had already had two movie offers, went to Denver in June at a modest salary of $125 a week, on the advice of her agent, Edith van Cleve, who thought she needed the acting experience before facing Hollywood. The work was hard and the living conditions modest. The ten actors of the company were expected to do ten plays in eleven weeks – a "rather gruelling schedule", Whitfield Connor, now producer of the company, then its leading man, recalls: "It was a question of forgetting one, rehearsing another and playing a third." Grace lived in one of the simply furnished rooms in a nearby house used by the actors of the company. She opened in *For Love or Money* and among the seven plays in which she appeared was, again, *Ring Round the Moon*.

She was well liked by the company and by the Elitch Gardens audience, Whitfield Connor remembers: "She was not a really seasoned actress, but she had a cool beauty, breeding and intelligence. As an actress she had already learned a most important lesson – what *not* to do."

For Grace that high summer of 1951 was a moment of great significance and in many ways a beginning, the threshold of a new life. At twenty-one she was about to embark on two important experiences – her first adult love affair, with a young fellow actor, Gene Lyons, who was also in Denver, and her first leading film role. On 10 August she received a telegram from producer Stanley Kramer: "Can you report Aug. 28, lead opposite Gary Cooper, tentative title *High Noon.*"

5
Grace and the King

Grace was cast for *High Noon* on the strength of a photograph and a young agent's recommendation. Jay Kanter of MCA became interested in her through Edith van Cleve. "Edie sent me some stills, talked about her, gave me a brief résumé of what she was doing and Grace kind of intrigued me," said Kanter, "and so I talked to the people at Stanley Kramer's company." Kanter had the confidence of the *High Noon* team, Stanley Kramer, producer, Fred Zinneman, director, and Carl Foreman, scriptwriter – he was the agent who had brought them the young Marlon Brando for his first film role in *The Men*.

"Kanter came round and said that he knew there was a part of a young Quaker bride", Zinneman recalls, "and that there was a young girl who was very pretty and had talent, working at the time in Denver in summer stock. And he produced a photograph of her and she looked very attractive." Kanter, Zinneman said, was an agent whose word you could trust and, what was important, Grace would not demand a high salary. "She was a new face and she had the kind of quality from the photograph that I thought was important ... with a kind of inhibition about it, very strait-laced and very virginal." When Grace flew in from Denver, Zinneman was the first to interview her and was astonished and delighted by her demure appearance – "the first actress I ever interviewed who wore white gloves", he said later. Otherwise the interview was halting: "I'm not terribly good at small talk", Zinneman admitted, "and she was terribly nervous. I would try to talk to her and she would answer 'yes' or 'no'."

Grace, her friends always said, led a charmed life. She was, as she herself recognized, lucky. Gary Cooper's performance as her husband, Marshal Will Kane, was central to the film's success, and *High Noon* began Grace's tradition of always working with the best directors and male stars.

At first Zinneman was worried by the great age difference between Grace, then twenty-one, and Cooper, who was well over twice her age, but as it turned out the contrast between his stern, lined looks and Grace's smooth, young face heightened the drama of the film. "Coop" was fifty when he played in *High Noon*, at a low ebb in his private life and professional career, and his health was poor. Temporarily separated from his wife Rocky, he was having a difficult affair with Patricia Neal, which was soon to end; he suffered from back trouble and, as if all this were not enough, after the shooting ended it was discovered that he had an ulcer and needed a hernia operation. Cooper played Will Kane as himself, almost without make-up, the pain and tension he was suffering etching lines on his face which made the role even more convincing.

Cooper was one of the few among Grace's leading men who did not fall in love with her, but, as one of the most sophisticated and certainly the best-dressed stars in Hollywood, he appreciated her qualities. "I thought she looked pretty and different," he said. "And that maybe she'd be somebody. She looked educated, and as if she came from a nice family. She was certainly a refreshing change from all these sexballs we'd been seeing so much of." Grace was chaperoned on location, in the country near Sonoma in northern California, by Lizanne, and the two Kelly girls enjoyed being driven round in "Coop's" sporty silver Jaguar, searching the mountain country for a good steak dinner.

Years later, when Grace was a big star, Hedda Hopper asked Cooper whether he had recognized her potential in *High Noon*. Cooper would only say, "I knew this: she was very serious about her work ... had her eyes and ears open. She was trying to learn, you could see that. You can tell if a person really wants to be an actress. She was one of those people you could get the feeling about." In other words, he thought that she had the potential to be an actress but, as far as *High Noon* was concerned, she was not one yet. Grace herself, when she saw the rushes, was unhappy with her performance in *High Noon* and felt that she was too inexperienced to get the direction she needed from Zinneman. She would have been mortified had she known that it was precisely her inexperience and lack of skill which appealed to the director. There was not a great deal any actor could have done with her part, Zinneman said, it had no dimensions to it, "but Gracie at that time wasn't equipped to do very much ... she'd just come out of school, so to speak". As far as he was concerned her failings as an actress gave the part of the marshal's Quaker bride the realism he was looking for. "She was very, very wooden ... which fitted perfectly, and her lack of experience and sort of gauche behaviour was to me very touching – to see this prim Easterner in the wilds of the Burbank Columbia back lot – it worked very well." Had he tried to give her more direction, he said, "I would have had an actorish performance, which was the last thing in the world I wanted, because I wanted the whole thing to look like a newsreel."

High Noon was a classic Western, the story of one day in the life of the small town of Hadleyville, where the retiring marshal, Will Kane, married that morning, awaits the arrival of a gunman bent upon revenge. The townspeople refuse to help him and his wife, as a Quaker, cannot support violence but at the climax of the duel in the main street she suddenly appears to take his side. *High Noon* restored Cooper's career, winning him an Oscar, but Grace failed to impress. Alfred Hitchcock, later to become the key director in Grace's career, saw the film and thought her performance "mousy" and for most men her quiet prettiness was eclipsed by the colourful sensuality of Katy Jurado as the gunman's mistress.

High Noon was the beginning, but, as Grace had the intelligence to see, it could easily have been the end of her Hollywood career. "After I saw *High Noon*", she told Hitchcock's biographer, Donald Spoto, "I thought, God, this poor girl may not make it unless she does something very quickly ... I was horrified. I rushed back to New York and started taking classes again. ... When we graduated from the Academy we'd sit and practise how we were going to sign our autographs. It was only a question of time – we were right there. There was nothing between me and stardom except a few city blocks." At nineteen it had all seemed so easy; now Grace, on the eve of her twenty-second birthday, realized that it was not, and that you have to take control of your life and make your own chances. Still immature as an actress and as a woman, Grace returned to New York, with both her confidence in herself and her faith in her destiny badly shaken, to work with Sanford Meisner at the Neighborhood Playhouse and to pursue her love affair with Gene Lyons.

"Sandy" Meisner was one of the three great teachers of the "Method" school of acting which had such a deep influence on the technique of the young stars of the 1950s like Paul Newman and Marlon Brando. If you were a serious actor, it was the done thing to take classes with Sandy Meisner even if you were working. "We weren't students," Bill Allyn said. "It was a professional class." Grace, comparing her performance in *High Noon* with Cooper's, observed, "When I look into his face I can see everything he is thinking. But when I look into my own face I see absolutely nothing. I know what I am thinking, but it just doesn't show." She meant that she was not yet capable of giving interior feelings outward expression. Working with Meisner would change that: as Allyn said, the "Method" school "deals with interior behaviour". Sandy Meisner later said that at the time he recognized that Grace was still "undeveloped as an actress", but that he felt she had real talent and would go on to do better and better things. "She was one of the most serious and hard-working students I ever had," he said. "She had an unusual personality – engaging, warm, appealing. She is a person you respond to immediately. She is sensitive and willing to learn."

Grace was learning about acting and expressing herself; at the same time she was also learning about love. Gene Lyons was her first serious love affair after her teenage romance with Harper Davis, now slowly dying of multiple sclerosis in the Veterans' Hospital in Wilmington. Lyons was almost the same age as Grace and, like her, he came from a Pennsylvania Irish background, the difference being that her Philadelphia parents were rich while the Lyons from Pittsburgh were poor. He was slender, tall and rangy with an abundance of reddish blond hair and finely moulded features. He had a stylish way of wearing his clothes, the overcoat always with the collar turned up. Like Grace, he had presence – when he came into a room, you noticed him. He was fun, charming and gentle, said Lee Grant, the actress with whom he had been in love previously, but he had a biting wit and high standards about people. Like Grace, he did not give his affections easily and, like her, he was reserved, private and secretive about himself. He was, as she was, passionate about acting and was a member of the Actors' Workshop on 6th Avenue.

In Denver, where they first met in the Elitch Gardens stock company, it was obvious to everybody that they were fond of each other, but, perhaps, nothing more. A leading member of the company recalls that "Grace and Gene spent a lot of time together – it was, to say the least, a romance. I cannot say it was an affair, let alone a serious affair. Grace was much too circumspect for that." Back east after *High Noon*, however, Grace and Gene made no attempt to conceal their passionate love – "they were just besotted with each other", a contemporary remembers, and they were often to be seen together, starry-eyed, in the Russian Tea Room. They talked of getting married and Grace went home to Philadelphia to tell her mother, "I think I'm in love." Mrs Kelly, always on the *qui vive*, had seen them both together in Denver and did not believe Grace was as serious as she claimed. Grace told her mother that "since she had gone out on her own she had found that her Philadelphia friends who were not in the theatre no longer interested her as much as they once had. Some of them told her frankly they thought she was foolish to want to be an actress." Gene, she said, was exactly the opposite – "He not only knew how she felt, but he felt the same way. He kept telling her that they could be stars in the theatre together, that they would stimulate each other to success and fame." Gene confessed the same thing to his closest friends. "He said he was really in love and that this was it ... at last he could step out and be himself." Alas for young love, the reality turned out to be very different.

On 10 February 1952 Grace and Gene played out in public what in some ways was to be the story of their love. They both appeared in *The Rich Boy*, a Scott Fitzgerald story adapted for *Philco Television Playhouse* by Walter Bernstein. Grace played Paula Legendre, débutante daughter of a wealthy California family, while Gene had the role of the rich boy of the title, Adson Hunter, spoiled scion of an East Coast dynasty. "From the beginning", runs the narrator's voice, "they were in love with each other." They meet at a party – "You drink a lot, don't you?" says Grace/Paula in her soft, creamy voice. Gene/Adson is entranced by her, and indeed Grace's beauty and sexiness comes through even the grainy tele-recording of early television. She is not yet the cool, groomed beauty of her Hollywood image; she is a little plumper, like a lovely calf in looks, with full lips, the strong jaw more apparent, her hair severely side-parted and drawn back in a bun. They become instantly engaged but Adson, drunk and self-destructive, misbehaves and Paula's mother disapproves. "You and Paula have been engaged for five minutes," she tells him icily, "and after what's just happened a slight separation might be a good idea." Adson continues to behave badly and Paula, on the rebound, marries a smooth nobody from Palm Beach, and later a man whom she genuinely loves. Meeting Adson by accident, she taunts him, "You see I am in love at last. I was only infatuated with you."

Mrs Kelly, like Mrs Legendre, thought Gene an unsuitable match for her daughter. She had detected an instability in his character –

about which she was later proved correct – and she had discovered that he had been married, although he was in the process of obtaining an annulment. Sadly, Gene certainly had a self-destructive element in him. When, just over a year later Grace dropped him for Jean-Pierre Aumont, he never recovered. He began drinking heavily and his acting career, which had been progressing so brilliantly, went gradually downhill. This may partly have been due to the strain of success – "Gene had a fragile psyche," a friend commented. "He was a very good actor, but he wasn't comfortable on centre stage." He had been a "golden boy", had enjoyed a rapid rise from his poor Pittsburgh background and was thrust into prominent roles. "Then, suddenly, the thing with Grace was over and so was he." While Grace's star continued to rise, Gene's dwindled. He played a supporting role in the *Ironside* television series and died an alcoholic down on his luck in 1975.

Although Grace was, with Rita Gam among others, named as one of the six busiest actresses on television in May 1952, the Broadway success she yearned for as her affirmation as an actress continued to elude her. In April Guthrie McClintic cast her in a new comedy, *To Be Continued*, which opened in Boston on 8 April and in New York at the Booth Theater on 23 April. The publicity handouts must have annoyed Grace deeply, describing her as "daughter of John B. and niece of playwright George". As far as the world of theatre public relations was concerned she had not yet made it on her own. *Variety* described her one scene as the Bryn Mawr undergraduate daughter as "played with real style", but the play was an inadequate drawing-room comedy and turned out to be yet another Broadway flop for Grace.

Meanwhile, on the West Coast, *High Noon* was gathering in no less than four Academy Awards, and Grace's connection with the Oscar-winning film was to prove the foundation for her future career. As a result of *High Noon* she was called in by Gregory Ratoff for a screen test for the film *Taxi*, which he was to shoot for Twentieth Century-Fox. Grace, on her way to a class with Sandy Meisner, was dressed for work in an old skirt and shirt, no make-up and hair uncurled, when the Fox New York office called her. When she arrived there, other girls, immaculately dressed and made up, were waiting and so was a representative from her agency, MCA, who was embarrassed at his client's appearance. Gregory Ratoff, on the other hand, was delighted.

"Perfect," he said. "What I like about this girl is she's not pretty."

Outraged, Grace's agent interrupted, "But, Mr Ratoff, she is pretty."

Ratoff would not be deflected. "No, no, she's not," he snapped, and to Grace, "Take off your coat." The sight of Grace's old clothes pleased him even more. "Magnificent," he declared. "Can you speak with an Irish accent?"

"Of course," Grace replied.

After the test, Ratoff very much wanted Grace to play the role of an immigrant Irish girl who bewitches a New York taxi driver, but his California bosses turned her down in favour of Constance Smith, who was already under contract to the studio. Grace was bitterly disappointed, as she later told Donald Spoto: "I was very eager to play it, as it was a one-picture kind of deal ... at that point in my career ... I wasn't really anxious to do picture work too much because it meant signing a seven-year contract with a studio, which I was trying to avoid, and this picture *Taxi* that was being done in New York had a very nice script and was a good part for me. ... I didn't get the part but that particular test won me two other parts." The *Taxi* test changed Grace's life: two great directors saw it and liked what they saw – John Ford and Alfred Hitchcock.

Veteran director John Ford was the first to recognize Grace's potential – his reaction to the *Taxi* test was, "This girl can act," and he invited her to test for a part in a big-budget African adventure film, *Mogambo*, for MGM starring Clark Gable and Ava Gardner. *Mogambo* was to be the turning-point in Grace's career, the film that was to launch her, aged only twenty-four, as a star. Grace's instinct, on which she placed so much reliance, told her that for this film she must drop her objection to seven-year contracts, that the chance to work with John Ford and Clark Gable on location in Africa was not to be passed up. Even then her reaction to the glittering prospect held out to her was cool and entirely individual. Before she flew to California to test for the part of Linda Nordley, the young English wife of a scientist on safari, Harry Friedman of MCA informed MGM that "there is one outstanding point which Miss Kelly has insisted upon and that is that Miss Kelly desires a limitation of three pictures per year during each year of the term contract ... it has been agreed that at the end of the second year of the term contract and at the end of the fifth year of the term contract, Miss Kelly has the right to return to the stage". Grace, even then, had no intention of being swallowed up by the Hollywood machine; success as a stage actress was still her principal goal and she regarded films as a means to that end. On 3 September 1952 Grace arrived in Los Angeles at MGM's expense to test for the part of Linda. John Ford and the producer, Sam Zimbalist, were satisfied with the result and Grace was signed at $850 a week.

Excited, Grace sat down to write to Bill Allyn, in the style of J. D. Salinger's then current cult novel *Catcher in the Rye*, which Allyn had given her for Christmas. "Sit down, catch your breath, I have some wonderful news," she wrote. "I'm going to do a picture in Africa with Old Clark Gable and Old Ava Gardner directed by Old John Ford." Then, within a few days of Grace's casting at the end of September, there was a serious hitch which almost destroyed her hopes of doing *Mogambo*. The film was an MGM British production and – apart from Ford, his assistant, the cameraman Robert Surtees and the three principal stars – the entire cast and crew were to be British. Moreover the film was to be shot on location in Kenya, Tanganyika and Uganda, which were then British colonies, and Grace, in order to work there, would need a permit. On 30 September Ben Goetz cabled from MGM at Borehamwood, asking for full data on Grace. "We expect resistance from Equity who will object to work permit on grounds part should be played by an English girl and unless she is well known star negotiations will undoubtedly be prolonged." Glumly the studio replied: "Only Motion Picture Credits High Noon Co-Star with Gary Cooper small role Quote Fourteen Hours Unquote Twentieth Century only other credits very important TV engagements." On 16 October, the day John Ford left London for Africa, they received the unwelcome news that the actors' union, Equity, had indeed objected to the granting of a work permit to Grace. MGM panicked; Zimbalist cabled Goetz telling him that if the ruling went against Grace he should make every effort to persuade Virginia McKenna, who had been tested for the part and had turned it down, to reconsider "even if we have to reimburse producer of her show for her release and possibly give her bonus for playing part". One anxious week later the crisis was somehow resolved; Grace's work permit was granted.

Mogambo was a remake of a 1932 Jean Harlow vehicle in which Gable had played the same part. Rewritten by the original scriptwriter, John Lee Mahin, and re-located in Africa from the original Malaysian rubber plantation, *Mogambo* was a torrid tale of two

women – the prim English Linda, played by Grace, and the glamorous lady of easy virtue, Honey Bear, played by Ava Gardner,
competing for the affections of Gable as the owner of an African
animal farm against a magnificent Technicolor background of African scenery, charging rhinos, gorilla hunts, menacing natives, etc.
The picture was to be more true to life than producer Sam Zimbalist
had imagined when he conceived *Mogambo* as a follow up to his
previous African success, *King Solomon's Mines*. The natives, or
rather some of them, were indeed menacing, for it was the period of
the Mau Mau guerrilla campaign against the white settlers of Kenya;
and, on a more personal level, Grace did indeed fall for Gable.

Gable, known in Hollywood as "the King", was the idol of millions
of women all over the world who had seen him as Rhett Butler in
Gone With The Wind. With three failed marriages and the tragic
death of his beloved wife Carole Lombard behind him, Gable's career,
like that of Grace's previous leading man, Gary Cooper, before *High
Noon*, had seemed to be slipping, and, unlike Cooper, his personal life
was often filled with booze and one-night stands. Nonetheless, as
Louella Parsons wrote in an ecstatic welcome for the film which was
to re-establish Gable's career, he was still "Hollywood's own king of
hearts". "Clark isn't always agreeable," she wrote. "He is not a fast
man with a buck. He is frequently lazy, and doesn't like to give interviews or dress up for parties. He often takes a few snorts too many.
But his warmth, charm and simplicity make you forgive him anything ... Clark is letting his hair go grey now," she concluded. "He's
grey in *Mogambo*. But he's still the great lover, off screen and on."

Gable was not a man who went in for platonic relationships, and
Grace was a romantic and passionate girl who had already fallen in
love with him in *Gone With The Wind*. Now he was her leading man
with a script full of suppressed passion and an exotic African background. Philadelphia was far away and Grace was on her own for the
first time – even the hyperprotective Kellys would not send a chaperone as a supernumerary on location to Africa. Whether or not it
was a physical affair, it developed into a friendship, and, as a romance,
it seems to have been one-sided. "Grace was very keen on Gable and
I guess he knew she liked him a lot," said one observer, adding
unkindly, "Grace was only a one-night stand for Gable ... she was
not really his type at all." Nor, under normal circumstances, would
one have said that he, apart from being Clark Gable, was Grace's
type of man. Generally popular with everyone, from stars to the

humblest member of the crew, he was, according to his friends, "a very direct, honest, very sweet person" but, even on his best friends' assessment, no conversationalist. As Ava Gardner quipped when someone asked her what Gable was like: "Clark? He's the sort of guy, if you say, 'Hiya, Clark, how are ya?' - he's stuck for an answer."

Grace could hardly have been more different from Gable's previous women - his great love, Carole Lombard, or the sexy waitresses and night-club girls he used to assuage his loneliness and his needs. Gable was not in love with her, but he was attracted by her and genuinely touched by her qualities. "She's an extraordinary girl, your friend," he later told Rupert Allan, recounting two stories about Grace on location which, he said, had touched him very much. When he went out on location in the African countryside Grace, even though she wasn't needed for filming, instead of staying in bed like Ava and the other actors, would often get up early and ride beside him on an uncomfortable wagon over miles of rutted dirt tracks in the heat.

"It's hell for me to bounce for miles with the bugs and the mosquitoes and everything - why do you do it?" he asked Grace one morning.

"Oh, I want to see things," she replied. "I want to have stories to tell my grandchildren."

On another occasion, when he had been out on location all day, Gable came back to the hotel where they were staying not far from the Indian Ocean to find no Grace. Someone told him she had been seen earlier that afternoon, walking with a book towards the sea. Gable was concerned; because of the Mau Mau guerrillas they had been instructed not to wander far from the hotel, so he followed the trail down to the shore, where he saw Grace sitting on some rocks against a long expanse of beach. She had a book open on her lap and she was crying. Startled, Gable ran down to her. "Why are you crying?"

She replied, "It's the most beautiful thing in the world. I'm reading Hemingway's *Snows of Kilimanjaro* about the leopard in the snow, and I looked up and I saw a lion walking along the sea-shore."

"She saw a lion walking along the shore and she wasn't frightened," Gable said wonderingly. "She was crying because it was so moving."

Publicly Grace and Gable would behave with great decorum. At the New Stanley Hotel in Nairobi, where all the crew and actors stayed, the wife of a crew member recalls them being "like a little old married couple – they would sit there eating ... he wearing glasses and she wearing glasses. They didn't look very glamorous." Indeed Grace could look frumpish at times. "She used to go round the hotel plain-looking and wearing glasses and we thought 'Poor little Grace Kelly ...' but when the Governor gave a cocktail party she dressed up and looked beautiful – all the men were around her and Ava Gardner was nowhere."

Yet, despite their discretion, people inevitably gossiped. Gable received a cable from a London newspaper columnist which read, "Rumours sweeping England about your romance with Grace Kelly. Please cable confirmation or denial." Gable's reaction, Grace told a reporter sweetly, was, "This is the greatest compliment I've ever had, I'm old enough to be your father," and this was to be the line both of them took – in public. Grace called Gable "Ba" – Swahili for father (she had actually taken the trouble to learn Swahili before arriving in Africa) – while Gable told the questioning Louella Parsons, "She's only a kid ... she should never have been allowed out without a chaperone." The most Grace would admit to was, as she told Anita Colby, having a "crush" on Gable, complaining ingenuously that "Hollywood can't seem to understand the degrees of a man-woman relationship." But Hollywood understood that very well; what it did not understand was the code of a Philadelphia gentleman, by which well-brought-up young ladies did not go to bed with men until they were married, a code which absolutely forbade "kiss and tell". Or, as "Jelly" Jehlinger had put it, "A lady will do anything, but only as a lady does it." Grace had normal sexual appetites and she was liberated enough in the context of her time to defy her middle-class Catholic Philadelphia upbringing to satisfy them if she felt the romantic urge to do so, but breaking the rules in private did not mean publicly advertising the fact. The cool blonde in white gloves was an image which suited Grace perfectly, a protective shield behind which the real, warm, sexy Irish Grace could operate in privacy. She was not promiscuous; each affair was a love affair, a starry-eyed romance which justified her following her instincts and helped her gloss over the fact that this was not the way well-brought-up Catholic girls in the 1950s were supposed to behave. Everything she did in private remained a closely guarded secret, because Grace was the kind of person who evoked absolute loyalty from lovers and friends – even after her death. It was a code of honour as rigorous – and less often broken – than that of the mythical Knights of the Round

Table. Later in life, when Grace was asked to compare her leading men, she replied, as the highest praise she could give, that "every one of them was a gentleman", and they in return, when asked what they remembered of Grace, would invariably mention the word "lady".

That Grace's code of behaviour was not Hollywood's was amply demonstrated by the legally married pair Ava Gardner and Frank Sinatra, who were together on location. Married for just a year and still deeply in love, they quarrelled incessantly. Much of the tension between them was caused by their careers – Ava was an actress much in demand, while Sinatra was at the lowest ebb of his professional life. Dropped by CBS from television and recording contracts, "box-office poison" in Hollywood and – the final indignity – dropped by his agents, MCA, his whole future career seemed to rest on the doubtful chance of playing Maggio in Columbia Pictures' projected *From Here to Eternity*. Sinatra was on tenterhooks over the part, flying a round trip to Los Angeles at his own expense to do a screen test of fifteen minutes with no promise of a contract. Grace, at first, was shocked by the couple's utter lack of restraint, contrasting it unfavourably with Gable's, who, she wrote, "is such a gentleman and nice to everyone and easy to get along with". But "Ava is such a mess it's unbelievable. Right now they are putting up a new tent for her – she just didn't like the other one because it was old – her tent is right next to mine – so I can hear all of the screaming and yelling." But Gable and Africa were widening Grace's horizons and, despite the "screaming and yelling", she and Ava and Frank became the closest friends and were to remain so throughout her life.

Christmas was spent on location in Uganda beside the Kagera River, where MGM made lavishly sure that stars and crew would not suffer too much in the bush. The stars' tents were equipped with bed, desk and chair and an extension complete with full-length canvas bath, with hot water provided morning and night, and a servant assigned to look after the tent and launder the clothes. An enormous generator provided electrical power for two huge entertainment tents with table tennis, darts and card tables and a cinema with twin sixteen-millimetre projectors showing a different film every night, and twelve mess/restaurant tents. Turkeys, champagne and Christmas puddings were flown in in the unit's Dakota DC3 and Sinatra sang at the Christmas party. While Frank gave Ava a diamond ring and a mink stole, Grace hung up for Gable a huge stocking filled with things she had filched from his tent.

The unit gave a party for the British Governor of Uganda, Sir Andrew Cohen, and his wife, at which Ford attempted a crude tease of Ava.

"Ava," he said, "why don't you tell the Governor what you see in this 120-pound runt you're married to?"

"Well," replied Ava, "there's only 10 pounds of Frank but there's 110 pounds of cock!"

Ford turned pale – "I'll never talk to that girl again" – but the Governor apparently loved it. Though Grace laughed at Ava's outspoken put-down, she was shocked and embarrassed on another occasion by Ford's uncouth behaviour at Government House in Entebbe, where the Governor had invited director and stars for the weekend. Gable and Donald Sinden, who played Grace's husband, equipped themselves with white dinner jackets from the wardrobe, while Grace and Ava took evening dresses, and the party flew up to Entebbe in the unit's Dakota. Ford, Irish-born and fiercely anti-British, arrived alone and late, appearing on the veranda of Government House, where the immaculately dressed party were taking tea with the Governor. Ford was dressed in creaseless, baggy, grey trousers, an ancient sports jacket, a washed-out blue shirt, dark blue tie with a dripping-egg motif on it, plimsolls on his feet and a baseball cap on his head. As Donald Sinden remarked, he must have borrowed the outfit purposely, because he was never seen in it again. At six the Governor suggested it was time to dress for dinner. "Dress for dinner?" said Ford. "This is all I've brought with me." After the briefest hesitation, Sir Andrew announced, "Very well. We will not dress for dinner." Grace, Sinden said, was particularly upset by Ford's behaviour, because she felt that he was letting down the Irish.

Ford was a great director, but an abrasive character who tended to treat his stars roughly and with scant respect. Sinden, who was on the receiving end of his anti-British prejudice, found him "the most dislikeable person I have ever met" and despite their initial enthusiasm for each other, Ford and Gable did not get on. According to Ford's nephew Dan, Gable "was careful, methodical and a notoriously slow study who didn't like spontaneity and change" and Ford's methods of direction did not suit him. Ford for his part was infuriated by Gable's passion for hunting and expeditions with Norman Read, their safari guide, into the Mau-Mau-haunted bush. Grace, more pliable and eager to learn, found working with him "quite an education". Once, while Ford was instructing the other

73

actors as to what he wanted them to do, Grace took it upon herself to move to a position indicated by the script. "Kelly, what the hell are you doing?" Ford screamed at her. "Well," Grace faltered, "in my script it says she walks over here . . ." He ran across the room to her, livid. "We are shooting a movie, not the script," he told her.

Ford was feeling irritable; he was ageing and his vision was becoming increasingly blurred by two as yet undiagnosed cataracts. In Tanganyika he came down with amoebic dysentery, and he was worn out by coping with the sheer scale of the picture and its sixty-seven-day shooting schedule. The problems were endless – with the heat, the dust, the weather, the animals and the hundreds of tribal extras, some of whom were imported from Angola and the Congo. A truck overturned, killing a young Englishman, John Hancock, aged only twenty-six, and when cameraman Robert Surtees tried to shoot a scene of a rhino charging Gable in a jeep, the animal attacked the camera truck instead. A crucial scene involved the capture of a black panther. When it was belatedly discovered that such animals were not to be found in Africa, one was hired, sight unseen, from an American zoo, but on delivery, says Sinden, "it proved very old, and nearly bald on its back. The make-up department was therefore required to spend hours sticking on false hair. Even then it refused to snarl. This we attributed to it probably being toothless." By late January 1953, Ford had had enough of Africa. Leaving a second unit to shoot the remaining animal scenes he flew to London to complete the film there.

Grace spent two months in London finishing *Mogambo* at MGM's studios at Borehamwood. It was her first experience of being treated like a star, staying at the luxurious Savoy Hotel and being escorted by MGM's top publicist, Virginian-born Morgan Hudgins. Rupert Allan, later to become her trusted aide, met her there for the first time. American-born, but educated in France and at New College, Oxford, where he won a rowing Blue, he was then editor-writer of *Look* magazine on the West Coast and was in London to cover the Coronation of Queen Elizabeth II.

In America it was already being rumoured that Grace Kelly was about to become a big star, but the girl Allan saw in the Savoy looked like an attractive college girl, with horn-rimmed glasses, dressed in a very English way in tweed skirt, sweater and brogues, and with the demure manner of a well-bred women's college graduate. Later, sitting on the floor of Ava's rented house in Hyde Park Gate, drinking champagne on a Sunday morning, he saw the real Grace Kelly behind the prim, "preppy" exterior. "She was very relaxed", he said, "because she knew all these people, she'd been working with them. And she told marvellous stories, especially about Ava, and she shocked Clark with stories he didn't know ... post-location talk."

For Gable and Grace it was the end of the affair. On 15 April 1953 Gable drove Grace to Heathrow Airport to catch a plane for New York. For the first – and the last – time, she gave reporters a public spectacle of her emotions. Grace – as they wrote gleefully – wept "a torrent of tears", but Gable, the old pro, gave the assembled reporters nothing to write about. He was still "the King", the masterful, masculine lover, and he was not prepared to play "father" roles even to a girl as lovely as Grace.

With the experience of a physical affair behind her which was also her first, and last, experience of being dropped by a man, Grace flew back to New York to find what her agent described as "a great big rumble going on about her". "How does it feel to be an overnight success?" Sinatra had wryly asked her when they were still in Africa. Rumours of her romance with Gable, her acting and her cinematic impact had been sweeping through show-business America and, as Bill Allyn, who escorted her to the Kraft Television Theater Ball at the Waldorf Astoria, confirmed, "There was a great furore about this beautiful, about-to-be-huge movie star" – except, it would appear, at MGM. The studio which, as Grace was to tell Hedda Hopper two years later, had "made such a fuss about signing her" after she returned from shooting *Mogambo* "couldn't have cared less about me ... and didn't know what the furore was about". "They seemed to want to hide the fact that I was in the picture," she said bitterly. "They called me into the New York office after I got back from Africa to show me a magazine layout. They were raving about what they were going to do with the picture. It was a 'Glamour in Africa' story. They had all the other people in the company – not a word that I'm along, not a mention of my name."

Grace's affair with Gable surely must have weakened Gene's hold on her affections by the time she met Jean-Pierre Aumont in the early summer of 1953, after her return from filming *Mogambo*. Aumont, a popular, dashing, French actor, attractive to women, was ten years older than Grace and a widower, his first wife, actress Maria Montez, having drowned after collapsing in her bath two years before. He and Grace met as co-stars in a television biography of the celebrated American ornithologist, Audubon; Grace, Aumont recalls in his autobiography, treated him with distant politeness refusing his invitations to lunch until, after four days, he finally succeeded in making her laugh and "the ice was broken". Although Aumont insists in gentlemanly fashion that they were "the best of friends", contemporaries remember that Grace dropped Gene for Jean-Pierre and that they had a brief romance until he left for other acting commitments and she for Hollywood. They were to meet again in a blaze of publicity two years later.

Whether the studio recognized it or not, as far as Grace was concerned the antennae of the film world were pointing sensitively in her direction. When *Mogambo* opened early in October 1953 it was well received and, although Gable and Gardner were the stars and took the major share of the reviews, Grace's notices justified the "rumble" about her. *Films in Review* praised the way "she, Director Ford and the cinematographer Surtees enable us to watch desire contend with integrity among the lineaments of that lovely face", while *Newsweek* was particularly perceptive:

> ... as [Ava's] rival, Grace Kelly makes one of the loveliest patricians to appear on the screen in a long time. Her particular quality is the suggestion that she is wellborn without being arrogant, cultivated without being stuffy, and highly charged emotionally without being blatant. It is a rare quality among the glossily packaged Hollywood beauties, and suggests that she might play some of the leading modern bewitchers – such as Daisy in *The Great Gatsby* ... She should enjoy a fine career.

"Emotionally charged without being blatant": the ability to convey sexual passion beneath a cool and cultivated exterior – the secret of Grace's magnetism both on and off the screen – was already apparent in *Mogambo* – apparent, that is, to those whose perceptions were particularly attuned. Alfred Hitchcock, searching for a leading lady to replace Ingrid Bergman, who had left Hollywood for Europe and Roberto Rossellini, had seen Grace in *High Noon* and found her "mousy". Grace's decision to set to work on improving her acting abilities after *High Noon* and to go for the part in *Mogambo* were rewarded. Hitchcock had seen the *Taxi* test and was interested; he saw a preview of *Mogambo* and was convinced. He wanted Grace Kelly.

76

6

Golden Girl

Hitchcock would make Grace a star, transforming a twenty-three-year-old actress of promise into Hollywood's golden girl. It was his image of her which cinema audiences would see and with which they would fall in love. Master film-maker that he was, Hitchcock understood the key role of fantasy in pictures and a great part of his success lay in his ability to project his private fantasy in a way that audiences could share and see as their own. Grace conformed perfectly to his ideal of a classy blonde whose cool exterior hinted teasingly at a hidden warmth and passion; it was these qualities in her which he alone recognized and had the ability to bring out. He did not create Grace; he had the perception to place her in the right setting so that, to use his own words, "she blossomed out" for him.

In just over a year Grace was to star in three major pictures for Hitchcock, *Dial M for Murder*, *Rear Window* and *To Catch a Thief*, but she was also during that same period to play the leading female roles in *The Bridges at Toko-Ri* and *The Country Girl* for William Perlberg and George Seaton, and in *Green Fire* for MGM. And this, moreover, was at a time dubbed "the frightened fifties" by cinema historians, when Hollywood was in a state of panic as audiences dropped sharply after the heyday of the forties. The challenge of television was beginning to bite hard and the movie moguls' answer was to make bigger, but fewer, pictures, cutting down on staff and salaries. In March 1954 MGM was to drop two of its biggest stars – Greer Garson and Clark Gable – and the prevailing mood in Hollywood was unusually hysterical even by its own high standards; the persecution of left-wing writers and actors by the House Un-American Activities Committee added to the general insecurity, fuelled by financial fears and falling audiences. "Fear", Grace told an interviewer, "covers everything out here like the smog."

It was against this unstable background that Grace was to carve out her film career, becoming the actress most in demand. While

77

other actors would do almost anything to get work, Grace made sure that she got the best parts with the best directors. She tackled Hollywood with the same cool-headed determination with which her father had won his rowing titles, treading her way carefully, although not always successfully, through the minefield of personal and professional jealousies, guarding herself as best she could against the sharp knives of the Hollywood wives and the gossip columnists, the vitriolic Hedda Hopper and the gentler but no less eagle-eyed Louella Parsons. Fortunately, Grace was no longer the gauche, prim Easterner which Fred Zinneman said she had been in *High Noon*. At twenty-three she was now a better actress and a more mature person. Sandy Meisner had improved her acting; New York, London and Africa had broadened her experience; Gene Lyons, Gable and, recently, the sophisticated Jean-Pierre Aumont had taught her about life. She had lost ten pounds in weight and gained a good deal in self-confidence. She was ready for Hollywood and Hitchcock.

On 13 June 1953 Harry Friedman of MCA formally notified MGM that Miss Grace Kelly had entered into an agreement with Warner Brothers to play Margot Wendice in *Dial M for Murder* for a minimum guaranteed eight weeks' engagement commencing on 9 July, compensation to MGM being a suggested $1,050 a week. Since the studio, as Grace had bitterly noted, had no plans for her, Hitchcock had obtained her for Warner Brothers for the duration of *Dial M*. The film was to be based on Frederick Knott's play and Knott was to supervise the script, Ray Milland was to play Tony Wendice, Grace's unscrupulous husband, Robert Cummings her lover, and John Williams the Detective-Inspector. *Dial M* was essentially a melodrama, in which Tony Wendice, the husband, discovers that his rich wife, Margot, has been having an affair. Afraid of losing her money if she leaves him he blackmails a disreputable former school-fellow into agreeing to kill her. The would-be murderer bungles the attempts and is himself stabbed by Margot in self-defence with a pair of scissors. She is arrested and charged with murder, but saved at the end by the alertness of the detective and a slip-up over the door keys by Wendice.

To Hitchcock's intense indignation, Warner Brothers insisted that *Dial M* should be shot in 3-D, the latest Hollywood fad, which, it was hoped, would stem the drift from the cinemas to television. Hitchcock, who had wanted to shoot the film in black and white, getting his dramatic effects from lighting and camera work, was, according to Grace, terribly encumbered by the huge camera necessary for three-dimensional film. As he sat on the set waiting for the monstrous machine to be manoeuvred, he liked to talk to Grace about his next project, *Rear Window*, which he was to make with James Stewart. For, although he was notorious for regarding actors as "cattle", Grace had already succeeded in winning Hitchcock's confidence and respect.

Professionally he found her the most co-operative actress he ever worked with, and he came to respect her judgment on wardrobe, which was always for him an important part of the image he wanted to create. For the murder scene, when Margot gets up in the middle of the night to answer a telephone call set up by her husband so that the murderer can step from behind a curtain and strangle her as she does so, Hitchcock wanted her to wear "a fancy velvet robe" for the effects of light and shadow on the velvet. Grace argued that no woman would take the time to struggle into "this great fancy robe" if she were getting up to answer a ringing telephone in her apartment – "I'd just get up and go to the phone in my nightgown," she told him. The scene was shot as she wanted it, and after that, Grace told Donald Spoto, "I had his confidence as far as wardrobe was concerned. He gave me a great deal of liberty in what I would wear in the next two pictures."

Always conscious of the effect of clothes and make-up, Grace "got into a fight" with the make-up man, who insisted that she wear a great deal of rouge – "Mr Warner likes a lot of rouge," he said. "She's just been imprisoned, she won't have rouge on, for heaven's sake," Grace told him. "I'm not going to put on rouge and if Mr Warner scolds you, tell him that I threw a fit and wouldn't have it."

Grace got on well with Hitchcock professionally and personally. "Working with Hitchcock was a tremendous experience and a very enriching one," she told Spoto. "As an actor, I learned a tremendous amount about motion-picture making. He gave me a great deal of confidence in myself. And also I have great affection and admiration for him, not only as a director but as a human being as well. ..., I have such affection for him and his wife that he can do no wrong." Hitchcock found that he could not play games with Grace, that there was a Kelly toughness beneath the ladylike exterior. Deliberately he tried to throw her off balance by telling Milland crude stories in front of her. "He turned to me and he said, 'Are you shocked, Miss Kelly?'" Grace remembered. "I said, 'No, I went to a girls' convent school, Mr

Hitchcock, I heard all those things when I was thirteen.' And of course he loved that sort of answer."

Hitchcock was a great gourmet and his wife Alma a superb cook; he was delighted to discover that Grace too loved food and she and her chaperone, Lizanne Kelly, were often invited up to the Hitchcock house on Bellagio Road for dinner at weekends. Hitchcock lost 40 pounds working on *Dial M*, slimming down to 219 pounds by cutting out lunch in favour of a cigar; Grace too dieted conscientiously, never drinking alcohol during the week because, as she told Hedda Hopper, she put on weight easily, but at weekends at Bellagio Road one very stiff dry martini would be followed by excellent wine and, according to Lizanne's recollections, "course after course of marvellous food".

Dial M was Grace's first leading role; although, as *Time* magazine remarked, she was not required to do much more than look beautiful and vulnerable, she "accomplishes both with patrician distinction". Playing the part of an Englishwoman for the first time since *Mogambo*, she sometimes let her accent slip, overdoing the clipped "Britishness" so that "bank" becomes "benk" while occasionally allowing a good old American "heere" to creep in in place of the British "here". Generally, however, her performance was rated a success: the Los Angeles *Daily News*, reviewing the film's Hollywood première in June 1954, described Grace as a "blonde, sexy newcomer" with "an earthy appeal that will give the boys something to think about".

Indeed that "earthy appeal" had been all too apparent on set – "All the men fell in love with Grace on *Dial M*," Lizanne recalled. "They were round her in scores – Tony Dawson [playing the murderer] and Frederick Knott [the author] really fell for her, they used to compete as to who could send her the most flowers until they ran out of vases and the place looked like a funeral home." But neither of them could compete with Grace's leading man, Ray Milland, nor was Lizanne, aged only twenty, an adequate chaperone for her sister. She could do little more than keep up appearances by sharing her apartment in the Château Marmont overlooking Sunset Boulevard; she could not prevent her sister from falling for the urbane charm of Ray Milland – "They were really taken with one another," she later admitted.

Ray Milland, star of countless films of the forties, including Grace's favourite, *The Lost Weekend*, was forty-eight, over twice Grace's age, when he met her on the set of *Dial M* but, as *Confidential* magazine put it, "after one look at Gracie he went into a tailspin that reverberated from Perino's to Ciro's. The whole town soon hee-hawed over the news that suave Milland, who had a wife and family at home, was ga-ga over Grace. Ray pursued her ardently and Hollywood cackled. Then mama Milland found out about it. She lowered the boom on ramblin' Ray and there followed one of the loudest, most tearful fights their Beverly Hills neighbors can remember." Milland moved out and his wife Mal told Louella Parsons that she planned to sue for divorce. But Mal was popular in Hollywood and the knives came out for Grace. Alerted by a family friend, public relations executive Scoop Conlon, who had promised to "keep an eye on Grace", Mrs Kelly flew out to Hollywood to lecture her daughter. "She and Scoop sat down and talked things over with Grace. They found her willing to listen," Jack Kelly told a reporter, while Louella Parsons wrote later that Grace "dropped Ray like a hot potato" when she heard about Mal Milland's divorce plans.

Family pressure and Hollywood scandal were too much for Grace: she fled back to New York at the end of September when shooting finished on *Dial M*. Hardly had she returned to her Manhattan House apartment when her agent called to tell her that Hitchcock wanted her for *Rear Window* to star opposite James Stewart and expected her back in Los Angeles in November. But "for some personal reasons", Grace later told Donald Spoto, "I really wanted to stay in New York," out of range of the Hollywood gossips. She was still, as she confessed to Oleg Cassini, the man with whom she was later to have a serious affair, "very fond" of Milland. "With public pressure you'll have to give him up," Cassini warned her. He was right. Grace could not face the scandal and within six months Cassini himself was to replace Milland in her affections.

Hitchcock was determined to get Grace for his cherished project, but she hesitated, not only out of reluctance to return to Hollywood but because there was a chance she might get the leading female role in *On the Waterfront*, which was to be shot in New York, produced by Sam Spiegel and directed by Elia Kazan with Marlon Brando as leading man. Grace told Donald Spoto that she was offered the part, later played by Eva Marie Saint, but that, forced to choose between Kazan and Hitchcock, she chose Hitchcock. Spiegel, however, remembers it differently and says that after he and Kazan had auditioned her for the part, he had to tell her that she had failed: "Elia

Kazan says you don't look hungry enough and I agree with him.'' And so Grace returned to Hollywood and Hitchcock.

Rear Window was to be a further projection of Hitchcock's image of Grace. Edith Head, Paramount's great designer, recalled the care with which he planned Grace's wardrobe, so that every costume she would wear was indicated when the designer received the finished script. "There was a reason for every colour, every style, and he was absolutely certain about everything he settled on," she said. "For one scene he saw her in pale green, for another in white chiffon, for another in gold. He was really putting a dream together in the studio." Grace was cast as a society-girl magazine editor who falls in love with a scruffy photographer, James Stewart. Stewart is insecure about her and believes that she thinks he isn't good enough for her. "Hitchcock told me that it was important that Grace's clothes help to establish some of the conflict in the story," Edith Head remembered. "Hitch wanted her to appear like a piece of Dresden china, something slightly untouchable." Edith rose to the challenge: Grace's suits were impeccably tailored and "her accessories looked as though they couldn't be worn by anyone else but her. She was perfect, and few actresses could have carried off the look the way Grace did."

All the action between Grace and Stewart happened within one room, where Stewart, confined to a wheelchair with a broken leg, watches his neighbours through the window, and concludes that one of them, a travelling salesman played by Raymond Burr, has murdered his wife. Grace's clothes were designed to have impact within that room and to build up the tension between the two characters. As she plays her first love scene with the impoverished photographer, the camera draws back from her face to show the beaded chiffon skirt of her dress, which "immediately told the audience that she was a rich girl". "Grace appeared in a nightgown and a peignoir in Jimmy's bedroom," Edith Head recalled. "Yet it was still a very innocent scene. Jimmy's leg was in a cast, and he was virtually helpless when it came to romance. Grace was just showing him what he was missing by not marrying her." It was, she concluded, a perfect example of Hitchcock's offbeat sense of humour, but it seems more likely to have been part of the director's build-up of his star, of his presentation of her as the lady of subtle sex. At one point during the filming Grace's small breasts did not fit the director's vision. Tactfully he whispered to Edith Head that "the bosom is not right. We're going to have to put something in there." When Edith suggested falsies, Grace refused. "It's going to show – and I'm not going to wear them." So, Grace remembered, "we quickly took it up here and made some adjustments there and I just did what I could and stood as straight as possible – without falsies. When I walked out onto the set Hitchcock looked at me and at Edith and said, 'See what a difference they make?' "

With each film Hitchcock was expanding his vision of Grace as the epitome of what he called "sexual elegance", luring the audience along with him to become helplessly bewitched by his star. In *Dial M* Grace as Margot Wendice had been beautiful, appealing in her helplessness, but it had been essentially a wooden part and Grace had been uncomfortable with her clipped "British" accent. Here, playing a Park Avenue society girl, her honeyed, mid-Atlantic "cream of tomato soup" voice came over seductively. It was her most accomplished performance to date and, as a later critic, Philip French of the *Observer* put it, she played the role "with charm and an easy erotic power".

James Stewart, recently and happily married to Gloria Stewart and one of the few among Grace's leading men who did not fall in love with her, nonetheless felt that "erotic power" and the teasing quality which made men lose their heads over her. "Grace, *cold*?" he said to an interviewer. "Why, Grace is anything but cold. She has those big warm eyes – and, well, if you ever have played a love scene with her, you'd know she's not cold. People who have inner confidence are not cold. Besides, Grace has that twinkle and touch of larceny in her eye."

But Grace, in public, was very circumspect. She had learned her lesson from the Ray Milland affair and, as Scoop Conlon put it, she had become "very cagey about doing anything the gossip columns can hop on". She was rarely seen on a date without a third person as a chaperone, either one of her sisters or one of her friends, Rita Gam or Prudie Wise. For *Rear Window* she rented a modest two-room apartment in a complex on Sweetzer Street, a palm-lined road off Sunset Boulevard, respectable enough during the day but haunted by prostitutes at night. Cecil Beaton, who visited her there to photograph her, was taken aback by the smallness and dullness of the place where she lived, describing it as "a modern apartment project where, rather like a reformatory, the inmates lived in cubicled apartments built around a courtyard ... a completely impersonal and modern background. The proportions of the two rooms were such that if one piece of furniture was moved, another would have to go out of place." The great photographer had no alternative but to take the young star wearing a little black dress sitting on the floor, lit by a reading lamp.

During the filming of *Rear Window* Grace shared the tiny apartment with Rita Gam, the dark-haired actress whom she had met in television when she was working for Rita's then husband, Sidney Lumet. Rita was in Hollywood making *The Sign of the Pagan*; she, like Grace, was New York-based and felt lonely in Hollywood, and when Grace invited her to join her in the apartment she accepted eagerly. The two girls, both working, would breakfast together in the kitchenette at 6 am, usually, Rita remembers, on prunes. They lunched at their respective studios, often had hamburgers at home in the evening, and on Sundays, exhausted, they would sleep all day then take turns to make the dinner. "One Sunday Grace did her spaghetti bit, with green salad. Or if in gourmet mood, her Beef Stroganoff. The next Sunday I'd do my duck à l'orange with wild rice. And always champagne. We would keep champagne in the house, nothing but champagne, we even had it with our hamburgers."

The sisters and the girl-friends were Grace's front line of defence against Hollywood. Although her telephone rang constantly, she hated to answer it herself and, according to Peggy, she would, after someone else had answered it, pick up the extension phone and listen in to find out who was calling before she would come on the line. "She almost never went out," Peggy said. "Even when she had a night off she would rather go out for a big dinner with me and have a lot of laughs. Family laughs." At parties she seemed so shy that she would often spend the evening talking to Peggy or to Rita or to whomever she had brought with her, and she had developed an infallible technique for freezing would-be wolves – sitting up primly straight, reaching in her bag for horn-rimmed glasses and adopting her clipped "British" accent. If she and Rita expected any trouble they would take Grace's old mustard-coloured Chevrolet – rented because Grace hated driving and never wanted to own a car – so that they could make their own getaway. Grace, said Rita Gam, was frightened of driving and avoided doing so whenever she could, and the only Hollywood thing about her was her longing for a car with a chauffeur so that she would never have to drive herself.

She protected herself from Hollywood by refusing to become part of it. "At times I think I actually hate Hollywood," she told a *Saturday Evening Post* interviewer. "I have many acquaintances here, but few friends." As with many Easterners, the West Coast and Los Angeles in particular was an alien land to her. "The East is home to me," she told Anita Colby. "It's where my family and friends are." She loved walking, but if she tried to walk anywhere in Los Angeles a policeman would stop her to ask where she was going; the soft climate made her feel lethargic and the smog irritated her sensitive sinuses, making her eyes pink and her nose run. Hollywood, for Grace, was just a place to work and to succeed. "It's just that she's a single-purpose girl," said a friend, explaining what Hollywood regarded as Grace's stand-offish attitudes. "And right now her purpose is to succeed as an actress."

Grace was not prepared to leave anything to chance – although she told Anita Colby that she thought luck had played a great part in her career, she took the greatest care to see that luck might come her way. Even before she had started filming *Rear Window* she had another part in view. On 13 November 1953, the day after MGM had signed another loan-out agreement with Hitchcock for Grace's services for *Rear Window*, the studio signed an agreement directly with Paramount to loan Grace to them for a Korean War picture, *The Bridges at Toko-Ri*, to be co-produced by William Perlberg and George Seaton, with William Holden in the lead role as a Navy pilot with a dangerous mission to destroy vital North Korean bridges. Grace was to play his wife.

"The part of the wife in *Toko-Ri* wasn't big enough to attract an important star," Perlberg told a *Saturday Evening Post* interviewer. "But there were a few spots in it which had to be right, and we needed more than just an ordinary actress who could get by with it. Our problem was to find an unknown with real talent. George and I interviewed a lot of girls. Among others we talked to was Grace." Grace, he said, was "dressed as if she were walking down the street window-shopping. She wore glasses and flat-heeled walking shoes." Grace knew perfectly well that a Navy pilot's wife should not look too glamorous and she had the sense to present herself in a way that looked believable for the role. Beyond that, Perlberg and Seaton were impressed by her seriousness. "She reminds me a lot of the girls at the Actors' Workshop in New York," Seaton said. "They're so intensely dedicated." Once they had talked to her they felt they had to have her, and there was no problem with MGM, who still had no plans for her. She was borrowable for $25,000, and as her salary for *Toko-Ri* was to be $10,000, MGM cleared $15,000 on the deal.

Much of *Toko-Ri* was shot on location in the Far East but Grace's scenes, as the wife spending a week in Tokyo with her husband before his departure on his mission to *Toko-Ri*, were shot in Hollywood on the Paramount lot. The filming naturally involved some intimate (by the standards of the day) scenes with Holden, including a shot in which they are seen in bed together, though modestly clad in nightclothes and forbidden to kiss each other.

William Holden, nicknamed "Golden Boy" for his rugged blond good looks and for the title of the film in which he had first made his name in 1939, was eleven years older than Grace. Born William Franklin Beedle in O'Fallon, Illinois, in 1918, he had had no acting experience before his looks brought him into pictures – since then, however, he had worked hard to learn his craft, almost too hard, with an intensity of concentration which triggered bouts of heavy drinking. He had been nominated for an Oscar for his part in *Sunset Boulevard* with Gloria Swanson in 1950 and had recently won acclaim for *Stalag 17*, which would win him an Oscar in 1954.

Holden was then at the height of his career, handsome, rich and famous, and, despite having a beautiful wife and two children at home, he was intensely susceptible to women who had what Hollywood calls "class". Recently filming *Sabrina Fair* with Humphrey Bogart and Audrey Hepburn, he had fallen heavily for Audrey – on *Toko-Ri* he fell for Grace. "Grace has the faculty of reminding me of my own wife," Holden is made to say in the Paramount publicity hand-out for *Toko-Ri*, but he was later and more believably to link her appeal with that of Audrey Hepburn – "Women like Grace Kelly and Audrey Hepburn help us to believe in the innate dignity of man." According to his biographer, Bob Thomas, Holden enjoyed "a brief but satisfactory romance" (whatever that may mean) with Grace during the shooting of *Toko-Ri* and they were to meet again on Grace's next film, *The Country Girl*. *Toko-Ri* won excellent notices as a war picture, but most of the attention was concentrated on the performances of Holden, Mickey Rooney and Fredric March, and very little on Grace's brief appearance. But as the New Year of 1954 opened Grace had a far more rewarding part in view, that of Georgie

Elgin in Perlberg and Seaton's next production, the film of Clifford Odets' Broadway hit, *The Country Girl*.

Grace's famous luck and also her determination played a part in landing her the coveted role which was to win her the Oscar. By January 1954 Perlberg and Seaton were set to film the play with Jennifer Jones in the role of Georgie, when they received a telephone call from her husband David Selznick, telling them that she was pregnant. As Perlberg remembered it – "George and I don't tear our hair at the news. We just look at each other. We're both thinking the same thing at the same time: *Grace Kelly*." They approached MGM to negotiate the loan of Grace but this time the studio told them that they had "big plans" for Grace and refused to let her go. "Somehow, we let Grace know we were negotiating for her," Perlberg said, "and somehow she got a copy of the *Country Girl* script ...'

Grace realized that this was the part that could make her as an actress, a serious dramatic role which could justify her professionally. The Kelly determination came to the fore; ten other top actresses might be manoeuvring for the role but she wanted it, and when Perlberg and Seaton told her that MGM would not release her because they wanted her for a projected adventure film called *Green Fire*, she summoned her agent and went to see the head of MGM, Dore Schary. To Schary she apparently delivered an ultimatum – either they loan her to Paramount for *The Country Girl*, after which she would do *Green Fire*, or she was going back to New York and the stage. Convinced that their new star meant what she said, MGM caved in, but they exacted a high price for their surrender: MGM were to be entitled to an extra, fourth, picture from Grace, for which they would pay her $20,000 on top of the salary agreed in the previous contract, with three separate options for three extra pictures at $25,000, $30,000 and $35,000; Paramount were to pay MGM $50,000 for Grace's services and were not to retain her beyond 4 April 1954. Grace's value had therefore doubled since the $25,000 levied for *Toko-Ri*.

There was another surprising hurdle to be cleared: Bing Crosby. He was to play the part of Frank Elgin, Georgie's alcoholic husband, and was opposed to Grace playing Georgie, not only because he thought her too glamorous and too inexperienced but also, as he later admitted, because the poisonous Hedda Hopper had told him Grace was a nymphomaniac. Bing's approval mattered, because he was a big and unpredictable star, and he had it in his contract that he could "OK" or "NG" his leading lady.

Arthur Jacobson, assistant producer on *Country Girl*, recalls the tense moment when Bing was to meet Grace for the first time at Perlberg's house in Palm Springs. "You never knew how Bing would react because he was very undemonstrative," Jacobson said. "Grace came in from playing tennis and she knew she had to meet Bing and what depended upon it. Bing came in from playing golf and they were introduced – 'Bing, this is Grace . . .' – and he just said 'Oh, hi,' and kept on walking past her with his pipe in his mouth. Grace was so disappointed she was almost in tears. But Bing said to me, 'If it's OK with Bill [Perlberg], it's OK with George [Seaton] and it's OK with you, what's the big deal?' Grace asked me what she should do and I told her, 'For God's sake don't make a fuss of him, it'll embarrass him.'"

Bing later said that he was so knocked out by Grace's beauty that he was speechless and shy; within a very short time of starting work on the film he, too, had fallen in love with her. William Holden was to play the other male lead as the theatrical director, Bernie Dodds, and according to Holden's biographer, Bob Thomas, an embarrassed Bing invited Holden into his dressing-room, where the following conversation took place:

"This Kelly girl, she's a knock-out, isn't she?" he said.

"She sure is," Holden agreed. "I've never known a young actress with so much know-how."

"I'm talking about her as a person. I don't mind telling you, Bill, I'm smitten with Grace. Daffy about her. And I was wondering if –"

"I felt the same way," Bill grinned. "What man wouldn't be overwhelmed by her? But look, Bing, I won't interfere."

"Bing was mad for her, really mad for her, taking her out all the time," Lizanne remembers. "She liked him very much, but she wasn't in love with him." Bing was a widower, his wife Dixie having died of cancer, and he too had been an idol of Grace's teenage years, but his magic did not work on Grace. Their evenings out were always accompanied by Lizanne or Peggy and, all too frequently, by a bevy of photographers who took some unflattering shots of a nervous and toupee-less Bing and an icy Grace. ("I look as though I was going to throw up," she said on seeing them.) She had plenty to be icy about; both she and Bing detested having their evenings ruined by publicity, and to make matters worse one well-known Hollywood playboy walked up to her in Mocambo's and said nastily, "Well, how about a date? I see you're going out with single men now." Grace gave him the famous look that could turn the unfortunate person on the receiving end to stone, but was nonetheless hurt by the insinuation.

And, indeed, another scandal of potentially Milland-like proportions was looming on her horizon. Bill Holden's highly recognizable white Cadillac Eldorado convertible had been seen several times outside her apartment on Sweetzer Street and soon the news was all around town that Holden, too, had "flipped over Gracie". Holden attempted to defuse the situation by telling Hedda Hopper that he had merely been picking up Grace to take her to dinner with his wife, Ardis, and that she had dined with them "about four times". "I don't understand all this publicity about Grace," he told Hopper ingenuously. "I like her, but I don't think she's the *femme fatale* she's built up to be." "She's pretty *femme*," Hopper quipped. "But she's not *fatale*," Holden retorted. But *fatale* she was as far as Holden was concerned; having given Bing his chance, he was pursuing Grace ardently. "I loved Grace and wanted to marry her," he is reported to have told Broderick Crawford and according to Bob Thomas, he succeeded in luring Grace, with a chaperone, for a weekend in Palm Springs, where they went on long midnight rides alone together.

What were Grace's own reactions to Holden – handsome, charming, famous and in love with her? Perhaps with his good looks, his seriousness about acting and his fatal instability he may have reminded her of Gene Lyons. It seems likely that she encouraged him – she was not above leading men on if she liked them – but how far she did so it is impossible to tell. Grace had learned her lessons well over Milland and she was not about to repeat her mistakes. At the tiny Sweetzer Street apartment she was now chaperoned by her delightful friend-secretary-companion, Prudie Wise, whom she had first met in her Barbizon days, and Prudie was seen accompanying her everywhere, even on the set, where the two girls were photographed tweaking Bing's ears. This time her precautions paid off. Support came from an unexpected quarter, the scandal magazine of the decade, *Confidential*. In an article headed "Memo: Hollywood wives stop biting your nails", the writer assured readers that "this new Hollywood heatwave . . . wasn't grabbing for a guy who already had a ball and chain". Citing the example of Grace "walking out cold" on the married Ray Milland, the article ridiculed Holden's visits to Sweetzer Street: "far from enjoying an ardent interlude, Holden was being given firm notice by Miss Kelly that he belonged at home." As for married men, the article concluded, "Keep off the grass!"

Confidential absolved Grace from having designs on married men, but even absolution is not pleasant as long as it is public; and, moreover, the magazine went on to discuss the nature of Grace's sex appeal. *Confidential*'s answer to the unspoken question "Does she or doesn't she?" was a heavy implication that, as long as the men were not officially married, she did. An anonymous Hollywood bachelor gave it as his opinion that "a lot of glamour girls like Monroe and Russell aren't as eager as you think. Their sex appeal goes into their looks. They use low-cut dresses and a wriggly walk for what they really don't have. Now that Gracie ...". Miss Kelly, the magazine concluded, was an example of still waters running deep: "behind that frigid exterior is a smouldering fire ... "And", they said, "what the older fellows go for – she looks like a lady and has the manners of one. In the Hollywood of the chippies and tramps, a lady is a rarity. That makes Grace Kelly the most dangerous dame in the movies today."

For Grace, to whom privacy was an obsession and whose secretiveness and reserve about her real feelings were so deep as to be remarked upon by her family and her friends, such speculation was painful. Publicly, and perhaps privately also, Holden's attention was putting too much pressure upon her; her solution to the situation was to summon Oleg Cassini to visit her while she was making *Country Girl*.

Oleg Cassini, slim, dark-haired and elegant, the son of aristocratic Russian parents, was the most sophisticated and cosmopolitan man Grace had yet encountered. Brought up in Florence, where his mother had a dress salon, he had played tennis for Italy in the Davis Cup team and, after emigrating to New York with his mother and brother, had set up his own design business there. Oleg and his brother, Igor, who wrote the Cholly Knickerbocker gossip column, were very much a part of the fashionable New York scene and destined to become even more so when, some six years later, Oleg was known as the friend and couturier to Jacqueline Kennedy. Cassini was, and is, fond of women, appreciative of them and successful with them; when he met Grace he had already been twice married, first to an heiress, Merry Fahrey, then to film star Gene Tierney. He had been determined to get Grace since the autumn of 1953 when, after seeing her in *Mogambo*, he had told a friend, "This is going to be my next girl-friend." "She was all that I wanted," he reminisced years later, "beautiful, clean-looking, ethereal enough, sexy enough ...." When he met her for the first time she was dining with Jean-Pierre Aumont in a fashionable French restaurant in New York, and, after asking Aumont to introduce them, he had pursued her with telephone calls and flowers. Finally he had persuaded her to make a date with him, only to hear her confess that she was in love with another man, Ray Milland. Predicting that Grace's infatuation for Milland would not last, he had never given up the idea of replacing him and, as he told Grace's biographer Gwen Robyns, when he received Grace's telephone call inviting him to California he was so excited that he dived into the empty swimming pool at his Long Island home, breaking his nose. When Grace saw him, his normally thin, aquiline nose swollen to an unsightly blob, she laughed. She was not yet in love with him - Oleg in Hollywood was no more than a charming and amusing escort.

Cassini, one of Grace's fellow actors recalls, visited her on the set of *Country Girl* "two or three times". On set the principals, Grace, Crosby and Holden, were total professionals and gave no inkling of any romantic involvement, and all three of them took their roles extremely seriously. For Grace as Georgie, the drab, unhappy wife of an alcoholic former matinée idol making his comeback, her acting would be all-important. Her beauty could not help her; she had, Arthur Jacobson said, to be "plained down" for the movie and Edith Head had the depressing task of "putting her in housedresses and skirts and blouses and making her look dumpy". She could only concentrate on her acting; but she had to do so in the knowledge that everybody would compare her performance with that of Uta Hagen, who had played Georgie with such power on Broadway in 1951. Crosby, too, was desperately nervous about his role and uncertain of himself as an actor, although the Frank Elgin part contained elements of his own life. He, too, had been a drinker as a young man before his wife Dixie helped him to cure himself of it, and he remained an insecure man with what he admitted was an exaggerated instinct for survival. Holden played Bernie, the director, who, convinced by Elgin to give him one last chance and believing that Elgin's problems are caused by his wife, tries to get Elgin away from her. In the process he discovers that Elgin is weak, an alcoholic and a hopeless liar and that Georgie is the strong one who is trying to protect her husband. He falls in love with her but, although she wants his love, in the end she rejects it to remain faithful to Elgin.

George Seaton, the director of *Country Girl*, was a perfectionist who took infinite trouble with his actors. Once, for one of Grace's most important scenes, he cleared the set of everybody except himself, Grace and Jacobson, and "by the time he got through rehearsing, analysing, talking about her relationships with Bing and Holden it must have been three hours' work". Seaton thought a great deal of Grace's acting ability; she had intensity, he said, "but on the other hand her intensity doesn't make her shoot her whole personality at you the first five minutes. With other stars, five seconds after they're on, you've seen all the personality they've got. With Grace you see different angles of her as the part develops."

Francisco ("Chico") Day, assistant director on the film, was impressed with her professionalism. "She was always ready to go, knew her lines, there was absolutely no problem, no matter what the scene was she had it pretty well in mind." He admired her concentration; even if Seaton were directing Holden and Bing "she was always right there with her entire attention ... she was so much involved in the scene, in the portrayal of the character – you knew that nothing bothered her, she was absolutely immune". Grace, he said, didn't behave like other stars did, chatting to anyone, kidding the crew; she would never over-react to anything that went on off the set. "She was just very, very calm and very sweet and gentle ... and always the same to everybody." When she first came to work in *Country Girl* the gaffers and electricians thought her just another blonde, Seaton said, "but as they got her full flavour, they fell for her". In the end they awarded her a plaque. Engraved on it was: "To our Country Girl. This will hold you until you get next year's Academy Award."

Gene Reynolds, who played Larry, the stage manager, in *Country Girl*, remembers that she was closest to the people who worked for her, particularly the women. "My first impression of Grace Kelly", he said, "was that she had a very close, kind of informal, chummy relationship with the people that worked closest with her like hairdressers and wardrobe people, the women on the set. ... I think they were crazy about her." Grace liked to develop a close relationship with people she could trust: the make-up artists, hairdressers, designers and wardrobe people, like Virginia Darcy, the hairdresser at MGM, who accompanied her to her wedding, and Edith Head, Paramount's chief dress designer, were among her few Hollywood friends. It was a pattern to be repeated when Grace became Princess of Monaco, when her hairdressers and couturiers were also to count themselves as her friends, and part of that discreet, loyal, personal bodyguard which Grace developed around herself.

Grace's performance as Georgie Elgin in *The Country Girl* was to win her an Oscar. When asked how her playing of the role compared with Uta Hagen's performance on stage, Gene Reynolds found it quite convincing. She was younger than Hagen and less powerful as an actress, but, he said, "I thought she was very good. She had a great sensibility and a sensitivity that was compelling." Grace herself said later that if she had been five years older she would really have known how to play Georgie; at twenty-four, having led a comparatively sheltered life, it required a considerable effort of imagination and acting skill to transform herself into the disillusioned, loyal wife of an alcoholic and a professional failure. It was to be Grace's first and last serious dramatic film role. Hitchcock wanted her for another comedy thriller, *To Catch a Thief*, and she was as determined as he was that she would play it, despite her studio's reluctance to release her yet again. But immediately the shooting of *Country Girl* was finished early in April 1954, she had first to pay the price MGM had demanded for allowing her to play Georgie, by fulfilling her promise to play opposite Stewart Granger in their South American adventure, *Green Fire*.

Green Fire, described in MGM's press release as "a modern story of dangerous adventure and romance against the unusual background of Colombia's fabulous four-century-old emerald mines", was in fact nothing more than a studio potboiler in an uncomfortable location. Curiously enough, it had originally been designated by MGM as a vehicle for their spurned star, Clark Gable, but in "the King's" place, co-starring with Grace, who played the owner of a coffee plantation, was the handsome English actor, Stewart Granger, then at the height of his swashbuckling career. "One of the peculiar attributes of Granger is his ability to look real mean when he is playing a character who is real mean," the *Los Angeles Times* commented. "But in spite of it, Miss Kelly cannot refrain from loving him. She is the owner of a coffee plantation and very much the lady, even when she is angry. She gets angry at Granger but not for long." Coincidentally the supporting role went to Paul Douglas, who had starred as the policeman in Grace's first film, *Fourteen Hours*.

It was an uncomfortable, even dangerous, film from the start. Since the producer Armand Deutsch and the director Andrew Marton had visited Colombia the previous year to reconnoitre locations, there had been a revolution and the company were escorted by six soldiers. The stars were appalled by the poverty they saw around them in the jungle villages and were nearly drowned on the upper Magdalena River when the steering on their boat went in a storm and they had to be rescued in dug-out canoes. "None of us really wanted to do the film," Stewart Granger recalled. Grace, he said, "was watching us all, she wasn't happy on the film because she knew she was in a potboiler. At the beginning she was rather looking down her nose at us. I felt sorry she was seeing us in this lousy movie." Despite being happily married to Jean Simmons, Granger felt "tempted a bit" by Grace. "She would look at me in a contemplative sort of way ..." And, he said, "She was very nice to kiss ... She was always cool and lovely and smelt nice."

Grace was yearning to finish *Green Fire* and be off to France, where she was due to start *To Catch a Thief* with Hitchcock and Cary Grant. She was exhausted, having worked on *Rear Window*, *Toko-Ri*, *Country Girl* and now *Green Fire* almost without intermission, but when they returned to California she would, after days spent shooting on the back lot at Culver City, rush to Edith Head's studio to discuss the all-important wardrobe for the new film. She even had a French teacher in attendance on the set so that she could use her spare moments practising the language in preparation for her visit to France. She was absolutely determined to go, even though MGM were making considerable difficulties about yet another loan-out of her services to Paramount. Hedda Hopper and Louella Parsons had already announced that the deal hadn't a chance of going through; only Grace and Hitchcock were sure that it would. "No matter what anyone says," Grace told Edith Head, "keep right on making my clothes for the picture. I'll be in it." In the end MGM yielded Grace up to Paramount yet again, this time for more hard cash and the promise of the loan of their top actor, William Holden, for an MGM picture.

The agreement was signed on 11 May 1954. By the end of the month Grace left for France, stopping off in Paris for a shopping spree for accessories at Hermès with Edith Head, before arriving in

Cannes to join Hitchcock and the rest of the company. At the Carlton Hotel she found Hitchcock and his wife Alma, Jessie Royce Landis, who was to play her mother in the film, John Williams, who had had the role of the detective in *Dial M*, her co-star Cary Grant and his wife, Betsy Drake.

As a film, *To Catch a Thief* was considerably below the high Hitchcock standard of *Rear Window*. It was essentially a fluffy comedy thriller, set against spectacular Riviera scenery, with two elegantly beautiful stars and designer Edith Head pulling out all the stops to make Grace look like a million dollars. It was, however, also Hitchcock's most strongly sexual presentation of Grace, with a script by John Michael Hayes loaded with *double entendres* and Grace taking the initiative in the affair with Cary Grant. It is Grace, the daring rich girl out for thrills, who seduces Grant, the retired cat burglar, in such scenes as those which follow. The first was shot while the two stars are sitting in an open white convertible high above Monte Carlo. Grace believes, wrongly, that Grant is "the Cat", a skilful burglar who has been terrorizing the Riviera's rich.

GRANT: What do you expect to get out of being so nice to me?
KELLY: Probably a lot more than you're willing to offer.
GRANT: Jewelry – you never wear any.
KELLY: I don't like cold things touching my skin.
GRANT: Why don't you invent some *hot* diamonds?
KELLY: I'd rather spend my money on more tangible excitement.
GRANT: Tell me, what do you get a thrill out of most?
KELLY: I'm still looking for that one....
GRANT: What you need is something I have neither the time nor the inclination to give you – two weeks with a good man at Niagara Falls.

KELLY (*later, at a picnic lunch*): I've never caught a jewel thief before. It's so stimulating! (*Offering him the cold chicken*) Do you want a leg or a breast?
GRANT: You make the choice.
KELLY: Tell me, how long has it been?
GRANT: Since what?
KELLY: Since you were in America last.

In the next sequence she invites Grant to her hotel suite for an intimate dinner and a good view of the fireworks, seen in the background over the horizon throughout the following exchange.

KELLY: If you really want to see fireworks, it's better with the lights off. I have a feeling that tonight you're going to see one of the Riviera's most fascinating sights. (*In her strapless, low evening gown she moves closer to him*) I'm talking about the fireworks, of course.

GRANT: May I have a brandy? May I fix you one?

KELLY: Some nights a person doesn't need to drink ...

GRANT: I have about the same interest in jewelry that I have in politics, horse racing, modern poetry and women who need weird excitement. None.

KELLY: (*as she sits seductively on the divan, her diamond-and-platinum necklace glittering above the bodice of her white strapless gown*) Give up - admit who you are. Even in this light I can tell where your eyes are looking. (*Close-up of her chest and necklace and generous décolletage*) Look - hold them - diamonds! The only thing in the world you can't resist. Then tell me you don't know what I'm talking about. (*The fireworks shoot intensely, seen in clear focus between them in the background. She kisses his fingers one by one, then places his hand underneath the necklace. Cut to close-up of raging fireworks*) Ever had a better offer in your whole life? One with everything!

GRANT: I've never had a crazier one. (*Cut to vast fireworks*)

KELLY: Just as long as you're satisfied! (*Fireworks again*)

GRANT: You know just as well as I do this necklace is imitation.

KELLY: Well, *I'm* not. (*They kiss: cut to fireworks, then back to the final frenzy of fireworks to the end of the scene*)

Paramount's publicity department was at pains to point out that Grace had been "kissed continuously by Grant for two and a half working days - 20 hours" and that Hitchcock was out to beat his own record for hot love scenes which he had established with Cary Grant and Ingrid Bergman in *Notorious*. As Hitchcock's biographer Donald Spoto remarks, it was surprising that there was no outcry of any kind when *To Catch a Thief* was released in 1955, since films with less obvious innuendo had run into trouble with Hollywood censors and religious groups.

Looking back now there is a poignancy about *To Catch a Thief*. It was to be the last film Grace made with Hitchcock and his most spectacular and loving celebration of her beauty. It was also set against the Riviera background which was to be her home for the rest of her life, and some of the most memorable shots were taken on the winding roads above Monte Carlo on which she was to meet her death almost thirty years later. Grace was still a bad driver and her extreme short-sightedness made things even more perilous during the scenes in the film where she is shown at the wheel of a white convertible driving Cary Grant along the Corniche. Spectacles were out of the question for this picture, and at the Philadelphia Retrospective in 1982 she recalled Cary Grant's terror when Hitchcock would insist "Faster, faster" as she manoeuvred the car round the perilous curves with the ground falling precipitously away below.

It was a happy time for Grace and her fellow stars in *To Catch a Thief*. Hitchcock, having lost over one hundred pounds on a diet of one meal a day and no alcohol, was determined to enjoy the food of the South of France. In the company of Grace, his favourite actress, and Cary Grant, his favourite actor, he was happy and amused and the Hitchcocks, the Grants, Grace and the other stars spent delightful evenings dining at restaurants along the coast and gambling in the Palm Beach Casino at Cannes. Later, when they returned to California in July to finish shooting the film at the studio, Grace and the Grants spent time together at the Hitchcocks' weekend retreat near Santa Cruz. The Grants gave her the miniature black poodle, Oliver, which was later, at the time of Grace's wedding, to become the most written about dog in the world.

For Grace, *To Catch a Thief* had an added element – Oleg Cassini. Cassini had not forgotten her while she was far away in Colombia and, when she returned to California, made sure that he was seen there too, but with a beautiful girl at a night-club. Grace saw him, talked to him, asked him why he hadn't called, told him she was going to Europe to do a film. Back in New York Cassini, according to himself, received a note challenging him to follow her to Cannes ("Those who want me, follow me"). He did; the result, in the romantic atmosphere of the South of France, was predictable. Staying in the Carlton at Cannes, dining at restaurants along the coast at night after filming, nothing, as P. G. Wodehouse remarked, "propinks like propinquity". Grace and Oleg fell in love. For her, Oleg in a European setting seemed infinitely more attractive than the men she had known at home in Philadelphia, New York or Hollywood, as, just under a year later, would Jean-Pierre Aumont when she met him again in Cannes. Oleg seemed to offer an international dimension to

97

her life which she had not known before, of travel, interesting people, a civilized, sophisticated way of life. Over dinner in romantic places they talked of marriage; far away as she was from Philadelphia, Grace minimized the difficulties they might encounter from the Kellys – Oleg's two marriages had taken place under Greek Orthodox rites and could be discounted, her father might be against it at first but her mother would soon bring him round. As she sat there, dreaming, on the Côte d'Azur, she underestimated the strength of her family's hold upon her, and she was unaware of the new pressures that would be put upon her. In America she was now a big, big star.

7

A Hollywood Crown

In June 1954 *Look* magazine devoted a cover story to Grace. Entitled "Hollywood's hottest property", it began; "In Hollywood, 1954 is likely to be known as this year of Grace." Four major films starring Grace were to come out in that year alone – *Dial M* in May, *Rear Window* in August, *Country Girl* and *Green Fire* in December. At the age of only twenty-four she had played opposite all Hollywood's top leading men, with the exception of Spencer Tracy – Gary Cooper, Clark Gable, Ray Milland, William Holden, Bing Crosby, Stewart Granger, James Stewart and Cary Grant – and had been directed by the most distinguished directors – Fred Zinneman, John Ford, George Seaton and, of course, Alfred Hitchcock. She had won the International Press Award for her performance in *Mogambo* and been nominated for an Oscar for Best Supporting Actress of 1953. Within less than six months she would be nominated for Best Actress in *Country Girl*, running a neck-and-neck race for the Oscar with Judy Garland, and make the cover of *Time*, an honour reserved for world personalities. "Hollywood is now eager to adopt actress Kelly, white gloves and all, and is trying hard, with the air of an ill-at-ease lumberjack worrying whether he is using the right spoon," *Time* scoffed. Their cover picture of Grace by Boris Chaliapin was captioned "Gentlemen prefer ladies" and the inside story was headed "The Girl in White Gloves".

By early November 1954 even *The New York Times* had become aware of this new celebrity. In an article entitled "Star on the Ascendant" the *Times* writer began his piece on Grace, "Every so often a personality will rocket to the top of the motion picture world in a dazzling ascent to success." She was becoming a star of the first magnitude, a status which in America is the equivalent of European royalty. To the public she was already a princess, earning the same adulation and the same reverential treatment as the daughter of a crowned head. As her films premièred one after another to critical and box office success so her photographs, profiles and interviews multiplied in the press. Girls everywhere copied the Grace Kelly look, the gleaming blonde hair in a short pageboy style, the classic clothes, even the white cotton gloves.

The spectacular rise was there for all to see, but the question puzzling the Hollywood pundits was – why? Grace did not conform to the "tintype" of a Hollywood star. "John Kelly's refined, almost distant daughter is something new to a town used to ambitious, bosomy cuties who willingly worship at the publicity shrine," the *Mirror News* of 15 February 1955 wrote. Grace, seen through Hitchcock's eyes, presented a new image of ideal woman, and one to which the cinema public, sated with what actor Van Johnson described as "a broadside of broads", responded.

Grace appealed to men and to women – to men because she appeared subtly alluring, never predatory or aggressively sexual. One of her leading men, who refused to be named, told reporter Joe Hyams what he thought was the secret of her appeal: "Every guy wants to make love to a lady. She's cool, clean and antiseptic, but you figure that's all a cover-up for the hell fire inside." For women she represented an easier ideal to follow than the sex-goddesses, Hayworth, Russell or Monroe; a romantic but not asexual figure, yet more than a mere sex object. In *Rear Window* and *To Catch a Thief* Hitchcock had shown Grace taking the sexual lead, teasing, baffling and seducing her leading men. It was an image which was all the more believable because it was a true reflection of how Grace was herself.

Perhaps the best description of Grace's appeal was given by Cecil Beaton, who, in the course of a lifetime spent photographing beautiful women, had become entitled to be considered an expert. First, and most obviously, she was photogenic; his photographic session with her when he visited her in her tiny apartment on Sweetzer Street was, he said, about the easiest he had ever done. As to her appeal, in the age of the atom bomb and of the violence of the Korean War, he said, people felt that the storm should be followed by a calm:

Miss Kelly's qualities are the serene ones ... she gives one a feeling of cool protection, while appealing to us with her infinite pathos ... she is captivating, but her lure is directed at our better instincts. Apart from her placid, calf-like beauty, she is a person of such dignity and independence and her fascination is so subtle that she is, as connoisseurs would say, an *objet d'art* of "the first order".

Questioned about her beauty, Beaton became lyrical: "Grace Kelly belongs to springtime. Pale primrose yellow, with her flaxen hair and dewy complexion, she evokes images of cowslips and curds and whey. Her eyes have a luminous, aquamarine beauty. They convey her sense of humour while having the wistfulness of a child."

Professionally he was fascinated by the contrast between her classically exquisite features, mouth, nose and nostrils, what he called her "muzzle", and the "rugged background" of her cheeks and jaw, which, he said, are "too square for classical perfection", and between the right side of her face, which he described as "very heavy, like a bull calf", and the left side, intensely feminine. Her face was saved from being "too classical and dull" by the little "amusement puffs" beneath her eyes. "The expressiveness of those little pockets of flesh is one of her important attributes," he wrote. But, he went on, "it goes without saying that an inherent part of Miss Kelly's appeal is the manner behind her face. She has unusually good taste and an unerring sense of comportment. Constance Collier once said of another woman, 'I know she is much too refined to be a lady' – but there is nothing too refined about Grace Kelly."

Charm and the power to attract are elusive qualities: there were other, more down-to-earth reasons for her success – her acting skill and her professionalism. Directors and the people who worked with her liked her because she was agreeable and easy to work with, always on time, always knowing her lines, never making scenes. "Grace knows her craft," director George Seaton told Hedda Hopper. "She comes to work with every line in the bag. She not only speaks her lines, she feels them."

Beyond that was her determination to succeed and her skill in shaping her career. William Holden said that hers was "the best calculated career in the history of the motion pictures". With the exception of *Green Fire*, which was the price she had to pay for *Country Girl*, Grace never accepted any part which would not do something for her; she had seen that *Country Girl* was the part of a lifetime for her and had gone after it with all the determination of which she, as a Kelly, was capable. She had kept Hollywood at arm's length until she was ready for it, turning down a standard movie starlet's contract offered her when she left the Academy, working to improve her craft after what she was professional enough to see was an immature performance in *High Noon*. She had accepted *Mogambo* because it meant three things: John Ford, Clark Gable and a trip to Africa. And she had had luck, the great good luck of being discovered by Hitchcock, at the height of his powers.

Grace, however, would have been a star even without Hitchcock. All her beauty, her acting skills and her personality might not have taken her to the top, might not have made her the screen idol which she became, had she not been possessed of that rare screen magnetism which all real stars project, whether on stage or on camera. "There are very few people that have some kind of a magnetism on the screen and she had it," Jay Kanter said. The crew on *Country Girl* recognized it – "when she gets in front of those cameras", one of them told Hedda Hopper, "something happens. She turns it on. She goes to work. And when you see her on that screen – wham! – she's with it." Stewart Granger said that while they were filming together he was not aware of her enormous talent, but, when he saw the rushes, "it came over like a – boom – she had this magic, of intense beauty", and he compared her screen presence with that of Spencer Tracy.

But while the cinema public, "like an old setter dog", as James Stewart put it, had detected Grace's star quality, not all Hollywood was at her feet and her studio remained uncertain of her appeal. MGM's view of what sold pictures and their somewhat ambivalent attitude to Grace's physical attributes was made all too clear in the poster they planned to advertise *Green Fire*, in which Grace's head was joined to a voluptuously curved body dressed in a clinging green dress.

In the movie colony there was, naturally, jealousy of Grace's success and resentment at her anti-Hollywood attitudes, which many of them regarded as hypocritical, as the *Mirror News* reported: "Grace Kelly doesn't mind being a big star, but at the same time she thinks she's too good for Hollywood," complained one man who had worked with her. "She won't live here and when she is here to make a picture she doesn't join in any of the movie colony's activities. She's supposed to be so terribly proper, but then look at all those whispers about her and Ray Milland."

Grace's dilemma was that of all celebrities, particularly Hollywood actors – of wanting public success and privacy at the same time. It is a dilemma which cannot be solved without some degree of deception. Grace's natural shyness and intense secretiveness about herself created a screen between herself and interviewers. "Chipping away at granite with a penknife" was how one would-be interviewer described his attempts to prise a story out of Grace. The "ice-cold Kelly" image was misleading but useful as a protective shield behind which Grace could operate as she pleased. The studios and the public paid her to be a beauty and an actress, beyond that they did not own her. If deception were necessary to protect her private freedom of action, then she would put up a smokescreen for the press – intimating to Anita Colby that her affair with Gable was nothing more than a "crush", denying that she and Cassini ever had any marriage plans.

Oleg Cassini indeed was to be a principal victim of what he himself called Grace's "emotional fragility", the conflict between her sexuality and her upbringing. Grace was like her father in her need for love and admiration; she had, like him, a healthy sexual drive and, just as he had done, would always in the end subordinate those feelings to what the Kellys saw as the "proper" and superior demands of her family and her position in life. She was, Cassini said, absolutely capable of rationalizing her emotions, as disciplined in her private life as she was in her work, even when making love. The passionate heat of their Riviera romance was doomed to fade away in the face of the Kellys' unrelenting hostility.

When Grace and Oleg returned from Cannes to California to finish shooting *To Catch a Thief* in the high summer of 1954 they were, according to chaperone Lizanne, "going very hot" and talking about getting married, but, towards the end of August, with the filming "wrapped", Grace flew East with Oliver, the newly-acquired poodle puppy, in her lap, to face the Kelly family and reality. Father Jack and brother Kell were not generally in favour of Grace's choice of men. "I don't approve of these oddballs she goes out with," Kell is reported to have "grumped" in *Time* magazine. "I wish she would go out with the more athletic type. But she doesn't listen to me any more." Oleg Cassini, a dress designer, twice married and described in the same *Time* article as a "professional man-about-ladies", was exactly the kind of man to make the Kellys "grump" a good deal. "Mother and Dad were not too fond of Oleg," said Lizanne. "Dad didn't like his track record too much."

According to Lizanne the affair between Grace and Oleg was already on the wane by the time Grace flew back East to join her family in Ocean City. Cassini remembers it differently but, whatever the state of Grace's feelings for him that September, the week which he spent with the Kellys at Wesley Avenue must have shown him that his cause was lost. Grace's father and brother made it quite clear that he was not part of their world nor would he be part of Grace's, and they were backed up by the Kelly friends, all of whom disliked the idea of Oleg even more perhaps than they disliked the man himself. Mrs Kelly could not bring herself to approve of a man who had been twice married, once to an heiress and the second time to a film star, as a husband for her daughter, even if both marriages could, from a Catholic point of view, be regarded as invalid. Only Grace's sisters were nice to the would-be fiancé, but they could not make up for the hostility of the senior members of the Kelly family.

Grace's family were very important to her; she might have outgrown them in some ways, evolving while they remained the same, but she was still, as her father told a reporter, "the most home- and family-loving person I've ever known". The bedroom of her Manhattan apartment was filled with photographs of her family and, when she was in New York, she spent most weekends in Philadelphia with them. Her father's approval was still the prize she vainly sought and his disapproval was very hard to bear. When he made it absolutely clear to her that if she went ahead and married Oleg she would be separating herself from her family and putting herself beyond the pale as far as the Kelly circle was concerned, she gave in. Oleg continued to be her escort into the early spring of 1955, but marriage was definitely out.

Grace spent the winter of 1954 in New York in her Manhattan House apartment, going to the theatre, visiting her gypsy fortune-teller and, above all, seeing her friends. She drew strength from her friends, needing them to give her the love and admiration she had been denied as a child, to satisfy her need to communicate, to exercise her undoubted power to attract and, just as her father had done, to gather round herself a loyal and devoted band. If she felt drawn to a person she would initiate the friendship, as she did with Judy Balaban Quine, daughter of the founder of Paramount and later the wife of Grace's agent, Jay Kanter. At first it was just a pleasant acquaintance – "we liked each other, that was clear," Judy said, "but it was sort of that we were there through Jay. Gradually we'd find each other really talking directly with one another about something personal." Then one night, as Grace and some friends were returning late to New York from Philadelphia on the milk train with a bottle of champagne, everyone else fell asleep, leaving Grace and Judy talking. Suddenly Grace, "out of the clear blue", said how glad she was that Jay and Judy had married each other, "because so often a friend will marry somebody and they're all right but you never make a connection beyond the fact of the person you were originally friendly with ... it's so wonderful for me that Jay married you because now we have our own independent friendship".

Grace, Judy said, took an incredible amount of time and trouble about her friendships; she had an extraordinary ability to concentrate on her friends even when she was the focus of some celebration, surrounded by photographers, interviewers and thousands of gawping spectators. "In the middle of the most dazzling event, which was centred and focused only on her, [she had this capacity] to do what she should do within that context and at the same time to be as sensitive to each of her friends who was there or involved in a way as though nothing was happening ... just tuned in to the immediate and important things to her, which I think is true for everything about her life."

She seemed, Judy said, to have learned young who she was and what was important to her and she held on to those things, without changing herself. "She was that way before she was famous as an actress and she was that way when she was a great movie star and she was that way when she was Princess of Monaco." Grace, she said, was a paradox in being "enormously strong and wildly vulnerable at the same time ... sensitive and caring and full of feeling for things, and easily and deeply touched and yet apparently self-contained and strong". She was vulnerable, too, about herself, yet with the ability to pick herself up and recover, to take a situation and to improve it. Religion, in a very personal way, was important to Grace and was to become more so as her life developed. Grace's religion, Judy said, was not just that of a practising Catholic but "a very genuine personal thing", which had nothing to do with mere conformity.

Instinctive religious feeling was part of Grace's Irish Catholic heritage, as was a strong interest in the supernatural, and in astrology in particular. She was a very superstitious woman, a friend said, with a deep belief in her destiny as predicted by astrology and in the personal characteristics of her sign, Scorpio. Astrologers had told her that she would achieve supreme good fortune through hard work, and that belief sustained her. She retained her interest in astrology to the end of her life: Carroll Righter of Los Angeles would regularly send her predictions. She also visited tarot-card readers or, in these early New York days, a particular gypsy fortune-teller.

She was in need of no gypsy fortune-teller, however, to advise her in her dealings with MGM; it was only too evident that the roles they had in mind for her were not ones which she would be likely to accept. As *Time* put it in an article of 31 January 1955, "Grace's admirers fear that MGM may do to her what the studio did to Deborah Kerr – lash her down to 'lady' roles and keep her there." Even after *Country Girl*, the writer pointed out, the best they could think of for her was *Green Fire*, and their next idea for her was an historical costume picture, *Quentin Durward*. Grace, who, as the magazine put it, "sees the satin-lined trap as clearly as anyone", turned down the part as soon as she read the script. "All the men can duel and fight," she explained. "But all I'd do would be to wear thirty-five different costumes, and look pretty and frightened. There are eight people chasing me: the old man, the robbers, the head gypsy and Durward. The stage directions on every page of the script say 'She clutches her jewel box and flees.' I just thought I'd be so bored. ...."

Relations between Grace and the studio deteriorated rapidly in the early months of 1955 as MGM continued to offer her parts which she described as "using me as scenery", while the roles she wanted were in films being made by other studios, such as the part of Leslie in Warner Brothers' *Giant*, which she would very much have liked to play, but which eventually went to another MGM star, Elizabeth Taylor. MGM, however, were not in lending mood as far as Grace was concerned; as Dore Schary explained: "Grace has made six pictures and only two of them have been for us – *Mogambo* and *Green Fire*. We want to keep her. We think she is a great artist and we are going to see she gets the right vehicle."

Unfortunately, however, MGM's idea of the right vehicle did not tally with Grace's. Although, on a fleeting twenty-four-hour visit to Los Angeles towards the end of January, she had in principle agreed to star in a Western, *Jeremy Rodock*, opposite Spencer Tracy, when the script finally arrived she turned it down. "I'm not trying to be difficult or temperamental," she told reporters. "I just don't feel I'm right for the part in *Jeremy Rodock*. My agent has told the studio the way I feel but they say I have to make the picture anyway." MGM was understandably hurt and angry at Grace's rejection of their project. "We feel Miss Kelly has certain obligations to us," Dore Schary said. "After all, we were the first to give her a chance." The studio put her on suspension as from 7 March. "So what?" was the reaction of Jay Kanter, when he heard the news. "It's not as if she were a hardship case." Rumours ran around Hollywood that Grace was trying to break her contract with MGM, which Jay Kanter denied. The only thing to do in Grace's case, he said, would have been to wait until the contract time was nearly up and then renegotiate a non-exclusive agreement which would have enabled her to make pictures outside the studio and keep the money she earned from them.

Grace, hating rows, was distressed, and the trouble with MGM came at a trying moment for her. In February she learned that she had been nominated for the Best Actress award and, added to the strain of waiting to know if she would win, she was in the process of moving to a new and larger apartment in New York on 80th Street and Fifth Avenue. She was, however, determined, and in the end it was the studio which caved in. Ten days before the Academy Award ceremony MGM had second thoughts; *Rodock* had been postponed until June and they had another project in mind for Grace, the role of the poetess Elizabeth Barrett in a re-make of *The Barretts of Wimpole Street*. Grace, still wary of committing herself, had indicated "informally that she felt it was too early for her to appear in that picture". A memorandum of a meeting of the studio heads at MGM on 18 March shows that they were still in menacing mood. "If she turns down *Barretts* we can suspend her again," it ran; but three days later they surrendered unconditionally and Grace's suspension was lifted as from 21 March. "We respect Grace," Dore Schary told the press, "and we want to do everything possible for her during this important time in her life when she is up for an Academy Award."

The press represented the nominations for the Best Actress award as a race for the Oscar between Grace for *Country Girl* and Judy Garland for *A Star is Born*. There was indeed a poignant contrast between Grace and Judy Garland, dark, petite, an agonized show-business genius with a talent as overwhelming as her ability to destroy herself and anyone who came close to her. Born literally backstage in Grand Rapids, Minnesota, of vaudeville parents, she had been part of the family act at the age of two and a movie star by the age of thirteen. With two unhappy marriages, a half-hearted suicide attempt and a public dismissal by her studio behind her, *A Star is Born* was Judy's enormously expensive comeback. Gossips wrote that "sentiment" would win Judy the Oscar but, as she wryly commented, "Hollywood is the least sentimental town in the world – and believe me, I know." Columnists naturally could not resist portraying Grace as the Philadelphia débutante, daughter of a millionaire father – "It's Judy Garland, born in a vaudeville trunk, versus Grace Kelly, born into a Philadelphia mansion."

There were other contenders, including Dorothy Dandridge for *Carmen Jones*, Jane Wyman for *Magnificent Obsession* and Audrey Hepburn for *Sabrina Fair*, but Hollywood insiders agreed that it must be a close race between Garland and Kelly. Both actresses desperately wanted to win. In the event it was Grace, sitting with her mother in the Pantages Theater, who heard her name called as the winner; Judy, in hospital after the birth of her child by Sidney Luft, who lost.

Grace, dressed in an ice-blue satin evening dress, wept with emotion as she received the Oscar on 30 March 1955. Even then, with eyes pink from crying and fingers shaking as she clutched the golden statuette, she retained enough presence of mind to refuse when photographers asked her to kiss Marlon Brando, winner of the Oscar for Best Actor. "I believe he should kiss me," she said, a Philadelphia lady even under stress. Brando, neatly dressed in a dinner jacket, beat Bing Crosby for the award and, curiously, *On the Waterfront*, the film with which Grace had almost become involved, swept the board, winning seven Oscars, including Eva Marie Saint's award for Best Supporting Actress. Grace and Marlon Brando, both anti-Hollywood stars, were the youngest ever award winners; Grace Kelly, no longer a Hollywood princess, had won a Hollywood crown.

In this moment of supreme triumph did she think that now at last her father must admit that she had reached the top through her own endeavour, as he himself had through his? Jack Kelly had recently, in public as well as in private, seemed reluctant to acknowledge Grace's success, although wryly admitting that she had become even more famous than he was. Recently, he told a reporter, he had placed a long-distance telephone call saying, "John B. Kelly of Philadelphia speaking." "Who?" the operator had replied in a bored voice. "Just say Grace Kelly's father is calling," Jack Kelly riposted. "The call went through", he said, "quick like a flash." When a reporter came to interview him about Grace, he could not resist introducing Peggy into the conversation. "You ought to see her," he said. "Peggy's the family extrovert. Just between us, I've always thought her the daughter with the most on the ball. You can't figure those things, can you?" In January 1955, two months before Grace won the Oscar, *McCall's* described her father's "bewilderment" at her stardom: "I thought it would be Peggy. Anything that Grace could do Peggy could always do better." Now, in the spring of 1955, less than eight years after Grace had left home to make her own way in New York, Peggy was a housewife while Grace stood at the pinnacle of her profession, an Oscar winner. She had become, as she had told Bill Allyn she would only three years before winning the award, "a big, big movie star".

She had achieved the first of her goals. Now, as she contemplated the future, the question facing her was – what next? An interview which she had given to *Collier's* magazine during a brief holiday in Jamaica just over a month before provided a clue to the direction in which her mind was turning: "One has different goals at different periods. . . . I'd love to get married and have children. But I hate to plan – for next year, even for next week. And there's a superstition of the theatre that if you want a thing badly, you mustn't talk about it. It's the sure way to lose."

She was seriously contemplating marriage, but the extent of her success and her huge celebrity posed its own problem – whom could she now find of sufficient stature that he would not lose his own identity in hers and become mere Mr Grace Kelly?

8
Enter the Prince

Early in March 1955 the telephone rang in Grace's New York apartment. It was Rupert Allan with an invitation to Grace from the French Government to attend the Cannes Film Festival as their guest of honour. "We've got to have Grace Kelly," the director of the Festival had told Allan. "Everybody in France is in love with her, she's the biggest star ever – and we can't talk to her because she's on suspension from MGM." Since Rupert Allan had first met Grace in London when she was finishing *Mogambo*, he had done three cover stories on her for *Look*. Grace liked and trusted him, but, wary as she was of involvements, her initial response to this invitation was cautious, even negative. "I'm changing apartments, I've got to get settled into this new apartment, I'm changing secretaries ... No, I don't want to go to France, it's the wrong time."

"Wrong thinking," Rupert told her. "You're young, you're attractive and I'm offering you spring in the south of France." Knowing how shy and how cautious she was, he promised her that he would be there to fend for her, to tell her what things to go to and what to avoid. Grace was still wary; she had read all the reports of the Festival two years ago when Robert Mitchum had been trapped in an embarrassing situation by a starlet who suddenly stripped off next to him in front of photographers. Moreover, in tune with the anti-Communist hysteria in the United States, the *Hollywood Reporter*'s Mike Connolly had represented Cannes under its Communist city administration as a violently anti-American Soviet front organization. Cannes, in fact, appeared to be everything that Grace abhorred, but she had confidence in Allan and she heeded his assurances that the French Government wanted her to go. "OK," she said. "I'll think about it. I don't think so, but I'll think about it."

When Allan called the next day, he was very forceful. "You've got to go," he told Grace. "OK, I'll go," she replied. Later he learned that Eric Johnston, head of the Motion Picture Association of

The Kelly clan: (*standing left to right*) Grace's uncles Charles and George, her father John B. ("Jack") and her uncle Patrick Henry; (*seated*) grandfather John H. and uncle Walter C.

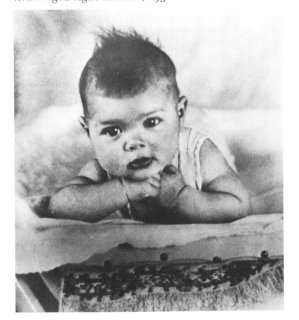

Grace aged eight months, 1930.

Aged two years.

In Henry Avenue: (*left to right*) Peggy aged eight, Grace four, their mother holding
Lizanne aged four months and John B. Jnr ("Kell") aged six.

At "the shore", Ocean City, New Jersey, c. 1934: (*left to right*) Lizanne, "Ma" Kelly,
Grace, Kell, Peggy and Jack Kelly.

At home, c. 1934: Grace and Peggy (*at back*), Kell, Jack Kelly, Lizanne and Margaret Kelly.

The Kellys setting off on holiday, 1936: (*left to right*) Grace, Peggy, their parents, Lizanne and Kell.

Class of '47: Grace in her graduation year, from the Stevens School yearbook.

Dear Doris —
Don't ever forget our days
at Stevens + our little
trip to N.Y. — Good Luck
at college Love Kelly

Grace in a "beanie" and Penn Charter sweater with three schoolfriends, c. 1947.

Stevens School hockey team, 1947: Grace (*front row, third from right*) and
Doris Snyder (*second row, second from right*).

Stevens School Student Council, 1947: Grace is third from right in the back row.

"After twenty-seven years of waiting and hoping, the name of John B. Kelly was on the Diamond Sculls": Grace with her parents, the triumphant Kell and Lizanne at Henley, 1947.

Grace in her teens (*right*) with her father and Lizanne at Ocean City.

A kiss for Kell on his departure for London and the Olympics, July 1949.

Graduation portrait, American Academy of
Dramatic Arts, class of 1948–9.

Her first commercial job: promoting
insecticide for the Bridgeport Brass
Company, 1948.

Her first professional stage appearance: Grace with Haila Stoddard and Carl White on
the opening night (25 July 1949) of *The Torch-Bearers* by her uncle George Kelly,
Bucks County Playhouse, New Hope, Pennsylvania.

To Aunt Marie
with love & kisses
Gracie —

One of her first publicity shots, c. 1949, inscribed to "Aunt" Marie Magee.

As a television leading lady in *The Borgia Lamp*, 1952,
in the *Lights Out* series.

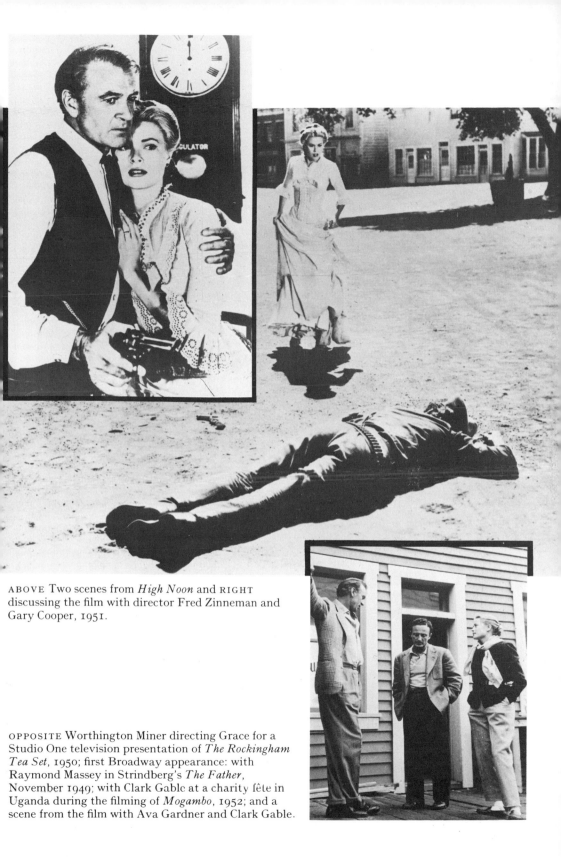

ABOVE Two scenes from *High Noon* and RIGHT discussing the film with director Fred Zinneman and Gary Cooper, 1951.

OPPOSITE Worthington Miner directing Grace for a Studio One television presentation of *The Rockingham Tea Set*, 1950; first Broadway appearance: with Raymond Massey in Strindberg's *The Father*, November 1949; with Clark Gable at a charity fête in Uganda during the filming of *Mogambo*, 1952; and a scene from the film with Ava Gardner and Clark Gable.

ABOVE Alfred Hitchcock directing Grace
and Robert Cummings in *Dial M for
Murder*; on the humorously decorated
bicycle given to her by Paramount, 1954;
and doing her own make-up at Paramount.

RIGHT Grace sharing a joke with Ray
Milland on the set of *Dial M for Murder*,
1953; sharing a cup of tea with Danny Kaye
on the set of *Rear Window*; and with her
co-star in the film James Stewart.

A publicity shot and two scenes from
Rear Window with James Stewart.

OPPOSITE ABOVE With Stewart
Granger in *Green Fire*; and "hair
mussed" – a make-up test for the
film.

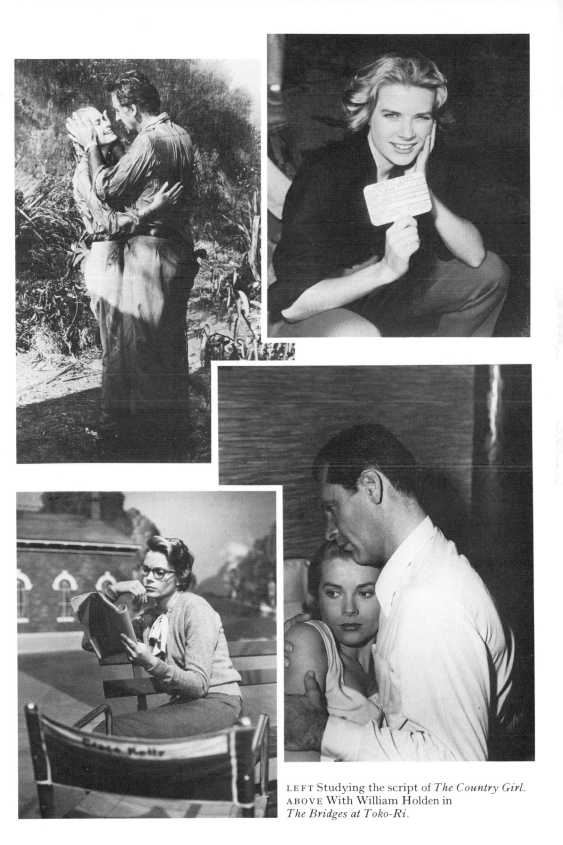

LEFT Studying the script of *The Country Girl*.
ABOVE With William Holden in
The Bridges at Toko-Ri.

Winning the Oscar: with William Holden in her prize-winning role of Georgie Elgin in *The Country Girl* (1954); making her tearful acceptance speech, 30 March 1955; and with fellow Oscar winner Marlon Brando: "I believe *he* should kiss *me*."

Filming Hitchcock's *To Catch A Thief*, Cary Grant turned "dead white under his tan", said Grace, as she drove him along the dangerous roads above Monte Carlo.

RIGHT Having afternoon tea on the set with Alfred Hitchcock.

OPPOSITE: TOP A tête-à-tête with Oleg Cassini in the South of France, summer 1954; CENTRE Shopping for souvenirs with Jean-Pierre Aumont, May 1955; and BELOW Grace's first meeting with Prince Rainier in the palace in Monaco, 6 May 1955.

Helen Rose showing Grace her costume designs for *The Swan*, and on location with Alec Guinness at the Biltmore, South Carolina, November–December 1955.

ABOVE The newly engaged couple at the
Night in Monte Carlo Ball at the Waldorf
Astoria hotel, New York, January 1956.
RIGHT 12 April 1956: wearing the much
criticized hat and clutching Oliver the poodle,
Grace disembarks in Monaco, followed by
Prince Rainier. FAR RIGHT 18 April 1956: the
civil marriage ceremony in the red and gold
Throne Room of the palace.

Two musical moments from *High Society*: "You're Sensational" with Frank Sinatra, and "True Love" with Bing Crosby.

19 April 1956: Grace and Prince Rainier
exchange rings during the religious
ceremony in the Cathedral of St Nicholas; a
formal wedding portrait; and at the
wedding breakfast with Grace's parents and
(*right*) bridesmaid Carolyn Scott Reybold.

With her first child, Princess Caroline, born on 23 January 1957.

Grace holds the heir to the throne, Prince Albert, born on 14 March 1958, while Prince Rainier amuses Princess Caroline.

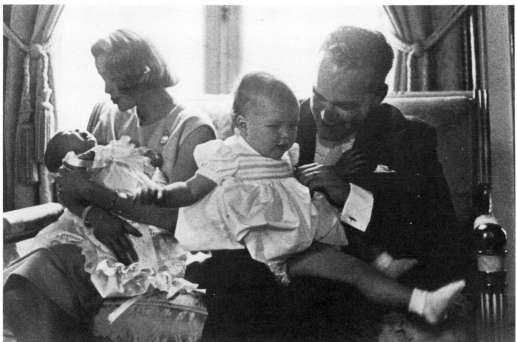

ABOVE Outside the former Kelly family home, Drumirla, Co. Mayo, on an official visit to Ireland in June 1961. ABOVE RIGHT Grace landing her fish off Westport, Co. Mayo. RIGHT The family with newly arrived Princess Stephanie, born 1 February 1965.

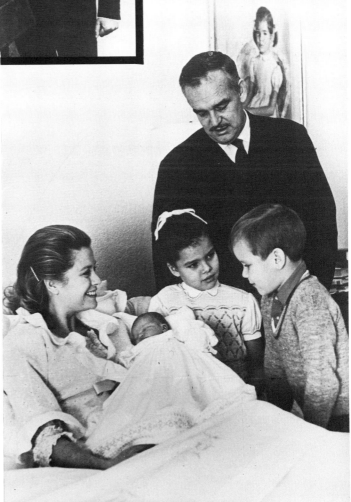

Wearing a dress given her by the flamenco dancers of Seville, Grace watches some gipsy dancers at the Feria with Prince Rainier, 26 April 1966.

With Prince Rainier at a fancy-dress ball in Monte Carlo, March 1969.

Dancing with Professor Christian Barnard, the famous South African heart surgeon, at the Red Cross Ball in Monte Carlo, August 1968.

The family on a winter holiday near Gstaad, Switzerland.

Preparing lunch in the galley of the family yacht.

Grace and Princess Caroline escorting Princess Stephanie from the family's Paris home on her first day at school, September 1976.

Princess Caroline, Prince Albert and Grace at
a Christmas party in the Red Cross children's
home in Monaco

Playing baseball during Monaco's American
Week against a team from a visiting US warship:
a strike – and she decides to run for it.

Ballet fan: backstage at the theatre in Vienna with members of the American Ballet Theater,
Mikhail Baryshnikov (*left*) and Gelsen Kirkian, June 1977.

In the family's Paris home with Princess Caroline.

Wedding procession in Monaco after the marriage of Princess Caroline and Philippe Junot, 29 June 1978: Prince Rainier and Grace on the left, the bridegroom's parents behind the bridal couple.

Standing before Shakespeare's presumed tomb in the church at Stratford-upon-Avon, where she performed a poetry reading, "A Remembrance of Shakespeare", in 1977.

Beside one of her pressed flower collages exhibited at the Galerie Drouant, Paris, June 1980.

With Prince Charles and his fiancée, Lady Diana Spencer, at the gala evening at Goldsmiths' Hall, London, in aid of the Royal Opera House, Covent Garden. Grace read poetry in "Themes and Variations", March 1981.

At Lourdes, France, with Prince Albert and other Monégasque pilgrims, July 1979.

"Tribute to Grace Kelly", 31 March 1982, with (*left to right*) Stewart Granger, Celeste Holm, Bob Hope, James Stewart, Rita Gam and Brian Aherne, Annenberg Center, Philadelphia.

The last Monaco Red Cross Gala attended by the whole family, 30 July 1982. Princess Stephanie is wearing a dress made by Dior for Grace in 1956, while Grace is wearing the dress in which she was later buried.

A fancy-dress party for family and friends aboard the *Mermoz*: (*left to right*) two unidentified friends, Princess Caroline, Grace (*above*), Prince Louis de Polignac, Prince Albert, Bettina Thompson Gray and M. Biancheri, Prince Rainier's private secretary.

At Roc Agel.

America, had called her too and emphasized that she would be going to represent America. For Grace, with her intense Irish-American patriotism and her sense of duty, that meant she could not refuse. And so, one evening in May, Grace arrived in Cannes from Paris accompanied by Gladys de Segonzac, who had acted as wardrobe mistress on *To Catch a Thief*. She was met by Allan and taken to the Carlton Hotel, where, just over a year ago, she had stayed with the cast of *To Catch a Thief* and Oleg Cassini.

Next morning at nine Allan called and was surprised to hear an unusually upset Grace.

'Rupert, this can't happen again. This is terrible. I'm going off to Monaco. Pierre Galante [film editor of *Paris Match*] wants to do a cover story on me and they've made arrangements already with the Prince of Monaco to show me around the palace, and it's a long way, I don't know how far it is." Not only was Monaco over an hour's drive from Cannes but the meeting with the Prince was scheduled for 3 pm and Grace was expected back for a reception at 5.30 pm that evening, and, to make matters worse, she had only unpacked late the evening before and none of her clothes were pressed. Nor could they be: Cannes was suffering the usual rash of strikes during the Festival and on that day there was an electricity strike. Moreover Grace, who had washed her hair, could not dry it.

"It's unbelievable," she told Rupert. "And now I'm committed."

"Well, don't do it. I told you to clear things through me. I'll tell *Paris Match* to drop dead."

"No, no, you can't get someone like the Prince of Monaco waiting there and not do it."

Pierre Galante was at that time married to Olivia de Havilland. The idea of doing a feature on Grace, picturing her with the Prince, had been the brainchild of his managing editor, Pierre Bonheur, who had commissioned Galante to set it up. Galante had "ambushed" Grace on the train from Paris, getting himself introduced to her through his wife, who knew Gladys de Segonzac. Grace, intrigued by the idea and unaware of the punishing schedule awaiting her at Cannes, had agreed to do it. Now she was faced with the prospect of a photographic session with a prince, her hair wet and with a wardrobe full of crumpled clothes.

Somehow, with the help of Gladys de Segonzac, she managed. Only one dress remained uncreased. It was a magnificent 1950s creation of black cotton satin splashed with a bold design of red and green cabbage roses, long-sleeved and tight to the hips, then bursting into a full skirt – spectacular but far too strong for photographs. However, there was no alternative: Grace put it on. While she scraped back her hair into a chignon, Gladys found a headband decorated with artificial flowers in Grace's luggage and fashioned it to fit over her hair in place of a hat.

Grace almost did not get to Monaco: the car in which she was travelling with Gladys, Pierre Galante and MGM's publicity man in Paris, Elias Lapinère, was crashed into from the back by the following car of *Paris Match* photographers. When finally, after snatching a quick sandwich at the Hôtel de Paris, they arrived at the palace, Prince Rainier, still at lunch at his villa at Cap Ferrat, was not there.

As she posed for the photographers against the rich background of the palace State Rooms Grace began to exhibit the first signs of nervousness, taking a mirror from her handbag and powdering her nose.

"What do I call him?" she asked Pierre Galante. "How old is he? Does he speak English?"

Prince Rainier III of Monaco was then not quite thirty-two, six years older than Grace, although he had already been reigning Prince of Monaco since 1949 on the death of his grandfather, Prince Louis. He was the son of Princess Charlotte, Prince Louis' daughter by Juliette Louvet – a washerwoman whom Louis had met in Algiers while he was serving with a French regiment but had, apparently, neglected to marry – and a French aristocrat, Comte Pierre de Polignac. His parents' marriage had been an arranged match and an unhappy one and, after their divorce in 1933, he and his older sister, Princess Antoinette, had lived a peripatetic life, mainly with their grandfather, Prince Louis, as he travelled between Monaco, where he rarely spent more than three months a year, Paris and Marchais, his hunting lodge in the Ardennes, or grouse-shooting in Scotland with his aristocratic cousins, the Hamiltons. Prince Rainier did indeed speak excellent English, having been brought up by an English nanny and educated at a succession of uncongenial English schools.

After a lonely, unsettled, unloved childhood, Prince Rainier had grown up into a young man who had intelligence and charm but could at the same time be difficult and moody, finding it easier to communicate with animals than with human beings. Indeed he had an intense rapport with animals and, in the private menagerie which he kept in the palace grounds, he would go into the panther's cage and play with it, or would pet a tiger given him by Emperor Bao-Dai of Indochina. He used to disrupt sedate dinner parties by throwing open his dinner jacket to reveal a large pet snake coiled round his waist in place of a cummerbund – he was given to practical jokes. He had a passion for the sea like his great-grandfather, Prince Albert, a celebrated oceanographer, and he loved boats and deep-sea diving, fast cars and rally driving. He liked women, and was attractive to them, and had had a long and serious affair with beautiful French actress Gisèle Pascal. This had ended in June 1953, apparently for reasons of state, because Gisèle seemed to be unable to bear the all-important heir for Monaco, although, in fact, she later married and had a child.

It was already 3.45 pm and Elias Lapinère, MGM's publicity representative, was looking at his watch. Grace was poised to depart. "I think he is very rude to keep us waiting like this," she told Pierre Galante. "Let's get out of here." But at that point the Prince arrived, having driven furiously from his villa at Cap Ferrat, where he had hosted a lunch party. Grace saw approaching her a young man of medium height, stocky, with dark hair and moustache, and very un-Mediterranean dark blue eyes. They were introduced, she curtsied, the Prince offered her a tour of the palace, which, having already seen it, she declined. They compromised on a walk round the gardens, including, of course, a visit to the private zoo. Grace surprised the Prince by being quite unlike the stereotype American film actress with her shyness and her quiet manners. He was, he admitted later, "very interested" in her and wanted to see her again. He already had plans to visit America the following winter and he and Grace promised to meet again then. And so, by the time Grace left Monaco for a hurried drive back to the hurly-burly of Cannes, the possibilities for the future were already in the air.

Characteristically, Grace was not very illuminating when interrogated by Rupert Allan that evening.

"How did it go in Monaco?"

"Oh, it went fine."

"How was the Prince?"

"Well, he was very sweet and very nice, very considerate, a very nice man. And certainly, as far as that goes, fine."

And that was all.

*   *   *

Grace's first, all-important meeting with Prince Rainier was to go almost unnoticed in the press furore over the re-appearance in her life of Jean-Pierre Aumont. They had kept in touch over the intervening two years and, knowing she was coming to the Festival, he joined her in the most public manner, at a dinner given by the celebrity-seeking party-giver Elsa Maxwell. Aumont arrived late and sat down beside Grace, immediately monopolizing her attention. They danced, they chatted, smiled into each other's eyes, and the world's press, assembled at Cannes, unaware that they already knew each other, jumped to the obvious conclusions. In an article headed "Is Grace Kelly in love?" Elsa Maxwell, described as "Confidante of International Society", reported a conversation she had had with Jean-Pierre at another dinner party he and Grace had attended but had left early. "Next morning he told me he had gone to sit and talk quietly with Grace because she had a headache."

"What is this, darling Jean-Pierre?" I asked excitedly. "Are you really falling in love?"

"Falling in love!" he exclaimed. "I'm desperate. Grace is the most adorable girl I've met since Maria died."

"But how does *she* feel?" I asked.

"Oh, I don't think she feels that way about me at all," he answered. *Time* magazine featured a photograph of Grace and Jean-Pierre dancing together – "Grace Kelly, commonly billed as an icy goddess, melted perceptibly in the company of French actor, Jean-Pierre Aumont . . . had Aumont, who came and thawed, actually conquered Grace?" it asked.

Grace was escorted everywhere at Cannes by Jean-Pierre, usually to public functions but also to one indiscreet private lunch at the Château de la Galère down the coast, where Grace was photographed with a long-distance zoom lens, holding and kissing Jean-Pierre's hand. After Cannes she spent six days in Paris en route to America, sightseeing with Jean-Pierre and pursued by an increasingly avid press. They went to the theatre together with friends and spent most of the weekend before she left with his family at his country house at Rueil-Malmaison. While Aumont's friends, and the world's press, gained the impression that he intended to marry her, Grace, on her arrival back in America, was smiling but absolutely definite that she and Aumont had no marriage plans. All she would say was the classic "we're just good friends".

Grace's non-committal attitude on the subject of Jean-Pierre may not have been unconnected with the publication in *Paris Match* a few days before her departure of the photographs of her romantic luncheon with him on the Riviera, pictures which also appeared in *Life*, blazoned across the United States. In his nationally syndicated column Igor Cassini weighed in with the charge that Jean-Pierre Aumont "had planned in advance to have their pictures taken" and that Grace was deeply upset about it. "Aumont, who was sort of forgotten all these years, now has received quite a shot of publicity in the arm – but Grace doesn't like to admit she was a guinea pig," he wrote. Igor Cassini can hardly be taken as an unbiased witness in the affair, but some substance was given to his allegations when it was discovered by one of Grace's friends that Aumont had borrowed the car in which he took Grace to the famous lunch from a *Paris Match* photographer. Grace, discreet as usual, said nothing, but when Philadelphia friends, interviewed on the subject of Jean-Pierre, innocently gave it as their opinion that he was very acceptable, as a Catholic and a widower, "Grace almost hit the roof. ... She didn't want anybody linking her with him."

Whatever the truth of the Aumont episode, the pictures and the rumours certainly upset the Kellys, to whom a French actor years older than Grace, even though Catholic and a widower, did not represent a suitable husband. And Jean-Pierre was far from being the only candidate for her hand. There was William Clothier, very much a part of Proper Philadelphia, who asked Grace to the exclusive Piccadilly ball as an out-of-town guest and wanted to marry her. Clothier, an upstanding, conservative young man and son of the National Tennis Champion, was a Philadelphia gentleman but hardly the fascinating cosmopolitan type that Grace now favoured. Then there was also socialite Gordon White, described by the press as "a rich young English film star addict who had once been the escort of Audrey Hepburn", and who was now Grace's eager suitor.

Grace, however, with Aumont definitely behind her, seemed to be more interested in returning to work. MGM had at last offered her a part, in a play by Ferenc Molnar, which she wanted to do and one which, apparently, had been suggested to her as suitable by her uncle George Kelly. The part, which she had already played before on television, was the romantic-*ingénue* role of Alexandra, princess of a make-believe Ruritanian nation, who is to save the family fortunes by marrying the rich Prince Albert, a plan which is almost shipwrecked by her falling in love with her younger brother's handsome tutor, played in the film by Louis Jourdan.

If Grace had entertained childhood fantasies of playing a princess, those dreams were amply fulfilled in the filming of *The Swan*. The location scenes for the film were shot at the Biltmore, the French Renaissance-style château built by George Vanderbilt near Asheville, North Carolina. "It's like a palace, I love it," Grace told Jay Kanter as she showed him round the huge house. The costumes for *The Swan*, set in the period around 1915, were, said designer Helen Rose, one of the best jobs she ever did. "I used beautiful fabrics on all the costumes," she wrote, "the finest I could find." Grace adored them. "I had never seen a star as thrilled as Grace was the day we fitted the white chiffon ball gown. She stood before the mirror, gently touching the embroidered camellias on the background of the gown, saying, 'How simply marvellous – what talented people you have here at MGM.'" Several skilled women had in fact spent weeks at embroidery frames carefully working each petal by hand. The image of Grace as a princess in *The Swan*, exquisitely beautiful with her perfect features and upswept blonde hair above the fragile white gown, is one of the most memorable and poignant of all her pictures.

Her studio, MGM, were certainly treating her as royalty, and Alec Guinness, then a relatively unknown English actor, playing opposite her as Prince Albert, was struck with the way she reacted to such treatment. Flying from Los Angeles to Asheville, North Carolina in a DC7 hired by MGM, the company were served a sumptuous meal which included steak, only for it to be discovered that the stewardess had forgotten the knives and forks. Grace and Alec Guinness enjoyed themselves sharing a penknife and scooping up the steak with a plastic spoon, but when they reached Asheville the airline executives, in paroxysms of obsequiousness, made profound apologies and declared that the stewardess would be sacked in consequence. "It was Grace who said, 'We can't let this thing happen,' and made us all sign a petition against the stewardess's dismissal, saying how sweet and apologetic she had been," Guinness remembered. Grace asked Guinness if he would like to share her car from the airport, and was embarrassed when it turned out to be an enormous limousine complete with outriders as if it were a presidential cavalcade. "After a while Grace found it too much and stopped the car and told the driver to please get rid of the outriders," Sir Alec said.

Sir Alec enjoyed working with Grace. "I thought she was terribly good in the range that she had. She had a sweet, cool quality, although she was very capable of having very endearing giggles. In our first scene together she rose from her curtsey and hit me under the chin so my teeth went clunk – we had to stop for five minutes to recover and Grace's make-up had to be redone." On another occasion director Charles Vidor wanted Grace's hair gently ruffled by air blown down a long tube – "it ruffled her hair but it blew my toupee off at the same time, which took about an hour out of filming – she was awfully good about it," Sir Alec recalls. He remembers too that someone, probably MGM, was still sensitive about Grace's reputation as "ice-cold Kelly", which, he said, "she wasn't at all". The script had a line in reference to her which ran: "How could you have anything to do with that frost-cake?" It was cut.

For the actors, the three weeks spent filming in Asheville, cooped up in each other's company in the Manor Hotel, were a time of silly games and hilarious fun. Apart from Guinness and Grace and Louis Jourdan there were Grace's friend from *To Catch a Thief*, Jessie Royce Landis, known as "Roycie", playing her screen mother, Brian Aherne, later a close friend, in the role of her wise screen uncle, a monk, and Estelle Winwood as a dotty spinster aunt. It was in this atmosphere that the now-famous "tomahawk story" began.

"Roycie" Landis visited an Indian reservation in the Smoky Mountains and came back with a tomahawk as a souvenir, a huge and hideous object some eighteen inches long and very weighty. She gave it to Guinness, who, as he was leaving the next day for New Orleans in a tiny plane, did not want to be loaded down with the thing. "I gave it to the hall porter," he said, "and told him to put it in Miss Kelly's bed." That was the last he heard or thought of the tomahawk until many years later he found it in his bed in his cottage in the country in England. "I didn't know who did it but I had a pretty shrewd suspicion," he said.

From then on it became an elaborate intermittent game between Grace and Guinness. The point was that, as he said, "We never mentioned it," never asking how one player had managed to per-suade some intermediary to place it in the other's bed. Guinness got his own back by arranging for Grace to find it in her bed when she was doing a poetry-reading tour in the States with the Royal Shake-speare Company actor, Richard Pasco. Finding the tomahawk in her her bed in the hotel in Minneapolis, she immediately suspected Pasco.

Casually she asked him: "You have so much experience in acting you must have come across Sir Alec Guinness some time or other, haven't you?"

"No, I haven't. Strangely enough, I've never met him," Pasco replied – sticking literally to the truth, although he was indeed the emissary through a mutual friend. Grace dropped the subject; it was an unwritten code that no direct questions could be asked.

Grace's greatest coup was to smuggle the tomahawk into Guinness's bed in the Beverly Wilshire Hotel in Beverly Hills when he was in Los Angeles to receive the Oscar. She called Rupert Allan. "Rupert, you're going to get a package from a messenger, and I want you to get it into Guinness's bed. You know what I'm talking about, don't you?" Allan found out where Guinness was staying and contacted his friend Helen Chaplin, executive assistant manager of the hotel, who mounted a complex operation to get it into the bed, via the floor manager, who kept watch to see when Guinness would leave for the ceremony and slipped it into the bed at the precise moment when the maid who came to turn down the bed would not discover it. When Guinness returned from the Oscar ceremony, alone and experiencing something of an anti-climax, since the organizers had forgotten to escort him to the Governors' Ball after the ceremony, he found the tomahawk waiting for him. "It made his evening," said Allan. The final exchange took place on Grace's last visit to England, at Chichester for a poetry reading. As she was leaving the place where she was staying, she opened her attaché case and found the unwieldy object with its stone head, painted with daisies and draped with hangings, nestling in her lingerie. It was the final round, nearly thirty years after the game had begun.

Grace, Guinness said, had been "very sweet" to him, even meeting him at Los Angeles airport when he first arrived from London and spending a good deal of time with him. He was struck by the pleasure and interest she took in reading poetry and the curiously childlike and naïve way she would talk about it. But, he said, she would only concentrate on one person at a time, and after two weeks she turned from him to Louis Jourdan. "Don't you realize", Louis Jourdan said when Guinness asked him about it, "I'm the one who's 'in'." Jourdan's attraction for Grace was that she could practise her French on him. She must have been thinking of the Prince's promise to meet again and saying to herself, "I'll show Rainier when he comes."

Sometime in December Grace received a call from Rupert Allan.

Bill Attwood, Paris editor of *Look*, had just done an interview with Prince Rainier and learned that he planned to make his first trip to America, and Rainier had told him he was going to New York, and maybe Florida and California if he had time. Attwood had asked him, "Is there any person you'd like to see in California?" and Prince Rainier replied that well, he had met a very attractive young actress named Grace Kelly and he thought if she were there he'd like to see her again. *Look* wanted pictures of Prince Rainier and Grace on the set of *The Swan* in Hollywood and Rupert was deputed to ask if she would pose for them.

Grace readily agreed. "Of course he was terribly nice to me and very sweet and polite, I'd be delighted to." Then she said, rather sharply, and one might think unnecessarily, "If you think there's anything else to this story, any kind of romance, you're wrong?" "I didn't think anything," Rupert said, taken aback. "Well," she said, "there's no romance, I've not heard one word from him. Never heard one word from him, one way or the other, and it was fine, just as I told you in Cannes when I got back from Monaco."

Was Grace irritated by the thought that anyone might start rumours of a romance or was it because she had not heard anything yet from Rainier despite his promise that he would get in touch? She had expected to see him again. There was a poignancy to the lines she addressed to the rejected young tutor in *The Swan*: "You see, I *want* to be a queen."

In the end Prince Rainier did not visit Grace on the Hollywood set of *The Swan*, but he had had her very much in mind when he planned his American trip. "The fact that I had met Grace here encouraged me more to go over there and we sort of combined to meet at Christmas," he said many years later when recalling their first meeting.

Marriage was also in the forefront of his thoughts when he planned the visit, as he revealed in an eve-of-departure interview which Grace may well have read, published in *Collier's* magazine on 9 December. Carefully he explained to journalist David Schoenbrun the reasons why, for the sake of Monaco, it was important that he should marry – going back to the treaty of 1918 between his great-grandfather, Prince Albert, and the French Government, which had been designed to protect French interests in Monaco against the pretensions of a German family to the Monégasque throne. The French offered Albert recognition of Monaco as an independent principality whose integrity would be guaranteed by France and whose sovereignty could not be ceded to any power but France. There was, however, a dynastic catch to the treaty in the form of a further clause stipulating that if the throne of Monaco ever became vacant, Monaco would become a "protectorate" of France. Moreover, since his mother, Princess Charlotte, relinquished to him her right to the throne in 1944, and in 1951 his sister, Princess Antoinette, had renounced all claims on behalf of herself and her children, only a child of Rainier's could succeed. If the Prince died without an heir or heiress, the Grimaldi family's centuries-old right to the principality would end, as would, almost certainly, the exceptional privileges and exemption from taxes of the citizens of Monaco. For Prince Rainier, at thirty-two, there was a dynastic imperative. It was his duty as Prince of Monaco to marry and have a child.

There were personal reasons, too, why he wanted to get married, as he told Schoenbrun. "A bachelor's life is lonely, empty – and particularly so for a prince." He would only marry for love, he said, vehemently denying that he was in any way "shopping for a bride", but added, "Of course it is not impossible that I might meet and fall in love with a girl on my trip. I am young, healthy and fancy-free and I want to get married . . . but please be fair and believe me I am not going to America for that purpose. I will get married just as soon as I meet the right girl, and I hope myself it will be very soon."

The Prince went on to describe his ideal girl, which in many ways was a blueprint of Grace. "I cannot stand flashy, spoiled girls. . . . She must be natural and charitable [with] a sincere, deep, Christian charity, a love for one's fellow human beings." As for the household duties of a princess, the Prince echoed almost word for word what Mrs Kelly used to say to her daughters:

How can she order dinner, or tell the cook what to make unless she herself knows how to cook? She must know how to decorate a table and arrange flowers in a living room . . . a princess must be a perfect hostess. I want to be proud of my wife, the way she receives people and keeps conversation moving at a reception, the way she decorates the house, her choice of furniture and paintings, the way she dresses herself and the children. She must be a woman of taste and refinement . . . to be the girl I love. I am certainly no expert on marriage, but the way I see it, marriage should be based on mutual respect as well as mutual love. I want a wife more than a princess. You can learn to be a prince or a princess, but you cannot learn to be a certain kind of human being. You either are or you are not naturally sweet and gentle.

So much for the character and personality of the ideal princess-wife, which the Prince put first, but when it came to her looks Grace might again have been the pattern. He liked natural-looking girls, he said, not "glamour girls or highly charged sexy wenches". He liked "a girl who is fair-haired and of light complexion, graceful and feminine". He could not bear intellectual snobs or snobs of any kind. "I just want a natural, ordinary girl who makes me feel that she is an extraordinary girl. I want a girl I can feel is mine, all mine, and that I belong to her. I suppose this is a very old-fashioned concept, but it is the way I feel. I must be the boss, or else I am not a man, but at the same time I am not a dictator. ... Marriage I think must be a give and take and that does not mean that one does all the giving and the other all the taking." He was very sure what sort of marriage he wanted. "I want both love and friendship from my wife, and that means a two-way exchange."

It was, in fact, a remarkable declaration of intent, by a man who was very sure who he was and what he wanted, and who, what is more, had taken the trouble to think long and deeply about it. He was not looking for money or blue blood or physical beauty on their own, but for personal qualities which would match not only his needs, but his own high standards. At thirty-two Prince Rainier had been through experiences which had marked him but also matured him so that he was very much his own man – including fighting in the Second World War; inheriting from his grandfather at the age of twenty-six quasi absolute power in his own principality; and last, but not least, a long and important relationship with a woman which was ended by reasons of state. For a woman like Grace, to whom the commanding figure of her father was an ideal, Prince Rainier could prove irresistible.

Grace may well have read Prince Rainier's declaration of intent in *Collier's* and pondered on its possible relation to herself; what she did not yet know was that a priestly Cupid had been working hard behind the scenes to organize the logistics of their meeting. The Cupid in question was Father Francis Tucker, a native of Wilmington, an ebullient, intelligent Irish-American who had been appointed by the Vatican, at Prince Rainier's request, to the parish of St Charles in Monaco. Tucker had become not only the Prince's father-confessor but also his friend and confidant, and he was credited in some circles not only with having prompted the Prince to break with Gisèle Pascal (although there were also rumours that Mademoiselle Pascal herself bravely took that decision) but also with having encouraged him to give up his bachelor playboy way of life in favour of the marriage which his subjects expected of him.

Father Tucker, Prince Rainier said, "was a great organizer and loved playing little parts", and when he heard from the Prince that he had met and been attracted to Grace Kelly, who was not only lovely and single but Irish-American and Catholic as well, Father Tucker was, said the Prince, "very pleased and helpful", throwing himself into the role of matchmaker with happy zeal. The business of arranging a further meeting between Grace and the Prince was to be managed through the Russell Austins of Margate, New Jersey, who were close friends of the Kellys and known to the children as "Aunt" Edie and "Uncle" Russ.

The Russell Austins had already met the Prince in a typically American way. They had been staying in Monte Carlo the previous summer, and Grace, hearing they were going, said in passing that she had met the Prince during the Cannes Film Festival. When they failed to get tickets for the Red Cross Gala at the Sporting Club, the Russell Austins simply called the palace and spoke to Rainier – "I am Grace Kelly's Uncle Russ and she told me to call you if I had a problem. [She had not done so.] I can't get tickets to this Gala." Prince Rainier replied that there was no problem and he would take care of it and get them two seats.

The next day they received a call from Father Tucker inviting them to the palace and there, Alice Waters, the Austins' niece, recalls, Father Tucker asked them, "How well do you know the Kellys?" and "If we come to the United States would it be possible for you to make sure that Rainier gets to see Grace Kelly again?" "No problem," replied "Uncle" Russ. They met the Prince and were very impressed with him and, naturally, when they got home "they told everybody about their adventures and how wonderful they were and that was the end of it".

"All of a sudden", Alice continued, "they get a letter from Father Tucker saying 'we are anticipating coming over, would it be possible to come and be with you on Christmas Eve and while we are there would we have an opportunity to go and see the Kellys?' So 'Aunt' Edie called 'Aunt' Margaret [Kelly] and said the Prince would like to see Gracie again but 'if she isn't going to be nice to him we won't bring him up because he is too delightful and Gracie could give anybody a cold shoulder'. So Aunt Margaret said, 'Well, I'll get in touch with Grace and see if it's all right with her,' and Grace said, fine, she would love to see him again."

In California *The Swan* was running late and it was only on Thursday 22 December that the director "wrapped" the final shots. Grace was working right up to the end and called on Rupert Allan to help her catch the plane for New York. "She was desperate to make a certain plane and it was very late," Allan remembers. She told Allan that she had to get to New York for the Kanters' Christmas party but, characteristically, she mentioned nothing about meeting Prince Rainier in Philadelphia on Christmas Eve. Allan and Grace packed frantically in the tiny house she had rented from Gayelord Hauser on Oriole Avenue, their progress impeded by Oliver the poodle, who was running around, grabbing her famous white gloves and anything else he could pounce upon. Together they finished all the splits of champagne, which Grace loved and with which the fridge was always full, and, with an extra suitcase borrowed from a friend, dashed to the airport to catch American Airlines flight No. 2 for Idlewild. It was 7.15 in the evening of 23 December when Grace arrived at Idlewild, where a studio limousine was waiting to take her to the Kanters' party. Next morning, 24 December, she left for Philadelphia.

Meanwhile Prince Rainier, accompanied by Father Tucker and a young doctor, Dr Donat, whom he was planning to take to Johns Hopkins in Baltimore to continue his medical studies, was making his way to Margate, New Jersey, to dine with the Russell Austins. That evening they drove up to Philadelphia to attend the Kellys' traditional Christmas Eve party at Henry Avenue. At the last moment Grace, faced with the actual prospect of seeing Prince Rainier again, panicked and called in her sister Peggy to help. Peggy remembers Grace saying, "That Aunt Edie is such a devil, she's bringing the Prince over. Come on, Peggy, be over here with me." The moment they met again, Peggy said, she could see the "sparks flying" between them.

After the party the Prince and Grace went to Peggy's house, where they played cards and games until four in the morning, and the Prince, Donat and Tucker spent what remained of the night at the Kellys' house wearing Kell's pyjamas, which were several sizes too large for them. The next day the Prince and Grace went driving alone through the romantic scenery of Bucks County, including New Hope, where she had made her first real stage appearance after the Academy. Marie Magee was there when Grace returned wearing a friendship ring the Prince had given her, a gold chain studded alternately with rubies and diamonds.

"Pa Kelly looked at that. He said, 'Is that an engagement ring?'

"'No, no, Daddy, this is only a friendship ring.'

"'Friendship hell!' he said.

"I tell you he was fit to be tied. He said, 'You cannot have that ring.'

"'Now Daddy. ...'

"He said, 'How come it fits so perfectly?' – which it did. And with that Mrs Kelly and I sat there and we didn't know what to do, and anyhow Gracie kept the ring. ...'"

Jack Kelly liked the Prince personally – as Peggy said, "they got on very well" – but he was not at all sure that he liked the idea of a European prince marrying his daughter. He might, after all, be after her money. So when Father Tucker had to go to Wilmington, twenty-five miles away, he offered to drive him, deciding it would be a good opportunity to check on the Prince with his personal chaplain. When he returned from the journey, he reported to his wife and Marie Magee.

"I certainly told that Father Tucker. I told him off. I said 'I didn't want any damn broken-down Prince who was a head of a country over there that nobody ever knew anything about to marry my daughter. I didn't want it and I didn't intend to get involved.'"

"Oh," Marie said. "He did really carry on. And he said, 'Father Tucker assured me that this was not the case, that this man had enough money to take care of Gracie.' He said, 'I don't believe it.'" Father Tucker then, he said, gave him enough figures to reassure him that the Prince of Monaco was well able to take care of John B. Kelly's daughter."

The Prince, however, had not yet put in a formal request for Grace's hand, although it was immediately obvious that he and Grace were, as her mother put it, "serious" about each other. They spent every day together and on Wednesday 28 December the Prince and Dr Donat drove Grace back to New York, where she had to see her agent and take singing lessons for her next film, *High Society*. Prince Rainier also stayed in New York, and on Thursday morning 29 December Grace telephoned her mother to tell her, "I'm very much in love", and that the Prince wanted to marry her. Father Tucker was summoned from Wilmington to New York and then despatched to the Kellys with the Prince's formal proposal. According to some reports, Jack Kelly's response was worthy of a staunch American democrat; he replied that "royalty didn't mean a thing to us" and that he certainly hoped the Prince "wouldn't run around the way some princes do, and that if he did he'd lose a mighty fine girl". European princes, to Jack Kelly, were a source of suspicion rather than awe. Perhaps, too, he subconsciously sensed that Grace had scored her final triumph and that in marrying someone as masculine as he was, but younger, richer and more powerful, she had somehow trumped him, moving at last irrevocably out of his orbit into a wider sphere. But he and Margaret Kelly naturally gave their consent, by telephone, and on that New Year's Eve of 1956, Prince Rainier III of Monaco and Grace Kelly of Philadelphia became formally, although still secretly, engaged.

The thirty-two-year-old Prince and the twenty-six-year-old movie star were madly, romantically in love with each other. "He was dazzled by her and she was dazzled by him," a friend said. "They were crazy about each other." Their romance had the inestimable advantage of perfect timing. Both of them wanted to get married, both of them knew that they would have to choose their partner very carefully, both of them were aware of the responsibilities which marriage would bring, and both of them had thought long and deeply about what it would entail in terms of personal commitment. Equally importantly, on the personal level that would make that commitment possible they had a great deal in common, not least of which was shared religion and a European view of marriage – Grace did not want a Mr Grace Kelly while Prince Rainier had made it clear that "the man should wear the pants!"

For both partners this marriage appeared to be the answer to their needs: for Prince Rainier a happy solution to his dynastic problem, his loneliness and his desire for a family life which he had never had; and for Grace to the dilemma of finding a husband who would match the position she had achieved. For Grace, however, marriage to Prince Rainier would involve abandoning the career at which she had worked so hard at a point when she had reached a pinnacle of success. Many people would find it difficult to understand how an actress could abandon such a career for what appeared to them a tinsel crown and a gilded cage.

Grace saw it differently. Having dreamed of being a princess, she was now about to become one in real life and she did not, and could not, conceive exactly what it would mean to be Princess of Monaco. All her instincts and the conventions of her background pointed towards marriage and motherhood as being the natural fulfilment of a woman's life; she had achieved independence and success in her work, now she saw marriage as her next goal.

Well aware that success was ephemeral, she could abandon her film career without regret. She had never liked being a movie star and she hated Hollywood, but marriage to Prince Rainier would also necessarily mean giving up all hope of fulfilling herself as an actress on the stage. Perhaps, deep down, she had doubts about herself: she admitted once to Oleg Cassini that she was not sure of her true ability as an actress. She had had very little stage success so far. No doubt she thought that marriage and motherhood would bring her fulfilment of a different kind and that, in realizing her childhood fantasy of being a princess, she would be playing the ultimate role. Only the future would reveal if the sacrifices she had to make would be worthwhile. On the brink of marriage, Grace saw it as a change of direction in her life which was both inevitable and desirable.

Grace made use of the few days of privacy left to her before her engagement became public knowledge to let her close friends into the secret. She also sat down and wrote to three men – Gene Lyons, Oleg Cassini and Jean-Pierre Aumont – telling them of her decision. Tidily, decisively, but also thoughtfully, she was closing the last chapters of her life as Grace Kelly; a whole new and different story was about to begin. To Oleg Cassini at their last meeting, after the announcement of her engagement, she said simply, "I have made my destiny."

9
Monaco Spectacular

On 5 January 1956 Jack Kelly announced his daughter's engagement to Prince Rainier at a pre-arranged luncheon party at the Philadelphia Country Club. Afterwards the family adjourned to Henry Avenue for a press conference and photography session. No one had bargained for the numbers or behaviour of the press as they scrambled for advantage in the Kellys' living-room, where Grace, dressed in a gold brocade shirt-dress and flanked by her mother, sat on a sofa holding the Prince's arm reassuringly. "They damn near broke the place down," Kell recalls; some of them stood on the piano and the pregnant Lizanne had to be ushered upstairs to be out of harm's way. Questions were fired mercilessly at the couple, including their plans for a family, which Mrs Kelly answered as Grace blushed. Finally the Prince had enough of what *Time* described as "the pressing of the press", muttering angrily to Father Tucker, "After all, I don't belong to MGM."

It was a foretaste of what the couple would have to endure throughout what was to become the media event of the decade, rivalling the Coronation of Queen Elizabeth II three years before. In New York to attend the charity Night in Monte Carlo ball at the Waldorf Astoria, accompanied by Jack and Margaret Kelly and the ubiquitous Father Tucker, Grace, dressed in a white satin gown by Dior with a corsage of white orchids, sat in what *Time* described as a "royal box" and "nibbled crystallized violets while the press howled at the door". Later they were seen dancing at the Harwyn Club until 4 am, where, *Time* reported, Grace "nibbled at Rainier's ear". When Grace, en route back to Hollywood, changed trains at Chicago to catch the Super Chief for Los Angeles, United Press reported proudly as the scoop of the week that their reporter had had the privilege of walking her poodle, Oliver, between trains.

Public reaction to the engagement was mixed: while most of the world's press, particularly in Europe, saw it as a fairytale romance, in France *Le Monde* wondered ominously whether Monaco would become an American base, and in America itself some of the comment was unfavourable. Some Americans felt that the ruler of a small Mediterranean principality known chiefly for its casino was not good enough for their queen, Grace Kelly, or indeed, any Kelly. "He's Not Good Enough For a Kelly", the *Chicago Tribune* headlined, stating flatly: "She is too well bred a girl to marry the silent partner in a gambling parlor." Even the Communist *Daily Worker* regretted that Grace had chosen a husband who "can't lay bricks ... or act ... or write plays ... or row a boat". While the *Denver Post* grumbled "Beneath Her Station", in England the *Manchester Guardian*, with a proper respect for protocol, headlined its story "Prince Rainier Engaged".

In Hollywood the reaction was one of stunned amazement. Hedda Hopper said bluntly, "Her friends are completely baffled; half of them don't believe she and the Prince will ever reach the altar." Almost no one on the West Coast had any idea of where Monaco was and some people thought that Grace was marrying the ruler of Morocco. The most that was generally known about the principality was that it contained Monte Carlo and the most famous casino in the world. Hollywood, and in fact show business in general, found it scarcely credible that Grace could abandon a spectacular career as actress and film star to go off and live in Europe as the wife of a prince of whom they had never heard. Many of them, even some of Grace's friends, thought that, dazzled by the glamour of being a princess, she was exchanging substance for shadow. Hitchcock, who privately regarded Grace's marriage as a betrayal on the scale of Bergman's departure with Rossellini, observed that "marrying a prince is in line with Grace's progression", but added, "She has bounced around with the ease of a girl on the trapeze. Whether the platform on which she has landed is too narrow, I don't know."

MGM's executives put a brave face on it and deferred releasing *The Swan* to time with Grace's real-life wedding to the Prince, which, it had been announced, would take place after Easter, some time in April; but they were worried, Aline Mosby of United Press reported, that their star would "fly off to Monte Carlo and be seen henceforth only on postage stamps". Grace had agreed to do two pictures for them, the first, due to start production on 17 January, being *High Society*, a musical version of *The Philadelphia Story*, and the second,

Designing Woman, with James Stewart, planned to follow on 1 June. Producer Sol C. Siegel had lined up an array of expensive talent to star in *High Society* with Grace, who was to play the part of the beautiful socialite Tracy Lord who flutters between ex-husband, prospective husband and newspaper reporter. Bing Crosby was to be C.K. Dexter-Haven, the aristocratic, jazz-loving ex-husband who plans to win her back, and Frank Sinatra the newspaper reporter sent to cover her wedding; while the musical success of the film was to be guaranteed by a Cole Porter score and the presence of Louis Armstrong as the bandleader friend of Dexter-Haven.

For Grace, *High Society*, made with her friend Frank Sinatra, and her former date, Bing Crosby, was a happy picture. Perhaps it was too happy. Looking dazzling wearing a series of Helen Rose gowns and sporting a huge diamond engagement ring from Prince Rainier, Grace's fluting voice mingled agreeably with the mellow tones of "Der Bingle" in the song "True Love", but her performance lacked the bite of Katharine Hepburn's in the previous straight film version of the play. Of the stars only Frank Sinatra and Louis Armstrong were to be absolved by the critics. Bing, wrote Bosley Crowther of *The New York Times*, was miscast and strolled through his role: "He wanders around the place like a mellow uncle ... stroking his pipe with more affection than he strokes Miss Kelly's porcelain arms," while Grace "makes the trenchant lady no more than a petulant, wistful girl". More kindly, the *Saturday Review* thought that "Her Serene Highness ... seemed preoccupied, as though her mind might have been on other things". Yet, despite the grumblings of the critics, *High Society*, with some good numbers by Cole Porter and the glittering names of Crosby, Sinatra, Armstrong and Kelly to help it ride the wave of Grace's romance, was a box office success, and Grace won a golden disc for selling a million copies of her duet with Bing, aptly named "True Love".

"True Love", shot on 6 March, was the last set-up of the film and, although no one was yet aware of it, the last scene that Grace Kelly would ever play for Hollywood. Producer Sol C. Siegel gave the traditional end-of-shooting party, which was also a farewell for Grace, who was due to leave for New York on 16 March but postponed her departure in order to present the Oscar on 21 March to Ernest Borgnine for his performance in the title-role of *Marty*.

Grace certainly had other things to think about during the

shooting of *High Society*. Prince Rainier spent six weeks in a rented villa in Bel Air in order to be near her and the two of them spent happy evenings together after she returned from the set. The Prince was reported as being "very impressed" with his fiancée's culinary skills, particularly her barbecuing. In February the Prince's father, Prince Pierre de Polignac, had arrived to meet Grace and to confer with the couple, Mrs Kelly and Father Tucker about wedding plans. Prince Pierre, tall, aristocratic, cultured and intellectual, forbidding to many and fastidious in his taste, became an immediate fan of Grace's and was to be of great help and comfort to her in her future life. Not everything, however, was pleasant. There was a chilly moment at a lunch given by MGM's executives for the engaged couple and Prince Pierre when Dore Schary asked Prince Rainier how big Monaco was and, on being told it was five square miles, commented tactlessly, "That's not as big as our back lot." Celeste Holm, who was present, remarked, "I knew that second that Grace Kelly would never make another picture."

Far worse as far as Grace was concerned was to see her private life exposed in the press across America in a series of articles entitled "My Daughter Grace Kelly – Her Life and Romances by Mrs John B. Kelly (as told to Richard Gehman)". The series, based on an interview given by Mrs Kelly to a reporter for the Hearst Organization's King Syndicate, appeared in newspapers from coast to coast. Day after day for ten days in mid-January Grace saw the private life she had striven so hard to keep private – Harper Davis, Peter Richardson, Gene Lyons, Clark Gable, Jean-Pierre Aumont, Oleg Cassini and, worst of all, an account of her engagement to Prince Rainier – paraded before the eyes of America. Hollywood was agog over the articles, which were featured in the *Los Angeles Examiner*. Mrs Kelly, innocent of the ways of the press, had agreed to give the interview in return for royalties to be donated to her cherished Women's Medical College, on the promise that she could check it before it was printed. Instead of showing it to her, the reporter telephoned Mrs Kelly in Philadelphia saying that he had a deadline and asking her if she would mind him reading the article to her over the telephone. Margaret Kelly, busy with preparations for a big dinner party, listened to the first – and most innocent – part then, according to Rupert Allan, told the reporter, "Well, look, I just have to trust you, if this is what I said, OK." And so the interview, stretched to ten articles by the reporter, appeared, shocking Grace and ruining Mrs Kelly's reputation with the press, who ever after liked to represent her as a brash, vulgar woman.

For Grace, who had so carefully built up her career and public persona on such very different lines, it was like being forcibly stripped in public. In her distress, she said something very revealing to one of her closest friends – "I've worked so hard and now my mother's going to destroy everything overnight." Even when she understood what had happened, it took her a long time to forgive her mother that indiscretion, which she regarded as having done irreparable damage to her image and reputation, offending against the gentlemanly code which she had been at such pains to follow, and bringing her down to Hollywood's own level.

She had worked hard to achieve success on her own terms, as a professional, with, she thought, the right to keep separate her public from her private life. For instance, when she was named "Best-dressed Woman" – she had appeared on that coveted list every year since 1953 and in 1956 tied for first place with Mrs William Paley – she would never admit that most of her clothes were designed by Oleg Cassini. When he accused her of disloyalty, she would say, "My personal life is nothing to do with my working life." It was a distinction which she had fought to preserve in the full glare of Hollywood stardom and one which she would continue to defend, as far as she could, as she raised her family behind the over-exposed walls of the Grimaldi palace in Monaco.

The time when she would have to give up any hope of privacy was rapidly approaching. On the day Grace finished *High Society*, Prince Rainier had slipped out of Los Angeles under an assumed name, C. Monte (for Monte Carlo). Reporters, however, were not to be fooled by such a transparent incognito and when he arrived in New York he found a posse of them waiting for him. Faced with the big question as to whether Grace would retire, he said that he and Grace had come to an agreement that she would not make any more films after her marriage and, having dropped this bombshell, boarded the liner *Ile de France* in falling snow to return to Europe. He was, he said, "a little bit weary" of all the publicity and wished more and more that he and Miss Kelly could marry quietly. It was a vain hope.

The Oscar ceremony, predictably, degenerated into a press stampede over Grace, who, driven into a corner by the crowd of reporters and photographers, cried plaintively, "But I haven't won anything," only to receive the wisecrack, "Yes, you have. You've won a prince." The next day Grace flew East, departing from Los Angeles for the last time as a film star.

Grace Kelly's last public appearance in America came on a misty morning in the first week of April 1956 at Manhattan's Pier 84. Crowds waited to see her as, dressed in a beige wool suit and a white, mushroom-like straw hat and the inevitable white gloves, she boarded the American Export liner *Constitution*. Sixty-six people had been refused bookings already made on the liner so that the Philadelphia Kellys and their friends could invade, *en masse*, the old world of Europe. Greatly outnumbering the Kelly party was, of course, the U.S. press in force, some 250 reporters, photographers, movie and television cameramen, in a regrettable farewell media mob scene in the confined quarters of the Pool Café. According to *Time*, Grace was backed up behind a table and, "crushed together, reporters shouted their questions; photographers climbed on the bar, on tables, on stools, railings, on each other's shoulders for height, and, with flashbulbs crunching underfoot, shouted orders at their victim: 'Hey, Grace! Looka me!' 'Stand up, Grace!' and 'Take it off, Grace [the hat]!' " The conference got so out of hand that the shipowners' press agent, standing on a chair and addressing the press, quite unwarrantably, as "Gentlemen", affirmed, with scant regard for accuracy, that "this is a press conference, not a riot", and warned the thronging reporters that if they did not "back up and give this lady air" it would end immediately. Grace, described as "unruffled, cool, completely gracious", said, "in an accent that is neither Philadelphia, London nor Hollywood, but seems to have traces of each", that she wished people would be more considerate of each other and that she found "the way you are stamping on each other ... quite frightening", but, said *Time*, "she never stopped smiling and all the while three dimples showed in each cheek". And so, with both Grace and the press running true to form, she played her last scene in America. When she had been ushered away by hired security guards to her special suite, and most of the press had been decanted less ceremoniously onto the dockside, the *SS Constitution* slid away into the fog, bearing Grace towards her new destiny.

With her went her father, mother and some seventy relations and friends, with selected reporters and photographers plus Grace's personal luggage of four trunks and fifty-six other pieces including twenty hat-boxes, her wedding-dress – a gift from MGM packed in a steel box so resembling a coffin that the doorman at her apartment had attempted to have it diverted to the nearest funeral parlour when it was delivered – Oliver the poodle and a large, untrained Weimaraner puppy, a present from Philadelphia friends. The Kelly guest list was a roll call of all the people who had been part of Grace's life both in New York and Philadelphia – "Flossie" Merckel, "Aunt" Edie and "Uncle" Russ Austin, "Uncle" Bill Godfrey and his wife and daughters, the Ralph Sitleys, her friend from Stevens, Maree Frisby Pamp, now to be a bridesmaid, Sally Parrish and Bettina Thompson, ex-Academy girls, both also bridesmaids, Marie Magee, Donald Buka, Broadway producer Gant Gaither, sister Peggy and her daughters Meg and Mary Lee, the Isaac Levys, the Leon Levys, Judy and Jay Kanter and Grace's hairdresser from MGM, Virginia Darcy. Grace had only eight days of her old life left with her family and friends, and she filled them with parties, games, charades and intimate chats with one friend or another. As they crossed the Atlantic in a noisy, friendly circle of togetherness, one thought was uppermost in all their minds. They would be returning to America, Grace would not; or when she did, it would be as a visitor, as Her Serene Highness, Princess Grace of Monaco.

At 9.45 on the morning of 12 April 1956 the *Constitution* dropped anchor in the Bay of Hercules beneath the Rock of Monaco topped by the pink Grimaldi palace, freshly painted in Grace's honour. This was to be her home for the rest of her life. Punctually, the Prince, who had been waiting aboard his private yacht, the 340-ton British-built *Deo Juvante II*, set out from the harbour to go alongside the liner. Grace, wearing a navy blue fitted coat, white corsage and gloves, pearls and a huge white organdie and Swiss lace hat, stepped across the gangplank, followed by her parents. She was clutching Oliver in her arms, thereby rendering it impossible for the Prince to do more than clasp her tightly by the hand – "Prince Gives Miss Kelly Kissless Hello in Monaco", the headlines ran – before they retired to the privacy of the saloon. As the yacht moved towards the shore cannon boomed on the *Constitution*, all the yachts in the harbour sounded their sirens and the 20,000-odd Monégasques and tourists assembled at vantage points cheered. Aristotle Onassis' private seaplane circled above, showering down red and white carnations, the colours of Monaco, and out of the grey clouds that had been brooding over the mountains behind the principality the sun shone for Grace to step ashore.

From the harbour the Prince drove her in his emerald green Chrysler up to the palace where, less than a year before, she had curtsied shyly to him at their first meeting. At a private luncheon for twenty-three people, Kellys met Grimaldis for the first time – Prince Rainier's father, Prince Pierre, his mother, Princess Charlotte, his sister, Princess Antoinette, and his stepmother, Princess Ghislaine, among them. Peggy's two daughters, Meg and Mary Lee, lunched separately with the three children of Princess Antoinette, Elisabeth, Christian and Christine Alix. Grace and her parents were to be lodged in apartments in the north wing of the palace while the Prince was to sleep at his villa at Cap Ferrat, the Villa Iberia; Kelly guests and bridesmaids and their families were put up at the luxurious Hôtel de Paris below in Monte Carlo. Already the separation was beginning.

Hardly had Grace set foot in her prospective principality than the sniping started, generated by the huge international press contingent, some 1800 strong, which, in columnist Art Buchwald's words, "have been standing elbow to elbow on a rock not half as solid as Gibraltar, waiting for something to happen". First to weigh in was the ebullient Lady Docker, whose taste for pink champagne and gold-plated Daimlers with zebra-skin seats was to lead to the downfall of her husband, Birmingham small-arms tycoon, Sir Bernard Docker. Reporting for International News Service and the *Los Angeles Examiner*, Lady Docker criticized Grace for the huge hat which hid her face and for her over-plain outfit. Had she been in Grace's place, she wrote, she'd have worn her ermine greatcoat with matching hat and handbag and have had a large "GK" embroidered on her dress. "The girl probably didn't know the size of Rainier's yacht," she sniffed. "It's only 135 feet long and 340 tons. My husband chartered that same ship before Rainier bought it and I'd call it a bit snug."

Tom Guinzburg, publisher husband of Grace's friend and bridesmaid, Rita Gam, described the scene in the lush Belle Epoque lobby of the Hôtel de Paris where they were lodged as "incredible wall-to-wall press". NBC commentator Jinx Falkenburg pointed out that NBC had used only nine reporters for the invasion of North Africa in World War II but was using thirteen for the invasion of Monaco. One French magazine alone had twenty-nine reporters and photographers on the assignment; the American contingent included such luminaries as Walter Cronkite, Art Buchwald and top social columnists Earl Wilson and Dorothy Kilgallen; while the British had the

Duchess of Westminster and Randolph Churchill, who, *Time* alleged, picked a fight with Lady Docker (never a difficult task) and "screamed aloud: 'I didn't come here to meet vulgar people like the Kellys.' "

As the days went by, heavy drizzle emptied the streets, driving reporters into bars to interview each other or waylay a wedding guest in a vain search for copy to send home. The press grew increasingly dyspeptic as it became evident that the principal actors in the drama, Grace and Prince Rainier, were rarely to be seen. There was a scene when the Prince and Grace, returning from lunch with Princess Antoinette at her house in Eze on 13 April, were ambushed by fifty photographers, one of whom lay down in the road pretending to have been run over in order to get pictures of the pair. Enraged, the Prince declared that he would ban press reporters from the civil wedding ceremony and he refused to allow pictures to be taken of himself and Grace when they arrived at the Casino for a dinner party and dance given by the Kellys the following night. Things were even worse the following evening at the gala given by the Société des Bains de Mer (SBM) at the Winter Sporting Club next to the Hôtel de Paris, when a Monégasque policeman broke a Frenchman's camera and the Frenchman bit him in return. In the ensuing mêlée between police and press two reporters were arrested and, when the Prince and Grace emerged, they were roundly booed by the dripping cohorts.

By this time Grace had been in the principality three days and the press "war" with Prince Rainier was worsening, as indeed was their behaviour. Reporters disguised themselves as waiters and members of the band to get into the Sporting Club Gala, and it was rumoured that two men had been seen fitting themselves out with clerical costumes in Villefranche in order to pass themselves off as priests and insinuate themselves into the Cathedral for the wedding. Grace's friends were persecuted, particularly the beautiful, recently-married Rita Gam, whose own wedding in New York the previous month had been turned into pandemonium by the press in pursuit of Grace, who was a witness. The British reporters, said Tom Guinzburg, Rita's husband, were the worst – "It was absolutely nothing for these fellows to shin up the drainpipes and peer into our room" – while Rita remembers two Turkish journalists bursting into her bathroom with requests for an interview. Almost the only "news" story was provided by the activities of an enterprising jewel thief or thieves in the Hôtel de Paris who stole a jewel box belonging to Mrs Matt

McCloskey, wife of Jack Kelly's old political ally, and three days later cleaned up on Grace's bridesmaid, Maree Pamp, enabling Art Buchwald to write a witty piece on the subject. Meanwhile the rain poured relentlessly down for five days, tempers flared and the Prince's unfortunate press officer, who spoke no language but French, locked himself up in a room and would not come out.

In desperation the Prince called in Morgan Hudgins, MGM's publicity chief, who had accompanied Grace on the *Constitution*. Hudgins recommended a daily press conference in English and French where a representative of the Prince could answer reporters' questions, and advised the Prince to allow himself and Grace to be photographed for at least a few minutes a day. "Rainier Calls in Publicist, War Ends", headlined the *Los Angeles Times*, and the improvement in Prince-press relations was immediately evident on the morning after the Sporting Gala riot, when the Prince and Grace rehearsed for their wedding at St Nicholas's Cathedral. Newsmen and photographers were invited to watch the rehearsal and when police started to shove them aside, Prince Rainier himself stepped in to prevent them. Reporter Dorothy Kilgallen conceded that the Prince had "talked genially" with the press, but felt that she and Grace's American friends were being given the cold shoulder. "The glass curtain of royal protocol is dropping between the movie star and her young friends. ... I feel Grace is slipping away from us," she wailed.

While star reporters like Kilgallen may have felt left out of things, Grace took particular care that her friends did not. On board the *Constitution* she had, Judy Quine remembers, taken the trouble to have private moments with each of her friends, "not only", Judy recalled, in a revealing phrase, "to include each person individually but also so that she could be really sure she had her own contact hooked".

In Monaco, after each event, Grace would be whisked off to the palace – "there she was up on the big rock", Judy said. But at each impressive function in her honour she would be, for her friends, "just as though you were having dinner at the neighbourhood restaurant. ... At all of those parties you could be sure she would come from the head table and stop by and say 'Have a trip to the ladies' room, Judy Bird?' And she would have a little conversation with you, keeping it small, immediate, personal, while all the big stuff was going on, and yet she was fabulous at that too." When they went up to the palace, Tom Guinzburg recalled, it was just the same as on the *Constitution*:

they would play games and Grace was as giggly as ever. But she **was**, he said, beginning to be "Serene" already.

For the time was fast approaching when she would indeed be "Her Serene Highness". On Tuesday 17 April the Monégasques held a "serenade" for the couple on the square in front of the palace. Red and white banners fluttering everywhere gave the scene a medieval air as the Monégasques sang and danced in native costume, followed by a boys' choir from Alsace, and dancers of the London Festival Ballet. As Grace retired at midnight fireworks shot into the sky, prompting wedding guest ex-King Farouk, who had only just emerged from his hotel for the first time after two days' seclusion with his bodyguards, to retreat once more, fearing an assassination attempt.

Wednesday 18 April was the day fixed for the civil marriage ceremony, held in the red and gold Throne Room of the palace. Grace, dressed in a rose beige lace suit with a close-fitting matching hat, sat stiff, strained and fragile on a throne-like gilt and damask chair, with the Prince, clearly also very nervous and ill at ease, beside her, as Monsieur Marcel Portanier, President of the Monaco Council of State, conducted the ceremony, beginning by asking Prince Rainier's permission to do so. Seated on gilt chairs around the walls were the Kellys and the Grimaldis and the diplomatic representatives of various Heads of State, a not very high-ranking selection with not a crowned head among them. The British royal family had sent Sir Guy Salisbury-Jones, head of the Diplomatic Service, and Lieutenant-Commander Weld-Forester, HM Consul in Nice; President Eisenhower had despatched hotel tycoon Conrad Hilton, while France was represented by François Mitterrand, then Minister of Justice. They listened to the lengthy recital of vows and the even lengthier recital of Prince Rainier's one hundred and forty-two titles, which included four dukedoms and the title, Duc de Valentinois, once borne by Cesare Borgia. It was a tense and formal occasion and the bride, looking dazed, did not relax until she sipped a glass of champagne with Rainier and the American reporters. Outside, the day, which had begun grey and muggy, burst into brilliant brightness as the couple appeared high up on a balcony to wave to the people waiting below. Grace would not officially become Princess of Monaco until the religious exchange of vows the next day, but she was, as her father remarked, "half-way there".

That night, indeed, she looked the part of a real princess. In a white evening dress by Lanvin of satin organza encrusted with pearls, rhinestones and opaque sequins, with a diamond tiara on her head and a diamond necklace "half an inch thick" round her neck, she attended a Gala at the Opera House. Across her breast was the red and white sash of the Order of St Charles presented to her by the Prince earlier in the evening. Prince Rainier appeared relaxed and smiling, although Grace, regally beautiful, could only manage a strained attempt at a smile before they watched a triumphant display by the London Festival Ballet starring Margot Fonteyn, Belinda Wright and John Gilpin (who, twenty-seven years later, was to marry the Prince's sister, Princess Antoinette). Afterwards the Prince and Grace went their separate ways for the last time; after dropping Grace at the palace, the Prince returned to Cap Ferrat.

The day of the wedding, Thursday 19 April, dawned with radiant sunshine; the drenching rain and the squabbles were seemingly a thing of the past. Glistening limestone-white, with its neo-Romanesque facade as ornately carved as a wedding cake, the Cathedral of St Nicholas stands on the cliff on which the old town of Monaco is built, the blue of the Mediterranean at its feet. A red carpet had been laid up the steps underneath a floating white silk canopy sustained by slim gilt columns topped with crowns, and opposite the entrance sailors from the French, British and American warships in the harbour stood at attention. Below in the town, the wedding guests prepared to leave the Hôtel de Paris – the huge shape of ex-King Farouk of Egypt in fez and dark glasses waddled down the steps, and, later, the elegant figure of Ava Gardner, flanked by Morgan Hudgins and Rupert Allan. Every available limousine in the area had been commandeered but the American guests were disagreeably surprised to find themselves obliged to abandon their cars at the foot of the Rock and board specially provided buses. "To a prince's wedding on a bus!" exclaimed one horrified woman, while Mrs Barney Balaban, wife of the founder of Paramount, was only persuaded to board such a plebeian vehicle when told that Somerset Maugham and the Duchess of Westminster had already been seen to do so.

Inside, the cathedral was decorated with white snapdragons hung in huge gilt baskets suspended from the chandeliers between each column along the aisle, and the altar itself, where the marriage was to take place, was banked with white lilies, lilacs and hydrangeas. Years later, Grace's main impression of her own wedding was of a battery of cameras and microphones peering at her through that very bank of flowers. The church was filling with celebrities – the swarthy, magnetic figure of Aristotle Onassis, then at the height of his power and influence as financial dictator of Monte Carlo; his attractive, blonde wife Tina, queen of international society; an even richer figure, the Aga Khan, with his soignée French Begum; Gloria Swanson, star of a different Hollywood generation from the bride, and Ava Gardner, Grace's friend and co-star. Beside Ava sat Rupert Allan and beyond him an empty seat – it was the seat reserved for Frank Sinatra. Sinatra decided not to attend the wedding, a gesture of his true friendship and respect for Grace. He had flown to London to equip himself with the white tie, top hat and tails required for the wedding when he realized that Ava, from whom he was estranged and soon to be divorced, would also be a guest. Knowing what the press would make of this juxtaposition, Sinatra, deciding that the publicity might detract from the true importance of Grace's wedding day, stayed away.

Meanwhile up at the palace Grace and the bridesmaids were getting dressed. Sister Peggy Davis, the matron of honour, and the six bridesmaids – Maree Frisby Pamp, Sally Parrish Richardson, Judy Kanter, Carolyn Scott Reybold, Rita Gam and Bettina Thompson Gray – were dressed in yellow silk organza with matching hats, designed by Helen Rose and made by Neiman Marcus. The four flower girls Elisabeth and Christine Alix, daughters of Princess Antoinette, and Peggy's daughters, Margaret and Mary Lee – were in white Swiss broderie anglaise, also from the Texas department store, although their shoes and socks had been ordered by the thrifty bride from the mail order chain, J.C. Penney. The wedding dress itself, the gift of MGM, was the *chef d'oeuvre* of Helen Rose and, according to her, the most expensive she had ever made. The lace for the bodice and the train was antique Rose Point, bought from a French museum at a cost of $2,500, and the skirt was of silk *gros de longre*, a fabric which is no longer made. Underneath it the petticoats were dotted with little blue satin bows ("something blue") and, according to the designer, so carefully made that they could have been worn separately as an evening dress. The bodice and the lace cap holding the veil in place were re-embroidered with seed pearls, as were the satin slippers and the white silk missal covered with lace and with a cross of pearls which Grace carried with a small spray of lilies of the valley in place of a cumbersome bouquet. Virginia Darcy, Grace's hairdresser from MGM, attended her as she had during the entire week.

Just after 10.30 am Grace walked up the aisle of St Nicholas on her father's arm, preceding the arrival of Prince Rainier, as protocol demanded. At the altar the bridesmaids were already waiting with Monsignor Gilles Barthe, Bishop of Monaco, who was to conduct the service, flanked by Father Tucker as Master of Ceremonies and the Kellys' parish priest from St Bridget's, Father Cartin. The two American priests were there, Father Tucker explained cheerfully, to see that "no one fumbled the ball at the match", and indeed their presence was highly necessary as far as the bridesmaids were concerned. None of them, with the exception of Peggy, were Catholics and all of them would be utterly dependent on Father Tucker's instructions – "Rise", "Kneel", "Sit" – throughout the ceremony. When Grace and her father reached the altar, Father Tucker whispered to Jack Kelly that he could go and sit down now. "No," was the characteristic reply, "I'll wait until he gets here. . . ."

A few minutes later the Prince joined Grace, wearing a uniform designed by himself and based on that of Napoleon's marshals – a decorated black tunic with gold leaf on the cuffs, sky blue trousers with a gold band down the sides and a midnight blue bicorne with white ostrich feathers. He was attended by three best men: his cousin, Comte Charles de Polignac, Grace's brother, Kell, and Lieutenant-Colonel Jean-Marie Ardant, the Prince's friend and governor of his household. There were a few hitches in the service as the bride and groom, visibly nervous, stood before the altar in the glare of the klieg lights necessary for the recording of the scene on film. The young page entrusted with the ring, six-year-old Sebastian von Furstenberg, dropped it and it had to be retrieved by the ever alert Father Tucker. Then Prince Rainier had difficulty placing the ring on Grace's finger, so that she had to assist him; trained actress as she was, she slipped the ring on to her finger with ease – recalling the announcement of their wedding in *Variety*: "bride, film star, groom, non-pro . . ." Just over an hour later it was all over. Grace and Rainier walked out of the Cathedral into brilliant sunlight.

As they entered the cream and black open Rolls-Royce waiting at the foot of the Cathedral steps, they smiled broadly at each other, as if realizing that their public ordeal was now almost over and that soon, as man and wife, they would be alone. The car carried them down the steep hill from the Rock to the little church of Ste Dévote by the harbour, shrine of the martyred virgin patroness of Monaco, where Grace, following tradition, laid down her bouquet, which was prudently retrieved and preserved by the priest minutes later. Then it was up to the palace for photographs and the wedding lunch, held in the courtyard of the palace with the family and bridesmaids sitting at tables in the enclosure formed by the sweeping double staircase, while the six hundred wedding guests served themselves from a buffet across the courtyard. At the end of lunch, the bridal couple, using Rainier's sword, cut the five-tier wedding cake decorated with the arms of Monaco, and at three o'clock they disappeared into the palace to change for their going away. Peggy and the brides-maids had one close last look at Grace when she came into the small anteroom next to her bedroom where they were waiting to say goodbye to her. "Come on, girls," said Virginia Darcy, "let's all curtsey to the new Princess!" "See you later, alligator," Peggy cracked facetiously to break the tension, as they all felt tears coming to their eyes. "In a while, crocodile," retorted the Prince, coming in to take his bride away.

Dressed in a neat grey suit and white hat, the inevitable Oliver tucked under her arm, Grace stood on the deck of the *Deo Juvante*, her husband by her side. As Rainier hugged her, they both waved goodbye, the yacht slipping out of the harbour towards the sunset. The swell was heavy and, once out of sight, the yacht anchored in the shelter of Villefranche for the night, but nonetheless it was the classic Hollywood finale. For Grace it was indeed an end as well as a beginning, the end of her role as Grace Kelly of Philadelphia, queen of Hollywood, and the beginning of a new life as Her Serene Highness, Grace Patricia Grimaldi, Princess of Monaco.

PART THREE

The Ultimate Role

IO

Learning a New Role

Grace returned from honeymoon to face the reality behind the fairytale. It was not only the beginning of a marriage, it was also the learning of a new craft, of what exactly it meant to be Princess of Monaco and a member of the oldest ruling family in Europe.

The Grimaldis had ruled Monaco, with a few minor interruptions, since 1297, when one Francisco Grimaldi, disguised as a monk, had succeeded in entering the citadel on the rock and seizing it from within. Originally one of the leading families of Genoa, the Grimaldis proved themselves masters in the arts of princely survival, murdering, marrying and fighting first for Spain and then for France, so that by the time the French Revolution shook the fabric of Europe they owned not only Monaco itself but the coastal strip including Menton and Roquebrune, large estates in France, and a string of titles to go with them. The French Revolution swept away all the substance of the Grimaldi inheritance and when, after the turmoil, they returned to their plundered, ruined palace they had lost everything but their titles and Monaco itself – an ancient town on a rock, a harbour backed by fertile orange groves, and a scrubby peninsula inhabited only by shepherds. It was then that they must have understood the cruel truth of the local saying:

> *Monaco io sono,*
> *Un scoglio.*
> *Del mio non ho,*
> *Quello d'altrui non toglio,*
> *Pur viver voglio....*

– "I am Monaco, a stray rock. I have nothing of my own, I do not plunder the goods of others and yet I want to keep alive."

Prince Charles III (1818–89) was almost blind and nearly bankrupt when the great financier and entrepreneur, François Blanc, who had made his fortune exploiting the casinos of Homburg and Baden,

145

moved into the principality. While he could do nothing to save the Prince's sight, he did everything to make his fortune. In 1863 he founded the *Société des Bains de Mer et Cercle des Etrangers* (Society of Sea-Bathing and Foreigners' Club), the shepherds were dispossessed of their hovels on the rocky promontory known as Les Spelugues across the bay from the Prince's palace, and Blanc began construction of the complex of Casino, luxury hotels and villas which within a few years would become known to the world as Monte Carlo.

By 1872 the Prince of Wales, incognito as "Captain White", had visited the Casino, as had the Emperor of Austria, Franz Joseph, and a clutch of fabulously rich Russian Grand Dukes. In the glittering two decades before the First World War, Monte Carlo in the winter was the most fashionable place in Europe; standards of dress were such that the Marquess of Salisbury, the British Foreign Secretary, was refused admittance to the Casino for looking too shabby, while famous courtesans like La Belle Otéro and Liane de Pougy vied with each other in the gaming rooms with dazzling displays of diamonds. The glorious Belle Epoque Opera House opened with a gala featuring Sarah Bernhardt, and in 1911 Diaghilev's Russian Ballet made their first appearance there and Nijinsky danced *Le Spectre de la Rose*. An English swindler named Charles Deville Wells became famous as "the Man who Broke the Bank at Monte Carlo" and newspapers headlined the suicides of desperate gamblers; meanwhile the Casino was making fifty million francs a year.

The First World War ruined the Grand Dukes and the courtesans were put out of work by the promiscuity of post-war society, but the Monte Carlo Casino survived, paying no less than seventy-three per cent of its receipts to the Monaco government, more than enough to keep the new Prince, Albert I, and his four thousand Monégasque subjects in taxation-free comfort. Albert I died in 1922, to be succeeded by his son, Prince Louis, grandfather of Prince Rainier, who, only two years after his accession, was subject to a bizarre attempt upon his throne by the sinister Levantine armaments millionaire, Sir Basil Zaharoff. Zaharoff had formed the secret plan of taking over not only the Casino company, the *Société des Bains de Mer*, but the principality itself as well, with his mistress of nearly forty years, the Spanish Duquesa de Marquena y Villafranca, as his official consort once her aged husband had died. Zaharoff's agents stealthily and steadily bought up shares in the company until by the spring of 1923 he owned the controlling interest. The following year the Duque died and Zaharoff married the widow. With the first part of his plan realized, Zaharoff began a campaign to topple Prince Louis. Fortunately for the Grimaldi succession, the new Lady Zaharoff died the next year and with her the millionaire's interest both in the Casino company and in the throne. Through the twenties and thirties the Monte Carlo Sporting Club continued to be one of the smartest places in Europe; but the way of life which supported it was to vanish in the cataclysm of the Second World War.

Prince Rainier III, aged only twenty-six, succeeded his grandfather, Prince Louis, in 1949. It was hardly a glorious inheritance; the palace, in which his grandfather had rarely spent more than three or four months a year, was dilapidated, a state which reflected the fortunes of the principality as a whole. An American visitor described Monaco as looking as though it were "on the point of death ... a slowly-expiring community of retired generals, drab gamblers and stray cats". Visitors to Monte Carlo had dropped to a quarter of their pre-war level and Casino takings to a tenth, so that by 1951 the company was running at a loss.

It was at this point that another apparent saviour appeared in the person of another Levantine millionaire, Aristotle Onassis. Onassis later recalled his first memory of Monte Carlo when, as a penniless sixteen-year-old refugee from the sack of his native town, Smyrna, he had sailed past in the night, a steerage passenger on a ship bound for Buenos Aires, where he was to make his fortune. "Every time I see the lights of Monte Carlo", he said, "I think how beautiful they looked that night as we passed – to me and to a thousand other seasick and homesick exiles." Now, thirty years later, he came back as a conqueror. In 1952 he decided that Monte Carlo, with its strategic position on the Mediterranean between Genoa and Marseilles, would be the ideal headquarters for his shipping company, put in a bid for the building of the old Sporting Club, and was refused. Onassis, however, was determined, and set about buying shares in the SBM, which owned the building, until by 1954 he had control of the company and all its properties, including, of course, the old Sporting Club, his original object.

Buying the SBM made Onassis an international celebrity – *International Who's Who* included his name for the first time as "the man who bought the bank at Monte Carlo", and *Time* magazine featured him as the man who "waterskis in the best international circles".

The flamboyant Onassis generated massive publicity with his twenty-six-year-old wife Tina, herself the daughter of a Greek millionaire, his worldwide fleet of tankers and his yacht, the *Christina*, which he had spent two and a half million dollars converting from a destroyer into a floating palace featuring, among other things, a bar with stools made from the scrotum of a whale. Headlines featured him as "the King of Monte Carlo" and Monte Carlo was nicknamed "Monte Greco". Monte Carlo made Onassis famous; Onassis in return made Monte Carlo glamorous again. Names like Greta Garbo and Sir Winston Churchill were featured in the newspapers as his guests; international celebrities and their followers swarmed to Monte Carlo, and the 1955 New Year's Eve party at the Hôtel de Paris saw a thousand people paying forty thousand francs a head to celebrate it in his company. For the first time in four years the SBM showed a profit.

Initially, Prince Rainier had actively encouraged Onassis's interest in the SBM. He was determined to modernize Monaco and was at loggerheads with the ageing counsellors bequeathed to him by his grandfather; to him, Onassis's dynamism and his money represented new hope and investment for Monaco. He was beguiled, too, by the shipowner's energy and overwhelming charm, while Onassis, for all his money and superior experience, needed the Prince's co-operation. Under the constitution of the SBM, the Prince had the right to veto the appointments of the senior officials of the company. The result was a compromise: the Prince's man, Pierre Rey, Comptroller of his household, was appointed President of the SBM, while the managing director was to be Charles Simon, an Onassis nominee.

On the surface, all seemed well; but the Prince was already beginning to resent the millionaire, who, he claimed, had misled him as far as his much-vaunted projects for the development of Monaco were concerned. He and Onassis, he told an interviewer in November 1955, had not spoken for over a year. Onassis, beset by international lawsuits, had indeed achieved little towards developing Monaco, but when asked by the mischievous reporter what Rainier had against him, he reacted sharply: "Did that kid have the nerve to say something nasty about me?" adding woundingly, "I thought when we got him that boat [he facilitated the purchase of the Prince's yacht *Deo Juvante*], he wouldn't talk so much." Onassis, however, was wise enough to make overtures; when the biggest bank in Monaco failed in the summer of 1955 in circumstances that touched members of the

Prince's household, mysterious "anonymous loans" subsequently appeared on its books which were rumoured to have come from Onassis. When the Prince's engagement to Grace was announced, Onassis, declaring himself to be "mad with joy", donated one million francs to the Prince's favourite charity, the Monégasque Red Cross, acceded to the Prince's request to stop the live pigeon shoot which was one of the more distasteful amenities of Monte Carlo, and loaded Grace with a bracelet and a tiara in diamonds and rubies – the colours of Monaco. The Prince's marriage to Grace signalled a *rapprochement* between himself and Onassis; in this case, as in so many others, her charm poured oil on troubled waters, but the signs for future dissension were already there.

Grace was aware, too, of the troubled marital history of the family into which she had married. Prince Rainier's great-grandfather, Prince Albert I, was a scientist of international repute, an oceanographer and archaeologist who founded the Institutes both of Oceanography and of Human Palaeontology. He was, however, a disastrous husband. His first marriage was an arranged match to a daughter of the Duke of Hamilton, Lady Mary-Victoria Douglas-Hamilton, a cousin of the Emperor Napoleon III. The wedding took place in September 1869; by the following February the Princess Mary-Victoria had left Monaco never to return. She gave birth to a son, Prince Louis, in Baden and after nine years the marriage was annulled. In 1889 the Prince married again, this time for love, an American girl, Alice Heine of New Orleans, who preceded Grace as the first American girl to marry a ruling European prince. Alice Heine, the widow of the Duc de Richelieu, was a pretty, petite blonde, and extremely rich, bringing Prince Albert a dowry of six million dollars. During the ten years Princess Alice remained in Monaco she was a great patroness of the arts – the theatre and opera in particular – but then, for some unspecified reason, she quarrelled violently with her stepson, Prince Louis, and she too left Monaco for ever, leaving behind her huge dowry. Prince Louis himself remained a bachelor until in 1946, at the age of sixty-two, he fell in love with and married an actress, Ghislaine Dommanget.

So much for the marital history of the family into which Grace, daughter of the Catholic Kellys, had married; the relationships of her more immediate in-laws were hardly less troubled. Prince Rainier's parents had separated in 1930, when he was seven years old, and were divorced in 1933. The beautiful, wilful and ultimately somewhat eccentric Princess Charlotte and the cultivated, handsome and austere aristocrat, Comte Pierre de Polignac (created Prince on their marriage in 1920), were completely temperamentally unsuited. When Princess Charlotte was ten, Prince Louis had taken her from her mother in Paris to Monaco, where she was, strictly brought up, but she was a free spirit unsuited to the confines of palace life. She became passionately interested in prison reform, spending her days working in the penitentiary at Pontoise outside Paris, and indeed shook her family by insisting on bringing as her chauffeur to her son's wedding an ex-crook named René the Swagger Cane. Her grand-daughter Elisabeth de Massy recalls that she was a delightful grandmother, although she never seems to have taken the same interest in her own children, and, indeed, rarely visited Monaco, spending most of her time at her house in Paris, or at the country château at Marchais in the Ardennes which she inherited from her father. When she did appear she was not sympathetic to Grace, and seems to have been the only one of the Grimaldis who resisted her charm. Prince Pierre, on the other hand, adored Grace from the first moment he met her.

Princess Antoinette, two years older than Prince Rainier, had shared his unhappy childhood. Princess Antoinette was very pretty, but petite, so much so that the irreverent international press at the wedding nicknamed her "Princess tiny-pants". Nine years before she had eloped with the handsome Alexandre "Alec" Noghes, a member of an old Monégasque family of Spanish descent, and had three children by him – Elisabeth, Christian and Christine Alix. Prince Rainier bestowed one of his titles, Baron de Massy, upon her and her children by Noghes, and she later married another Monégasque, the powerful and distinguished Jean Charles Rey. Princess Antoinette, like her brother, was endowed with a fiery temper and had frequent rows with him; after the wedding the press liked to represent her as estranged from her brother and his wife out of jealousy. In fact, Grace and her sister-in-law got on extremely well; Antoinette adored her brother even though they quarrelled and Grace was the calming influence which brought them together. To Grace, family links were of primary importance; she was determined to create with the quarrelling, difficult Grimaldis a family as united and close to each other as the Kelly circle into which she had been born. Ultimately she was to succeed triumphantly; she was, like Margaret Kelly, a natural "mother-hen", aware of everyone in the family, their problems and their whereabouts. "She knew where everyone was and when they were coming back," Elisabeth de Massy said. "She would never push herself on to you but she was always there if you wanted her to be. She occupied an enormous place in our lives."

But for Grace, newly-wed American bride in an unfamiliar European family, all this lay in the future. Her first concern was for the marriage on which she and the Prince had staked so much, a personal commitment that must succeed. It would not always be easy; Prince Rainer had, as he admitted openly to American newsmen on his first trip to America, what he called "a terrible character". Restless and easily bored, intelligent and witty yet sometimes finding it difficult to communicate with people, he had a quick, fierce temper which would lead him to explode in sudden anger only to subside, repentant, before Grace's serenity. He was sensitive, moody and could be difficult, characteristics arising out of insecurity bred by an unhappy, rootless and largely loveless childhood. In Grace he found the stability that came from the close-knit clan environment in which she had been brought up.

Prince Rainier's background had been very different. After his parents' divorce in 1933, when he was ten years old, he and his sister had been shuttled between, and bitterly contested by, their father and mother. Prince Pierre had even attempted to kidnap his son and had to be deterred by litigation. In practice the war between father and mother resulted in the children spending most of their time with their grandfather – "He was a kind of no-man's land," Prince Rainier said. The only stability in their lives was provided by their English nanny, Miss Kathleen Churchill Wanstall, who claimed proud relationship with the Churchills of Blenheim and whose contempt for the French language and things French was expressed in her determination to speak French only to the dogs.

The Prince's early education can only be described as cruel in the best English traditions. At the age of about ten he was despatched to a small English preparatory school, Summerfields, which the Prince describes as "dreadful", situated in the dismal tedium of a small English coastal town, St Leonard's-on-Sea, near Hastings. From there, he was sent to public school - Stowe in Buckinghamshire, - which he said, "I disliked thoroughly and ran away from promptly the first term." To be a foreigner and a Catholic in a Protestant English public school before the war marked you out as "different", a cardinal sin in the eyes of your fellow boys; to be chubby and insecure gave them ammunition with which to torture you. An older boy remembers that Prince Rainier was known as "fat little Monaco" at Stowe and that even the only other Catholic boy at the school, taller and older than the Prince, would bicycle as fast as he could to get away from him when they went on their lonely expeditions to Sunday mass at a church outside the school. Fortunately for the Prince's future, he was taken away from Stowe and sent to Le Rosey in Switzerland, a school which he remembers with affection and admiration.

The outbreak of World War II ended his time at Le Rosey and he returned to Monaco, where his grandfather, Prince Louis, gave him a brief induction into the art of princely government, and he then went on to finish his education at the university of Montpellier and at the Ecole des Sciences Politiques in Paris. In 1944, aged twenty-one, he volunteered as a foreigner with the Free French forces and fought in the Alsace campaign, winning the Croix de Guerre; after the armistice he was sent to Berlin to work in the Economic Section of the French military mission, and in 1949 he returned to Monaco as its ruler. The army had taught him the habit of command, which, added to the experience of power, strengthened a naturally auto-cratic temperament – ideal for a ruling prince, less so, perhaps, for a modern husband.

Monaco, the tiny principality of which Prince Rainier is absolute ruler, is a city state, less than four hundred acres in area – roughly the size of Hyde Park in London, half that of Central Park in New York and considerably smaller than the Bois de Boulogne in Paris. Almost every inch is built over and some 27,000 people, of whom 4982 are Monégasque citizens, live there, with a floating population of several thousand French and Italian workers who flood in every day, and tourists – the poor to spend the day and the rich who come to stay.

Monaco, the principality, which seen from the sea looks like a single town built up the lower slopes of the towering cliffs of the mountain known as the Tête du Chien, is actually divided into several different quarters. Monaco today looks very different from what Grace saw when she came to the Grimaldi palace as a bride. High-rise buildings crowd against each other, replacing the ornate stucco villas built during the first expansion of Monte Carlo early this century, and, on the extreme west of the principality, a huge land-fill project, Fontvielle, has claimed several precious new acres from the sea to form a yacht marina, sites for residential projects and light industry. To the east of Fontvielle stands *Le Rocher*, the Rock, dominated by the pink and cream Grimaldi palace with its turrets and white limestone crenellations, surrounded by the old Monaco Ville, a charming Mediterranean town of narrow, light-filled streets paved with cobbles or granite blocks. On the edge of the cliff above the Mediterranean stands the dazzling white limestone Cathedral of St Nicholas, where Grace and the Prince were married and the Grimaldis lie buried, and, to the east, the huge bulk of the Oceanographic Museum built by Prince Albert I, Prince Rainier's great-grand-father and the ancestor whom he most admires. Below the Rocher is the harbour where millionaires' yachts are berthed in serried ranks like an ungainly shoal of fish. Behind the harbour the bustling business quarter is called La Condamine, where, dwarfed beneath a huge viaduct, stands the little chapel-shrine of Monaco's patron saint, the virgin martyr Ste Dévote, whose body miraculously appeared here after her death at the hands of the Romans in Corsica in AD 304.

But to most outsiders Monaco means Monte Carlo. Founded by François Blanc on the promontory opposite the Rocher, where the Casino and the two grand hotels, the Hôtel de Paris and the Hermitage, still form perhaps the most beautiful complex of "Belle Epoque" buildings in Europe, this is the Monte Carlo of the Grand Dukes and the great gamblers – the wonderful gilded Opera House (inside the Casino building, of course) where Nijinsky danced and Sarah Bernhardt performed, the lavish gambling rooms with ceiling paintings depicting Monte Carlo as it used to be, a deserted, tree-lined shore where ladies in wide-brimmed hats picnicked elegantly under the trees. It was this elegant past of Monte Carlo which Grace was to strive to preserve as the principality's increasing prosperity fuelled the pace of modernity. When the SBM (which owns the Casino, the two grand hotels and the Sporting Club with other facilities) under Onassis's ownership planned to pull down the Hermitage hotel to make use of its site for more profitable real estate, Grace threatened to nail herself to the door. The project was abandoned.

Over all this Prince Rainier reigns supreme – he *is* the Government, and since in theory all power in Monaco both executive and judicial derives from him, in practice what he says, goes. He runs the Government with a Minister of State, who is always a Frenchman, and three counsellors for finance and home affairs, public works and social questions. There is a Parliament, called the National Council, of eighteen members elected by Monégasque citizens every five years, tribunals, a generous social welfare system, police and security forces – all the trappings of a modern state. Monaco is strictly controlled and strongly policed; the streets are safe for the rich foreign residents, tourists and companies upon which much of the state's prosperity depends. The Monégasque citizens are a privileged band, paying no personal income tax and enjoying all the benefits of a welfare state, with preferential status as far as employment in state companies like the SBM goes and the comfort of close personal links with the ruling family such as exist on the best-run great estates. Their privileged way of life is financed by an income of which only a very small percentage comes from gambling, less than 4%, and which is mainly derived from taxes on real estate development and company profits and money from tourism and public utilities. Over the years of Grace's life in Monaco, the principality would, under her husband's modernizing influence, become a mini-Switzerland, prosperous, money-orientated, a refuge for foreigners, mainly Italian and Anglo-Saxon, from the fiscal exactions of their native countries. Grace's job would be to soften this commercial aspect, making Monte Carlo once again a cultural centre as it had been under her predecessor as an American princess, Princess Alice, and, above all, to care for her husband's subjects, the Monégasques.

Monaco, a miniature state, behaves as if it were a country of larger dimensions. The Prince maintains consulates in the capital cities of Europe and in the United States with officials who are usually personal friends whom he has found sympathetic and can trust.

And so Grace found herself in the curious position of living in a town ruled by her husband and in a home, too, where he was supreme. As an ex-queen of Hollywood, accustomed to ordering her own life and career, she had to adjust to living in a palace, which is rather like a medieval city. Self-contained, it has its own teams of maintenance men, electricians and plumbers, cleaners, workmen and two upholsterers under the command of a *régisseur* (director), while some thirty women work in the laundry room alone – pressers, embroiderers, experts in starching and linen-mending, and dressmakers – without counting the numerous palace servants.

The Government is run from the palace, so there is an extensive executive suite of offices, as well as the state rooms and private apartments. Built by Prince Rainier's ancestors in the days of their glory before the French Revolution, the palace is mainly of the sixteenth and seventeenth centuries. It is constructed round a central courtyard, the Cour d'Honneur, which is frescoed and galleried, and has a fine sweeping central staircase of Carrara marble. All the rich collections of paintings, silver and furniture held by the Grimaldis vanished in the Revolution. Today state rooms are furnished with what remained to the family after 1789 together with the objects they have collected since – mainly standard palace furniture of the eighteenth century of gilded wood, with some Venetian ebony pieces. The walls are lined with silk brocade and family portraits which are almost indistinguishable one from the other and depict many of the aristocratic European (mainly French) ladies whom the Grimaldis married. Dominating the Throne Room, with its gilt throne, red velvet curtains and canopy, is a portrait of a uniformed and moustachioed figure of commanding presence, Prince Rainier's grandfather, Prince Louis II, whom he greatly resembles.

When Grace arrived she found the palace in a constant process of transformation. Prince Rainier was the first ruling prince to make the palace his home. When he succeeded his grandfather, Prince Rainier told his biographer, Peter Hawkins, "all the roofs needed to be re-done – they hadn't been looked at for sixty years. And a lot of the rooms were rather run down, sad and decrepit. ... I wanted to get the palace re-equipped so that it would be a nice place to live in as well as efficient and easy to run." And so the huge cistern under the central courtyard was drained of the thousands of gallons of water originally intended to enable the Grimaldis to withstand a siege but which in practice only tended to cause rising damp in the palace walls, rooms were cleaned and restored, brocade was ordered from factories in Lille to match the original eighteenth-century hangings, paintings were restored and furniture re-gilded.

In the Prince's view, his wife's first job was, as he had told David Schoenbrun, to run the palace household, no easy task in view of its size, Grace's lack of French and the inborn resistance to change of a number of old servants who had been doing things the same way since Prince Louis' day. The old majordomo, in charge of the wine cellar, the silver, crystal, and the setting of the table, the head of a team of ten footmen, presented the first major obstacle. He was determined to assert himself from the beginning and his response to Grace's gentle suggestions would be "Oh, we never do things that way." He might conform to her wishes once, out of politeness, as when she asked him to turn off the dazzling bulbs in the dining-room chandeliers, but the next time it would be back to the old ways. The head gardener, responsible for the flowers to decorate the tables, had been there for forty years and was equally unprepared to change his ways.

Grace's task was made easier by the appointment of an English-woman, Mrs Christine Plaistow, as housekeeper in the spring of 1957. Mrs Plaistow's task was to take care of the guests, many of them English-speaking; she had four chambermaids working under her. She was responsible for the linen and for the flowers in the guest rooms, and she worked with the gardeners over the flower arrangements in the state reception rooms, while the gardeners did the flowers for the tables for dinner and lunches.

Each maid, under Mrs Plaistow's direction, was assigned to particular guest suites of bed-, bath- and sitting-room, and when the guests arrived the maids were introduced to them by Mrs Plaistow and they would then unpack the guests' clothes. For the private apartments there was a butler, two maids and a personal maid, Honorine, for the Princess, who looked after her clothes and helped her dress. Gradually, Mrs Plaistow said, the Princess took over the household, tactfully making suggestions to the staff: "She was always so kind and courteous herself that they didn't mind."

Grace, as the Prince's hostess, would oversee arrangements for the dinners and luncheon parties. In the big dining-room, the table had leaves to seat up to thirty-six people and white damask tablecloths, embroidered with the Prince's arms, to fit every size. If there were to be more than thirty-six guests, Grace would have small tables seating eight each, for which she bought pretty pink, yellow or green under-skirts with tops of white organdie or lace. The little dining-room in the state apartments would seat up to twelve people, the hand-embroidered tablecloths being made in the palace linen rooms. "The palace's embroidered linen", Mrs Plaistow said, "is out of this world." The dining-room in the private apartments was even smaller and seated about ten people, and in the summer the Princess liked to seat people in the garden at large round tables covered with flower-printed cloths from Madame Porthault in Paris. Each morning she would discuss the menus with the chef.

She also chose the colours for the maids' morning uniforms, sewn in the palace linen room. They were made of poplin with white piqué collars and aprons, and the colours were different each year – yellow, pink, blue, turquoise or pale green. In the afternoons and in winter the maids changed to black uniforms with white collars, cuffs and aprons. As the guest rooms were redecorated the Princess chose the paint colours and the materials to be used, and scoured the palace store-rooms for pieces of furniture or objects which she liked.

Grace and the Prince lived, not in the grand rooms of the palace, which were mostly shut or in process of restoration, but in the Prince's bachelor rooms off the courtyard on the ground floor over-looking the garden facing west. They were, a friend recalls, rather dank, dark and gloomy, contributing to the misery of Grace's first year as Princess. In a foreign country, far away from her family and friends, Grace would spend long hours alone with only Oliver for company, waiting for her husband to come down from his office. She was isolated by language – the French that she had worked so hard to learn was still not adequate for real conversation – and she was surrounded by strangers at official functions. Even the palace ser-vants, although not hostile, were reserved and wary of her as a foreigner and a newcomer, waiting for her to prove herself worthy of their regard. The same was true of her husband's subjects, whose only contact hitherto with Americans, Prince Rainier said, had been with GIs, sailors and the less sophisticated tourists. They were not at all sure, he said, how an American woman would behave and so their attitude was "let's wait and see how she is going to do". It took about two years, he said, for the Monégasques to make up their mind about Grace; then "they opened up and completely adopted her and she became tremendously popular".

But in Grace's first year in Monaco such whole-hearted acceptance was still in the future. Lonely and in an alien environment, she suffered a personality crisis as she struggled to find an identity and a role. In the seven hard-driven years since she had left Philadelphia to become an actress, she had had little time for reflection, concen-trating her entire energies with single-minded passion on achieving success in her career. Now that motivation had ceased to exist; she no longer had to get up early in the morning to work long hours in the studio. The sudden and absolute cessation of working on the job she loved came as a shock and she had not yet found a new channel for her energies. Now she was cast in a subordinate role for which the script seemed both intimidating and obscure; moreover it was a part from which she would never be able to escape, the negation of that freedom and independence which she had struggled so hard to achieve. She had to learn what it meant to be a princess and to make of that role what she could.

She had to learn that a palace can be like a prison: because you are constantly under observation, you cannot just walk out of the door and go where you like. You are not free, because you must be attended by a lady-in-waiting and a security guard when you go out in public, even if all you want to do is to visit a shop. For Grace, who had always defended her private life so tenaciously, the glare of publicity under which she was forced to live was particularly painful. She had to learn, too, that a princess cannot have intimate friends in a palace, that there can be no equality of relationship except within the princely family. No subject must be allowed to become too intimate or too familiar otherwise you will lose their respect and become an object of gossip and intrigue in the small, enclosed world that is a palace – and in the equally small world of Monaco outside.

For Grace, who was, like her husband, by nature shy, to whom walking into a room full of strangers was a nerve-racking experience, the public duties of a princess were particularly hard. At public functions she was at first criticized for being too regal, her icy poise concealing her private terror. Almost thirty years later, long after she had mastered her craft as princess and learned to cope supremely well with the public pressures, she told her friend Bill Allyn: "I wouldn't have been able to do my job as well as I do it now had I not been an actress." Discipline, the awareness of the role you are playing and the capacity to project an image of that role to the public, are all part of an actor's trade. Grace learned to play the part to perfection, looking and behaving more like a princess than many who were born in a palace, but you have only to compare photographs of Grace in her first formal portraits as Princess with those of her later, mature years to see the difference. In the early pictures the tenseness is apparent, the beautiful eyes wide and staring; in the photographs of Grace's last years all her warmth and intelligence shines through – she is herself.

At twenty-six, Grace was sometimes uncertain, moody, sleepless and frightened. Alone in a foreign environment, she had still to learn the confidence to develop her personality. "There is no real Grace yet," she told a reporter.

As Princess, Grace was even more famous than she had been as a film star, a world celebrity on a grand scale. The public circumstances of her becoming a princess and her wedding made everyone curious to see her, even to touch her. The consequences could be frightening for Grace, who admitted that sometimes she suffered from claustrophobia in crowds. When she and the Prince visited Genoa early in her marriage, the crowds pressed so closely round the automobile that the sides began to buckle.

Grace's task of adjusting herself to her new role was not made easier by the press, scanning her activities with eagle eye, seeking for cracks in the façade of the fairy-tale which they themselves had helped to create. "Grace has hit a dead-end with her subjects, who are not very impressed with her performance in the role of Fairy Princess," an English newspaper reported, quoting an "anonymous citizen" as saying, "Our Princess acts more like a Queen than any Queen does." Even the Catholic Church, annoyed by the ballyhoo surrounding the wedding, implied that the marriage of Grace and the Prince was basically inspired by materialist calculation: "The romance, if not an imposed one, was certainly advised by experts who had watched the Monégasque tourist trade dwindling and badly needed some unexpected sensation to put it back in the public eye," the Catholic news agency DIS reported.

Grace's difficulties in her first months in Monaco were increased by her pregnancy; almost as soon as they returned from their honeymoon she realized that she was expecting a child. As she admitted in an interview with Olga Curtis of INS when she and Prince Rainier visited New York that September, she had been "pretty sick" for the first three months. "They told me about morning sickness," she complained, "but they didn't tell me you could be sick all day every day." Now, feeling better, she found it difficult to control her appetite and had put on twenty-six pounds. "I wake up hungry at night," she said. "The Prince is excellent at scrambled eggs, but I had to teach him how to make sandwiches. Now he invents new ones for me." She confessed to having had a craving for noodles and spaghetti – "My doctor says I eat too much." Grace was what the French call a trifle *gourmande*; she loved food and now that she was pregnant she felt that for the first time she could abandon the self-discipline she had exercised in keeping herself pencil-slim as model and movie star.

Grace spent some of that September packing up the last vestiges of her old life, the contents of her apartment on Fifth Avenue and 80th Street, and arranging to have them shipped to Monaco. She and the Prince paid a formal visit to President Eisenhower in the White House, but for her the greatest pleasure was seeing her family and her friends again. She had confessed to her husband how much she missed her women friends, missed being able to call them up, have lunch or go to a film together. For their part, none of them seem to have realized at the time how lonely she had been, that the constant letters they received from her were not, Judy Quine said, "just a question of Grace being good about writing but needing desperately to have a kind of communication. I think a number of us felt that things would happen to her that would not so much elevate her above us ... but remove her in some way. But she just had no intention of ever being removed and would not let any of us do that." Yet however much Grace tried to keep things as they were, it came as a shock to her friends to realize that as a princess her life could never be quite normal again. When Tom and Rita Guinzburg took Grace and Prince Rainier to dinner at Orsini's restaurant in New York, two tables had to be booked – one for their party, the other for the Secret Service agents guarding them.

Returning to Monaco in mid-November, she and decorator George Stacey, who had done the Fifth Avenue apartment for her, set about transforming her rooms in the palace. The private apartments consisted of a drawing-room, library, dining-room, bedroom, bar-club-room and a small kitchen. Here she and Stacey arranged the things he had bought for the New York apartment – what he described as "pretty French country château things", among them a favourite nineteenth-century love seat upholstered in a blue fabric woven with the motif "I love you". "Only the French", Prince Rainier remarked when he saw it, "could design a love seat for three people...." Opposite the apartments, down a marble staircase, a huge empty room where the Prince had once kept two lion cubs was being converted into a nursery suite, with an enormous playroom which could be screened off to make one or more children's bedrooms, a bedroom and bathroom for the nurse, a bathroom for the children and a kitchenette. The rooms were painted with a mural of Disney animals, the fitted cupboards and woodwork in yellow and white and it was furnished with wicker chairs.

Grace was making herself at home. Gradually, too, she was making her influence felt in the palace, where, Prince Rainier said, she succeeded in winning over the staff by the end of her first year there, although it was to be a further year before she would be fully accepted by all the Monégasques. But, in Mrs Plaistow's words, "the first of her triumphs" was to be the birth of her first child.

As the new year of 1957 opened and the birth of Grace's first child became imminent, there was a new invasion of Monaco by the world's press. There were, remembered Rupert Allan, who had been called in to deal with the English-speaking press, "two hundred and fifty or sixty members of the press there waiting. And not average press – top men." Once again Art Buchwald, the *New York Herald Tribune*'s star columnist, found himself sitting in Monaco waiting for something to happen. With editors in London, Paris, Bonn, New York and all over the world worrying about their reporters' expenses and demanding results to show for them, the newspapermen were looking for anything they could find to make a story.

Each day Rupert and Emile Cornet, a charming, debonair ex-rally colleague of the Prince's who had been hired to deal with the French reporters, gave separate press conferences, trying desperately to feed them facts, well aware that a newsman with no information is going to invent it. Even then ludicrous rumours took hold. Someone discovered that the Prince had bought a pony from a farmer up in the mountains and interpreted this to mean that he was expecting a boy. Questions about the pony and its significance were asked every day until Rupert Allan was forced to discover the truth about it from the Prince. "Did you", he asked, "buy a pony for your heir, for the child to be born?" Prince Rainier replied that he had only bought the pony, which he had never seen, because someone had told him that it was abandoned and was to be slaughtered and that he was paying a farmer to take care of it until he decided what to do with it. Allan decided that nothing would satisfy the press but an actual sight of the animal so, having wheedled a reluctant farmer into allowing the press on to his property, he arrived at the mountain field with a contingent fifty-strong to photograph the pony. "They wanted something tricky, though," Allan recalled. "There was a pretty girl, a friend of the farmer's daughter or something, who was dressed up for the occasion and the press wanted to take pictures of her and the pony. I said 'No.' I could see the headlines – 'Prince's mistress looking after pony while Princess Grace in labour...'."

As the birth of the child, predicted to arrive a fortnight early, drew near, Mrs Kelly hurried over from Philadelphia to be with her daughter, and Grace's gynaecologist, Dr Emile Hervet, arrived from Paris. To the annoyance of the press, although Grace had initially planned to have the baby in hospital it was decided to follow the tradition that the Grimaldi heir should be born in the palace, and that only in the case of a difficult birth would it take place in hospital. At this the television networks put in a request to Rupert Allan to alert them so that they could have the cameras ready if Grace had to leave the palace; they even asked for the driver to slow down opposite the cameras so that they could get shots of Grace in labour going down to the hospital. The cameramen were to be disappointed: in the library of the private apartments, converted into a delivery room, Grace gave birth to a daughter on 23 January 1957, nine months and four days after her wedding. The baby, delivered without anaesthetic as Grace had wished, weighed 8 lbs 11 oz and had her father's deep blue eyes. She was named Caroline Louise Marguerite.

Cradling her daughter in her arms and sipping champagne, Grace knew that she had achieved the first goal of her new life – the succession to Monaco was assured. Even then, back in Philadelphia, her father was disappointed; he had been waiting eagerly for the first Kelly grandson. "Aw, shucks, I'd been hoping for a boy," he is reported to have said. Peggy had two daughters, Lizanne's first child was a girl, as was Kell's – "I suppose it is up to me to break the boy barrier," Grace wrote to Marie Magee. "If I have a boy before Kell he will kill me. . . ."

Within fourteen months of the birth of Caroline, she had achieved even this, with the birth, on 14 March 1958, of her son, Albert Alexandre Louis Pierre, a beautiful, blond, blue-eyed baby who, like his sister Caroline, weighed 8 lbs 11 oz. Monaco now had a male heir and Jack Kelly a grandson. Prince Rainier, who had also secretly been hoping for a boy, was overjoyed. "It was one of the most wonderful experiences of my life," he said.

II

Private Life and Public Relations

With the birth of Prince Albert, the long-awaited male heir, Grace had fulfilled the public and private purpose of her marriage. Now, with her first two pregnancies successfully behind her, she could concentrate on her dual role as mother and princess. For her and for her husband, one job was at least as important as the other; indeed their golden rule was that the children came first. "Childhood passes so quickly," Grace said.

For her and for Prince Rainier one of the most important things was to bring up the children to lead as normal and happy lives as possible despite the pressures round them. For Grace it was a question of re-creating the close family atmosphere she had known at Henry Avenue, adding to it all the demonstrative affection she had not received from her mother and avoiding the competitive stress induced by her father. Prince Rainier simply wanted the children to have the secure, happy childhood that he himself had never known. There were to be no stern English nannies in starched uniforms, no isolation of the children from their parents, and no enforced exile to far-away boarding schools.

Grace, who had had no personal experience of such a creature, had heard of the authoritarian ways of the traditional English nanny from her husband and from her father-in-law. "I was never allowed into the nursery to see my children," Prince Pierre remembered of the reign of Miss Wanstall. "I want to be in charge of my children," Grace said, and she engaged, as nurses, first a young Swiss maternity nurse, Margaret Stahl, and then a young Englishwoman from Rugby, Maureen King. Maureen had never had any formal training as a nanny, although she had worked for an aristocratic family in Belgium, then for the playwright, Jean Anouilh. When Grace was expecting Albert, Maureen's sister had, unbeknown to her, written to Monaco recommending her. Maureen had all the qualities Grace was looking for: she was cheerful, informal as far as training was concerned, but she had experience, spoke English, which was important since Grace's French was not yet very fluent, and also spoke French. Maureen arrived in 1958 when Albert, always known as "Albie", was three months old; she first looked after Caroline and then Albert as well, when Margaret Stahl left, staying for seven years until 1965, when Stephanie, the last baby, was born.

Grace and Prince Rainier organized their working schedules so that they would have time to be with the children, always breakfasting with them, lunching with them whenever they were able, and always seeing them at bedtime. Breakfast was at 8.30 every morning, although the children would have erupted into their parents' room half an hour earlier. They ate at the oval mahogany table in the dining-room: grilled grapefruit, egg and toast with tea for Grace and coffee for Prince Rainier. Often the children would be there when their mother was dressing, with Caroline in particular taking an intense interest in what her mother should wear. At bedtime Prince Rainier would romp with the children and get them thoroughly over-excited until Grace read them bedtime stories. If the Prince was too busy to go down to the nursery at bedtime, the children would always ring his office to say goodnight to him.

They were brought up to be completely bilingual, speaking French in the nursery, English to their parents; later they would always speak English to their mother and French to their father. There was a certain amount of discipline, with definite times for rests after lunch and for going to bed – always half-past six when they were very young. They had to eat the food they were given or else go hungry – Caroline developed a lifelong hatred of sweetbreads. "However much you disguised them we always recognized them," she told "Nanna" King years later. If they were naughty – disobedient or cheeky – they were smacked, and when Caroline went through a phase of trying to bite her brother, Grace took her arm and bit it to show how much it hurt. "That stopped it," said Maureen King.

People were to be treated with respect and once, when Albert said haughtily to the butler, "You may take my plate away," Grace told him sharply to do it himself. "I don't think they realized they were anything special for a long time," Maureen King said. Grace tried hard to give them a normal childhood, bringing them into contact with other children as much as possible. When Caroline was four, Grace started a palace class with lessons given by a primary school teacher, Francine Vincent, for Caroline and two other little girls, later to be joined by Albie with boys of his own age.

Caroline was a very spirited child, outgoing, domineering and very aware of how she looked. She used to order her younger brother about, for Albie was sweet-tempered, quiet and very affectionate. She was intensely feminine and, like Grace, loved dolls, the favourite being a battered rag doll known as "poor pitiful Pearl", while Albert followed his father in his passion for cars, his favourite toys being a collection of Dinky toys (miniature cars and trucks). Caroline had inherited her father's intense rapport with animals and used to frighten her mother by fearlessly approaching any animal she saw. Although the Prince's menagerie was kept at the bottom of the cliff on which the palace stood, there would always be animals brought up for "rest and recreation" in the garden outside the apartment. The Prince kept a lemur, which he dearly loved, in a cage in the dining-room and there, too, was Coco the parrot, who would whistle the Monégasque national anthem whenever anyone came into the room.

Coco would also be moved to the library, which was the real family living-room for the first ten years of Grace's married life. Her former lady-in-waiting, Australian Mrs Madge Tivey-Faucon, described the big round table in the centre of the room as being in indescribable but charming disorder – "buried under a heap of papers, magazines, all sorts of parcels, toys, opened boxes of chocolates and vases of flowers". The room would always be full of dogs – the Prince's pugs and Grace's poodles, particularly the famous Oliver, who always slept at the foot of her bed and never left her side. Grace, Prince Rainier said, thought of Oliver more as a person than an animal; the Prince thought of all his animals that way. Once, Mrs Tivey-Faucon records, as she and Grace were deep in conversation in the library the Prince swept in, obviously with an important announcement for his wife as he tried to interrupt her. Grace was quite impatient, the Prince also, and in the end he said, very loudly: "You don't seem to understand how important it is. Tanagra is pregnant!" Tanagra was his chimpanzee and, according to Mrs Tivey, no favourite of Grace's. The Prince, however, continued, raising his voice: "It's very rare for a chimpanzee to breed in captivity."

"All *rightie*," snapped Grace. "I'll knit her something. . . ."

Curiously, Madge Tivey-Faucon, known familiarly as "Tiv", had come to work at the Palace through Gisèle Pascal, who had introduced her to Prince Rainier. She had initially been engaged to act as his English-speaking secretary and after his marriage the Prince asked her to stay on as lady-in-waiting to Grace and to teach her French.

After she left, she fell out of favour as a result of writing about her experiences in an article for *Cosmopolitan* in 1964.

Early in their married life the Prince and Grace came to the decision that it was essential for them and for their children to have a private refuge where they could relax away from the palace and from Monaco, where they were cooped up under constant scrutiny. The answer was to be Roc Agel, an old farmhouse on a green ledge high up on the slopes of Mont Agel above Monaco. The Prince bought the property with its sixty acres in 1957. By 1959 the old house had been transformed and enlarged, with Grace personally supervising the building, keeping the style simple like that of a Provençal *mas* or farmhouse – brown tiled roof, massive beams, sturdy stone walls and carefully carved woodwork. The plumbing was, however, American and so was the kitchen, in Grace's favourite colour, aquamarine, fitted up with her equipment from New York. One cloakroom-lavatory, its walls covered with stills from Grace's movies, was a reminder of her film star past.

The locals dubbed Roc Agel "the Ranch", and it was equipped with outbuildings and a growing collection of animals – riding horses for the Prince and Grace, ponies for the children, plus an assortment of cows, goats, rabbits etc. The house was looked after by an Italian couple, but at weekends Grace liked to do the cooking, experimenting with Chinese or Indian dishes while the Prince worked in the fields with his tractor or in his workshop doing carpentry or ironwork. Often there would be barbecues, with the Prince, like any American husband, in charge of the cooking. "They would be home on Sunday barbecuing and Rainier would play the drums, and somebody would go and chase the chickens out of the yard, and Grace would chop the salad," Judy Quine recalled. "They had a strong sense of family as a rock ... that was a good strong bond between them and she carried over a lot of the traditions of her American family." Roc Agel was sacred as far as their privacy was concerned – it was only for the family and a few close friends. It was for weekends and for the heat of late summer, when the fresh, cool mountain air was a tonic after the simmering heat of Monaco below.

At the Palace, too, they were making improvements to create more of a home for the children. In 1962 they put in an enormous swimming-pool in the garden and, when their third and last child, Stephanie, arrived on 1 February 1965, and it became obvious that their present quarters would soon be far too small for them, they began making a new family home, rebuilding a wing of the palace which had been destroyed in the French Revolution.

The pattern of their family life became established: living in the palace during the week, spending weekends and the high summer months of August and September at Roc Agel, often spending October in Paris, where at first the family crammed into the Prince's bachelor flat. The Paris flat had only three bedrooms and a living-cum-dining-room. The children's laundry had to be strung along the passages, to the surprise of anyone who came through the service entrance; later they moved to a larger and more suitable apartment on the smart, expensive Avenue Foch.

The official year in Monaco would start again in November, with the National Day on 19 November, followed by Christmas parties for Monégasque children at the palace, and the International Circus Festival, initiated by the Prince, after Christmas. Towards the end of January they would go to a rented chalet at Schoenried near Gstaad. That was, Maureen King said, "a treasured holiday" because they all had more freedom there than they did in Monaco, and the children rapidly became expert skiers. Here, one year, Oliver, her last tangible link with her life in America, was savaged to death by a neighbour's dog. Grace was heartbroken.

The summer of 1960 brought anguish for Grace when her father died suddenly of stomach cancer. Almost his last public appearance was to get up from his sick-bed after his first exploratory operation and appear in a courtroom to testify as a character witness for a friend. A second exploratory operation revealed that the cancer was too advanced to be operable. Jack Kelly died at home on 20 June.

Flags flew at half mast throughout Philadelphia and, less predictably, within days copies of Jack Kelly's will were selling at $7 a copy. Jack Kelly had always had a sneaking fondness for expressing himself on paper and had written his autobiography and even a play, but his will was destined to be his only published work. Dated 1953, it was written in plain American English without legal obscurities: "Kids will be called 'kids' and not 'issue' and it will not be cluttered up with 'Parties of the first part' ... and a lot of other terms that I am sure are only used to confuse those for whose benefit it is written. ...." Sons-in-law were specifically excluded from benefiting under the will – either through legacies or by buying stock in John B. Kelly, Inc. As far as company stock was concerned, Jack Kelly said he preferred to see his employees as stockholders rather than some future sons-in-law of whom he might not approve:

> Since I have chosen my employees ... I would rather see them as stock-holders than many of the Romeos that I see presenting their charms to the tunes of their mandolins under the windows at 3901 Henry Avenue. There is also the possibility that some Burlesque girl with a sweater may sell Kell [sic] a bill of goods ...

The conclusion was full of phrases characteristic of Jack Kelly's beliefs and his code of behaviour. There were to be no extravagant displays of grief at his death, he stipulated: "As for me, just shed a respectful tear if you think I merit it ... the thoroughbred grieves in the heart." He was leaving them his possessions, but if he had the choice between worldly goods and character "I would give you character. The reason I say that is with character you will get worldly goods because character is loyalty, honesty, ability, sportsmanship and, I hope, a sense of humor.... If I don't stop soon," he concluded, "this will be as long as *Gone With the Wind* so just remember, when I shove off for greener pastures or whatever it is on the other side of the curtain, that I do it unafraid and if you must know, a little curious."

Jack Kelly's estate amounted to just under $2 million, a third of which was to go to his wife, the rest to be divided equally between the children. Three years later, in 1963, Philadelphia raised a monument to John B. Kelly which, appropriately, depicted him sitting in a bronze rowing shell, and was sited beside the Schuylkill River on which his great rowing career had begun.

Jack Kelly, despite having a prince as a son-in-law, remained the rugged Irish-American. democrat to the end. While his brother George took happily to palace life, Jack, according to his nephew Charles, "hated Monaco, where you'd have servants all over you.... My Uncle George adored the palace and the life that went with it. But Uncle Jack couldn't bear the protocol in Monaco." Even at the time of Grace's wedding, columnist Earl Wilson reported Jack Kelly as remarking in the lobby of the Hôtel de Paris, "We're staying at the palace but I'd rather be down here. There are too many servants underfoot at the palace. It's very regal."

Jack Kelly was ill at ease in the palace and not only because of the numbers of servants "underfoot". By nature dominant and accustomed to being the boss in his own house, he could not feel comfortable in a place where his daughter and son-in-law were treated like royalty whereas he was definitely of a lower rank. While Margaret Kelly often stayed at the palace and got on extremely well with her son-in-law, who both liked and respected her, Jack Kelly's reactions to Prince Rainier were more complex. It was in many ways difficult for him to feel totally relaxed with a man who was more powerful than he, younger than he and yet who with his sporting prowess was in no way his masculine inferior. The Jack Kelly whom Prince Rainier saw in Monaco, quiet and reserved, would have been unfamiliar to his friends in Philadelphia.

Moreover, Grace, the daughter who had striven so hard and in vain to gain his approval, whom he had always declared to be inferior to his beloved Peggy, had revealed an intelligence, determination, discipline and will-power like his own. In marrying a man as masculine but more powerful than her father, she had ended the contest between them with the upper hand.

Whether Grace was aware of her father's reactions or not is impossible to tell. As Princess she remained awed by his looks, his character and his achievements, worshipping him just as much as she had when a child. Years after his death she would impress her father's qualities on sympathetic listeners – "He obviously meant a great deal to her," one commented. No doubt she grieved for him, undemonstratively and in private, as he had wished.

The death of her father was not the only private sadness for Grace during the 1960s. She suffered two miscarriages before the birth of her second daughter, Stephanie Marie Elisabeth, on 1 February 1965. Stephanie was to be the last child; Grace had a very serious miscarriage in 1967 in Montreal, where she and the Prince had gone for Expo '67. She was driven to the Montreal Royal Victory Hospital after being taken ill after a banquet, but the baby was dead and had been so for some time. And so Stephanie, seven years younger than Albert, was the baby of the family, and treated as such, petted, spoiled and indulged. With her father's dark hair but with the Kelly jaw and athletic ability, Stephanie was to grow up slowly, clinging to her "baby" status, always holding her mother's hand, sucking her thumb even as a teenager. She was also to be the tomboy of the family, a gifted gymnast, a girl for blue jeans and scooters who, unlike her elder sister Caroline, did not enjoy being a princess.

Family concerns apart, Grace had a busy, glamorous life as public relations Princess of Monaco. Both she and Prince Rainier hated the comic-opera image of Monaco in the press and resented the widespread belief that the fortunes of the principality rested on the spin of a roulette wheel. Somerset Maugham had described Monte Carlo as "a sunny place for shady people", as if it were a haunt of international crooks, con-men and seedy gamblers. The Prince was determined to modernize Monaco, to increase its tourist potential, and to augment its revenue by attracting business and light industry; and both he and Grace dreamed of making it once again the centre of the arts which it had been in the first decades of the century.

Grace's arrival in Monaco provided a much-needed boost to Monaco's international image; as an international celebrity whose glamour exceeded even that of Onassis, she was a magnet for the rich visitors Monte Carlo needed. Elsa Maxwell, court jester and confidante to the international rich and famous, moved in. Short, fat and ugly, Elsa was an unlikely leader for the Beautiful People, but with her irrepressible energy, real kindness and insatiable appetite for parties and celebrities she was a focus of the international social scene. As a connoisseur of celebrities and friend of princes and millionaires, Elsa recognized that Grace had what it takes. "I recognized the qualities in Grace – talent, courage and the depth and strength to live up to celebrity – when I first met her on the Riviera," she wrote in her book *The Celebrity Circus* in 1964, ranking Grace with Elizabeth Taylor and Jacqueline Kennedy on the international celebrity scale. "Grace showed from the first a natural aptitude for being a princess, a quality of belonging that I've found to be rare in people who suddenly rise to such a position."

Grace loved parties – she was, a friend said, quite childlike about them, adoring the dressing-up, the glitter and the fun. She and Rainier went to Elsa Maxwell's parties, including a fancy-dress dinner party to celebrate the opening of the new indoor pool at the Hôtel de Paris, at which the Prince arrived disguised with a fierce black moustache and bald wig and Grace came in a rubber mask with fat cheeks and braids, wearing a floppy straw hat and big flippers. Both of them dived into the pool like the rest of the guests and although most people left at five in the morning, they stayed on for breakfast with David Niven and Elsa Maxwell, sitting quietly together watching dawn break over the Mediterranean. Grace's social stamina was remarkable. If a party was fun, she would always be among the last to leave, and among her own friends at the palace she would stay up drinking champagne, playing games or just talking, until dawn.

Elsa Maxwell and Aristotle Onassis were the social life and soul of parties along the Mediterranean, and Grace and the Prince were often with them. On one occasion there was a big social weekend on Majorca for the opening of the Hôtel Son Vida. Onassis was there, then in the full blaze of his affair with Maria Callas, Elsa, of course, the Prince, Grace and the New York dress designer Vera Maxwell, who had recently become a friend. One evening the party took over from the hotel orchestra on "Ari's" initiative. Elsa played the piano, Maria Callas took the maracas and Prince Rainier the drums, while Grace conducted and Ari sang French and Italian love songs.

Although a gulf was widening between the Prince and Onassis over the development of Monaco and the affairs of the SBM, in private life the Prince and Grace liked him for his dynamic charm and life-enhancing energy. He would do things like inviting them on the spot to fly to London with him on a private plane, and hiring a dance band from Monte Carlo to accompany him on the plane as he danced with Grace's American secretary, the tall, rangy Phyllis Blum, who towered over him. But while the relationship with Onassis was soon to be disrupted by a bitter quarrel over Monaco, Grace remained friends with Callas for the rest of Maria's tragic life. Grace, often held up as an archetype of chilly prudishness, had no qualms about accepting invitations to cruise with Ari and Maria on the *Christina*, on which Callas lived as his mistress after his divorce from Tina. Grace admired Callas for her genius and her passion, liked her for her directness and, although she was saddened by the effect of her affair with Onassis on her singing career, she remained a loyal admirer after the affair, and indeed Maria's career, had ended. She saw her frequently in Monaco and Paris and forgave her eccentricities and selfishness. When Onassis died Grace was one of the few people to realize what this meant to Callas and to write to her sympathizing with her pain.

Private friendship could not, however, forestall what was bound to be an escalating struggle between the Prince and Onassis for the control of Monaco. Relations between the two men deteriorated steadily from 1960, when Tina Onassis divorced her husband and Onassis, according to the Prince, began increasingly to lose interest in Monte Carlo. "I have two toys," Onassis is reported to have said, "the *Christina* and the SBM." Now he was spending more and more time on the *Christina*, less and less, both of his time and of his money, on the SBM. The Prince accused Onassis of doing nothing to improve the facilities of the SBM (the hotel and casino company), of having no interest in such improvements, while Onassis dubbed the Prince's projects ostentatious and ruinously expensive. The quarrel came out into the open in 1965 when the Prince, in an interview with *Le Monde*, publicly accused Onassis of neglecting Monaco's interests and concentrating only on money-spinning projects, while Onassis's board of directors counter-charged that their activities were being sabotaged by deliberate administrative inaction.

Onassis proposed dividing the SBM into three companies, the gambling, other tourist amenities and the real estate, the first two to be farmed out to other businessmen while Onassis would maintain control of the holding company and concentrate on making huge profits from the SBM's real estate, which he proposed to use for the construction of middle-income apartments to be sold to foreigners. The SBM, through its ownership of the Casino, the Winter and Summer Sporting Clubs, the Hôtel de Paris and the Hermitage, is responsible for all the principal amenities and entertainments of Monte Carlo as well as owning the heart of its real estate. Prince Rainier saw this project of splitting up the SBM's interests and speculating in its real estate (including such projects as demolishing the Hermitage hotel) as "the ruin of the SBM", which would shatter the whole economy of the principality.

Prince Rainier charged Onassis with failing to keep up the cultural obligations of the SBM, and of the opera season in particular – a curious defect in the lover of Maria Callas. "There are supposed to be eighteen opera presentations a year here," he told his biographer Peter Hawkins, "but now I can do only eight each season. I tried to get Mr Onassis to do something about this, but he could not see the importance. He told me: 'No, no, no. We must do away with opera. People are not interested any more.' "

Monte Carlo had lost its glamour for Onassis, who saw himself increasingly as a modern Odysseus, a Captain Nemo based on his own island kingdom, Skorpios, ranging the seas on his floating palace, the *Christina*. His attitude towards Monte Carlo and the SBM was simply that of capitalizing on his investment.

For Rainier the future development of Monaco was at stake. As absolute ruler he decided on absolutist action. In 1966 the National

Assembly passed a law to force the SBM to increase its capital from five to eight million francs by the creation of 600,000 new shares at five new francs each, to be issued to the State and paid for by the Government; the law also provided that owners of shares purchased previously could sell them to the Government at average quotation prices on the Paris Stock Exchange over the period 1 January to 30 April 1967. The State was to have preferential rights to acquire stock in the event of any further increases in SBM capital. The Bill was approved by the National Council, thus giving the State a little over a third of the total shares, which, given the holdings of the Prince and others, meant that Onassis was no longer the majority share-holder. Onassis resigned from the administration of the SBM and contested the law as unconstitutional in the Monaco Supreme Court, but, to no one's surprise, on 5 March 1967, while he was cruising in the Caribbean with Callas, the Supreme Court decided against him. As a result of this defeat he withdrew all his interests in the SBM and on 17 March the Monaco Treasury paid into his account a cheque for $10,000,000, representing the value of his shares in the SBM. Onassis claimed he should have got over $30,000,000, but he had no alternative but to accept the *fait accompli*. Monte Carlo was no longer "Monte Greco".

The sixties, the heyday of the "Beautiful People" of the International Set, was the decade of ostentatious parties, faithfully, even reverentially recorded in columns of newsprint, of charity balls like the famous *Bal des Petits Lits Blancs* which brought the rich, the famous and the beautiful jetting in wherever they might be held. As social ambassadress for Monaco, Grace was a prominent figure on this glittering social carousel. She and the Prince were hosts to one such ball, held in the courtyard of the palace, a medieval feast attended by all the "names" of Europe and America.

The most sensational occasion was undoubtedly in April 1966 at the Feria (the Spring Fair) in Seville, then an essential jet-stop on the international social calendar. Guests of honour were Grace and Jacqueline Kennedy, and the international press portrayed their encounter as a week-long social duel, even interpreting their different styles of dress as a challenge match. Grace opened the Feria wearing a ruffled pink lace Andalusian dress presented to her by the local flamenco dancers and was accompanied by a bearded Prince Rainier, while Jacqueline Kennedy, the President's widow, was dark and svelte in the black and white of traditional Andalusian riding costume. The climax of the week's festivities for guests and press came at the Débutantes' Ball, held in one of the most beautiful houses in Europe, the fifteenth-century Casa dos Pilatos, owned by the Duquesa de Medinaceli, with its courtyards and fountains, Greek statues, coloured tiles and intricate gilded ceilings.

That evening Jacqueline Kennedy had to fight her way through a giant posse of photographers and celebrity-seeking guests to reach her table, then face twenty minutes of flashbulbs until she took refuge at a bar in the corner of the ball-room. Grace arrived some forty minutes late, protected by soldiers in plumed helmets who shoved the photographers out of the way, knocking some of them down, and by the time Mrs Kennedy succeeded in fighting her way back to her table the débutantes' presentation ceremony had begun. Grace put out her hand for a quick handshake, and then they both sat, silent and fatigued, on either side of their host, the Duque de Medinaceli. The result was a front page picture in the *New York Herald Tribune* for 19 April captioned: "Cool Conversation ... Princess Grace of Monaco and Mrs John F. Kennedy seem to have little to say to each other at the Seville, Spain, Red Cross Ball." Grace was so upset that she wrote an open letter to the newspaper denying that there was any coolness between herself and Jacqueline Kennedy, "for whom I have a great respect and admiration", blaming "the many dozens of photographers who pushed, shoved and relentlessly pursued us all night".

Jacqueline Kennedy and Grace were not soul-mates, as the press readily sensed, but they were neither of them insecure celebrity-seekers indulging in petty rivalry. Very probably Jacqueline Kennedy, besieged by photographers, had been angered by Grace's late arrival, which had contributed to her ordeal. Had she known the real reason, she would have understood. Grace's short-sightedness had always been a problem for her; since she could not recognize, indeed hardly see, anybody at a range beyond about eight feet, it had contributed greatly to her reputation for being cold and distant. The perils of her myopia had recently been brought home to her on a state visit to the President of Italy in the Quirinale when, reaching the top of an immense formal flight of steps, she had been unable to distinguish between the formally dressed official photographers and the official party until steered in the right direction by her husband – "Grace, those are the photographers, the President is to the left."

Recognizing General de Gaulle on their state visit to Paris in 1959 had been easier. "I just made for the tallest *chapeau* [hat]," said Grace.

Since a princess who is also a famous beauty would disappoint her public if she were to wear her spectacles on public occasions, Grace had decided to try contact lenses. Seville was the first big occasion on which she wore them, and it was a disaster. Someone, possibly herself or her maid, had dropped them out of their cases and then had replaced the left lens in the case for the right eye and vice versa, so that, when she came to put them in, they were wrong and hurt her eyes so that they watered and she could not see. They had to be jettisoned, leaving Grace uncomfortable, upset and late to face the glare of the flashbulbs and the press of the crowds. She never wore them again.

"Although Grace and the Prince both love parties", Elsa Maxwell wrote, "I doubt that they'll ever really become active in international society." Grace did what was expected of her as representative of a state to which those people were important. Liking people, she charmed them, but she was not a committed, paid-up member of that international set. She was still shy and wary of people who were in Society: she could respond to people, but as people and not as sophisticates. She needed directness, genuineness and a real personal warmth before she could open herself up to someone. Initially "international society" frightened her – Contessa Donnina Cicogna remembers that the first time she asked Grace to one of her Monte Carlo parties, many years ago, David Niven brought her. "It needed a bottle of champagne to get her here," he confided to Donnina as they arrived. As a Philadelphia Kelly Grace had not been part of "proper Philadelphia". In Europe she and Prince Rainier, despite his family connections, were not surrounded by personal friends drawn from that most exclusive of social and genealogical handbooks, the *Almanach de Gotha*. Nor could they afford to have intimate friends in the small world of international Monte Carlo society, as enclosed and as visible as a goldfish bowl, in which petty rows such as the famous Docker affair of 1958 could erupt into hurricane proportions.

The central figure in this row was none other than the flamboyant Norah Docker who had been so critical of Grace's quiet wardrobe and behaviour when she first stepped ashore from the *Constitution*. It was not the first row in which Norah Docker had been concerned in the principality but it was to be the last. At the time of the wedding Sir Bernard and Lady Docker had complained bitterly to the palace when they found themselves excluded from the Casino night club when it had been reserved for the Kellys' party in honour of the Prince and Grace. Their objections had been noted, and resented, but, as big-spending habitués of Monte Carlo, the Dockers had been invited to all the public wedding functions.

The final row had occurred two years later, when Norah Docker had demanded that her nineteen-year-old son, Lance, be added to the list of guests for the reception honouring the christening of Prince Albert. Their request was refused and in dudgeon the Dockers not only refused to attend the christening of the heir to the principality, but held a press conference at the Hôtel Majestic in Cannes. There followed a dinner at the Hôtel de Paris where Lady Docker, her indignation perhaps heightened by her favourite pink champagne, was reported to have said some disagreeable things on the subject of Their Serene Highnesses and to have insulted the Monaco flag by breaking in two a small paper replica of the flag and throwing it to the floor.

By now Prince Rainier had had enough; he banned the Dockers from Monaco, which, under the terms of his treaty with France, meant that they were also forbidden to enter the entire department of the Alpes Maritimes. The Dockers were thus effectively excluded from the Riviera from Cannes to the Italian border. Lady Docker riposted in characteristic fashion in the *Daily Express*. As far as she was concerned the Prince could go and jump in the sea, she said: "I am signing my own decree that I will never enter that Hyde Park principality again.... I will not take my yacht within shooting distance of the palace.... They will miss us more than we will miss them."

It is hardly surprising that Grace and the Prince limited their close friends to those very few people whom they knew they could trust – principally David and Hjordis Niven, whom Grace had known since her Hollywood days, and the writer Paul Gallico and his English wife, Virginia.

The Docker episode was a mere storm in a teacup. Far more serious in its implications for Monaco was the confrontation which took place in 1962 between the Prince and the mighty General de Gaulle.

Relations with France loom large on the horizon of Monaco. Physically there is little to distinguish the territory of the municipality from that of its neighbours. France is Big Brother, standing in much the same territorial relation to Monaco as China does to Macao and

Hong Kong, the important difference being that Monaco has been an independent entity for more than six centuries, long before France itself assumed its final shape. The natives of Monaco naturally speak French, but their own language, Monégasque, owes nothing to Northern France, everything to the Mediterranean shore, to Provençal and to Italian. Absorption by France remains a potential nightmare for Monégasques and for non-French residents of Monaco, who would lose the happy privileges, fiscal and otherwise, which they enjoy. Grace, in marrying the Prince and producing healthy heirs, had ensured the independent existence of Monaco for years to come, and her very presence as an international personality was reassuring. The crisis of 1962, when France threatened Monaco with virtual extinction, came, therefore, as a painful shock.

Grace and Prince Rainier had paid a state visit to Paris in 1959, when they had been royally received by General and Madame de Gaulle and the General had shown himself clearly enchanted by the Princess of Monaco. The following year the de Gaulles had visited Monaco, where the General had complimented the Prince upon the technical advances he had initiated there. Ironically though, the explosion which took place in January 1962 was fuelled by the Prince's successes in bolstering Monaco's economy. With the help of a young American adviser, Martin Dale, former US Consul in Nice, the Prince formed the Monaco Economic Development Corporation 'MEDEC' to bring new business to Monaco, and in 1961 alone no less than forty-six companies registered, several of them American. France suspected that American influence was being substituted for her own in Monaco, that Monaco's business interests were expanding at the expense of France and that French citizens were avoiding paying French tax by running their companies from, and residing in, Monaco.

Matters came to a head in a complicated financial battle over a communications company, Images et Son, which controlled both Radio Monte Carlo and Radio Luxembourg. When France attempted to acquire control of the company by buying up the shares through a third party, Prince Rainier issued an ordinance forbidding resale of the shares. Emile Pelletier, the Prince's French Minister of State, approved the ordinance, but, when the French Government issued an ultimatum to Monaco to abrogate the ordinance or face reprisals in all fields, Pelletier sided with France. Prince Rainier fired him and the French Government riposted by threatening that unless Monaco accepted the full French tax system by October, France would cut off the principality's supplies of gas, water and electricity, and impose customs and immigration controls on its borders.

Monaco's foreign residents were in a state of panic, and Grace, interviewed by the *Saturday Evening Post* in the summer of 1962, admitted to being "very concerned, very anxious and worried". Prince Rainier recalled his parliament, which he had dissolved three years previously over a budgetary dispute, and announced a new constitution and a general election for October with women's suffrage for the first time. After a brief "siege" by the French customs authorities in October, negotiations began. A compromise was eventually reached whereby French residents of Monaco would be subject to the financial laws of France, thus calming French fears that the principality was being used as a haven for money flowing out of the troubled French North African colonies.

The confrontation with de Gaulle coincided with a bitter personal disappointment for Grace. Alfred Hitchcock had never given up dreaming that his favourite leading lady would one day return to work for him. He was not alone in hoping to lure Grace back to Hollywood; two years earlier, while Grace was on the *Christina* with Onassis and Callas, Spyros Skouras, putting together *The Greatest Story Ever Told*, had what seemed to him to be a brainwave. He sent a cable to Onassis: "Please help me. I'm offering a million dollars to Princess Grace if she will do the Virgin Mary in this picture and a million dollars to Maria Callas if she will do Mary Magdalene." Onassis read the cable to Princess Grace, Prince Rainier and Callas at lunch. They all thought it was hysterical – "The Virgin Mary – no way," Grace said giggling; "Mary Magdalene, yes. . . ."

Hitchcock, however, was a different matter. Both the Prince and Grace loved and trusted him, and when he sent Grace Winston Graham's *Marnie* early in 1962 with the suggestion that she should play the title role, she liked it. In her heart of hearts Grace had never given up the idea of acting again, even if she had no intention of returning to Hollywood. She was tempted, and the Prince encouraged her to agree. "I think that anyone who has spent so much time on their craft as the Princess has, and she's so good at it, it's a waste," he told a friend. "And she gets pleasure in doing it," he continued, "she should do it . . . it would be right for her to do it. Why should a talent like that go?" It was agreed that the film should be shot at the end of the summer, during the time the family normally spent away from Monaco before official duties recommenced in November. They would rent a house in Virginia, where the outside scenes were to be shot, and Grace would receive a fee of $375,000, which she would donate to Monégasque charities. On 19 March the palace announced that "Princess Grace has accepted to appear during her summer vacation in a motion picture for Mr Alfred Hitchcock to be made in the United States".

There was an immediate public furore – "Grace Returns to Hollywood", the headlines screamed worldwide. The Monégasques, nervous and confused by the political situation with France, jumped to the conclusion that their Princess was abandoning them and returning to America, and worse, since the press release neglected to mention that her fee was to be donated to charity, that she was doing it for the money. Together with their feeling of betrayal went the sense that the wife of their sovereign Prince would be demeaning herself by appearing in a commercial film. Perhaps they were right: the part of Marnie, a thief with psychological hang-ups to whom stealing is a substitute for love, was hardly a suitable one.

The project was dropped, but it had had a traumatic effect upon Grace, brutally demonstrating to her the limitations that her position had placed on her life. Her intentions were just as open to misinterpretation as they had ever been in Hollywood, but her ability to do what she liked was even more restricted. With that avenue of self-expression definitely closed, the success of her role in bringing up her family and as Princess of Monaco became even more important to her. More than ever she realized that her dynamic energy and creative instincts would have to be exercised within the confines of the life that she herself had chosen.

"Are you happy?" an interviewer asked her four years later. "I don't expect to be," she replied. "I don't look for happiness. So perhaps I am very content in life, in a way . . ." How, the interviewer pressed her, would she define happiness? "I suppose being at peace with yourself," she said. "Not anxiously seeking for something, not being frantic about not having something."

"Are you at peace with yourself?"

"Well, I understand myself. But I argue with myself all the time, so I guess I'm not really at peace. . . ."

"Since you haven't found peace of mind, what do you think will help you achieve it?"

"Well, I have many unfulfilled ambitions in life . . . ," Grace replied.

When asked that same question – "Was Grace happy?" – a close friend answered enigmatically, "She made her own life." Grace found a number of small avenues for creative expression – painting, drawing, sculpting, embroidery, learning pottery, Italian, the guitar, and reading during the long quiet evenings after dinner when her husband fell asleep. She would read late into the night, history books, biographies, often of women in a similar position to herself, finding out how they coped; Queen Victoria was a particular favourite.

Grace and Prince Rainier, intent upon improving the international image of Monaco, were not only ambassadors for their country, they were also – and this represented a considerable step up in personal status – becoming acquainted with, and accepted by, European royalty. Europe's royal houses had been conspicuous by their absence at the Monaco wedding. The young bachelor Prince of Monaco had not counted for much in royal circles, but gradually Grace's beauty and charm, and indeed her excellent playing of the regal role, made the Prince and Princess of Monaco desirable and welcome guests in other palaces. Grace and the Prince were on friendly terms with the King and Queen of the Belgians and the young King and Queen of Spain. They were invited to royal events such as the wedding of King Constantine of Greece to Princess Anne-Marie of Denmark in Athens in 1964, and to the wedding of the daughter of the Queen of England, Princess Anne, to Captain Mark Phillips in 1973. Earl Mountbatten, great-uncle of the Prince of Wales, was to become one of Grace's most fervent admirers, even, it was rumoured, to the extent of writing anonymously in *Time* magazine on the occasion of Prince Charles's thirtieth birthday of the ideal bride for the Prince – "there is only one Grace Kelly". When Prince Charles finally chose his bride, Lady Diana Spencer, Grace and her son Prince Albert were honoured guests at the wedding in the summer of 1981. It was all quite an achievement for a girl from Germantown, Philadelphia, daughter of an Irish bricklayer.

One state occasion was to have particular significance for Grace: the visit which she and Prince Rainier paid to President and Mrs de Valera of Ireland in 1961. Grace's Irishness was central to her identity; her Catholic religion had helped her to understand the Catholic Europeans among whom she now lived; coming back to her Irish roots made her feel that she was also part of Europe by blood and tradition. As she struggled to work out an identity, to be American and yet be a part of Europe, her Irish roots and the cultural background of Ireland were to become ever more important to her. Going to Ireland, the land where her grandparents were born, was a personal rite of passage: a Kelly was coming home.

That was the way the twenty thousand people saw it who waited to greet Grace as she stepped off the plane at Dublin airport wearing a Dior suit of Kelly green. As she appeared an enormous roar went up. "My God," said Rupert Allan, who met her, "everyone yelled as if they were going to burst their blood vessels, men, women and children. . . ." In Dublin itself the crowds were unbelievable; the press of people in the streets en route for the Gresham Hotel, where President de Valera was waiting for them at a reception, was so great that it actually stopped and rocked the solid old Rolls in which they were travelling. It was an immense outpouring of affection and pride – pride that Ireland had produced not only America's first Catholic President, a Kennedy, but also Princess Grace. At the hotel in Cork where Grace, Prince Rainier and the children, attended by Maureen King, were staying, a huge crowd waited outside, only dispersing after Grace appeared to wave goodbye; and as they drove through Ireland, first to County Kerry, where they were to have a few days' rest, and then on Grace's own private pilgrimage to County Mayo, the country roads were lined with schoolchildren waving Monégasque flags that they had made themselves and screaming "Princess Grace! Princess Grace!"

Visiting Drumirla for the first time must have been an emotional experience for Grace and, as she sat in the cottage which had been the Kelly ancestral home enjoying the Irish tea and scones offered her by the then owner, white-haired Mrs Ellen Mulchrone, she must have reflected on the spin of the wheel of fortune which had brought her, grand-daughter of a poor emigrant farm boy, back to Drumirla as a princess. This, she felt, was her land, and these people, the warm, witty and not at all reverential Mayo people, were her people, men like her cousin, boat-builder Paddy Quinn, and his family, who live on one of the soft green hump-backed islets rising out of the misty grey sea off the coast between Westport and Newport. Grace and the Prince had tea with the Quinns, went sea-fishing around the islands and stayed in the charming local fishing hotel.

Drumirla, with its simple house overlooking the brooding lake and the bare moorlands, and the lonely Mayo coast where the landscape melts into the sea, satisfied a central need in Grace, giving her not only physical, tangible roots but an explanation and a *raison d'être* of her romantic, poetic soul. The Irish experience was for her a germinal one, providing an East Coast American girl planted on a Mediterranean shore with roots in Catholic Europe and a logical cultural tradition to follow. Far away in Monte Carlo she would cherish that tradition, buying a remarkable library of books on Irish poetry and music, and instigating, in the unlikely setting of Monte Carlo, a celebration of that uniquely Irish genius, James Joyce. Nearly fifteen years later, after Mrs Mulchrone died, Grace would buy the house which her Kelly grandfather had left just over one hundred years before, and the wheel of fortune would come full circle.

Indeed through the 1960s Grace was putting down her roots in Europe, gathering around her, on that side of the Atlantic, a band of devoted friends, followers and helpers such as she had had in her previous life in America. At first her immediate palace circle had included her American secretary Phyllis Blum, whom she had met through Rupert Allan in September 1956, when Phyllis helped her pack up her Fifth Avenue apartment, and who joined her later in Monaco as her secretary in August 1958. Phyllis left in 1962 to marry Julian Earl, Somerset Maugham's nephew, but she remained close to Grace, who would often ask her to accompany her on her travels and would stay at her London house. Phyllis Blum and Maureen King, as the two English speakers in the palace, formed a happy partnership, pitting their wits in inventing practical jokes aimed at Prince Rainier, who would retaliate in kind. Maureen King, who was then a plump, jolly girl – Caroline called her "Big, fat Nanna" – had a healthy appetite and Prince Rainier nicknamed her "Killer", claiming that feeding her cost him more than paying Grace's hospital bills when she had an appendectomy in Lausanne.

Among the closest and most loyal of the palace people were Colonel and Madame Ardant. Colonel Ardant, who had spent two years as "Governor of the Prince" with Prince Rainier at Montpellier, had been appointed Governor of his Household when he left the army in 1960. His wife, a few years later, became the Princess's lady-in-waiting and devoted friend. "In twenty years of service," said Madame Ardant, "I never had the slightest difficulty with the Princess. She had a very equable character, no 'caprices' and great self-control, she never made a scene if something was wrong." If it was, she would quietly let Madame Ardant know afterwards and ask her to tell the person concerned. She was, said Madame Ardant, "a truly extraordinary person, with a great tolerance and understanding of people". "My princess" was the way she referred to Grace and that was how those who served her liked to think of her: people like Paul Ramundo, ex-Resistance fighter and, until his retirement, Grace's personal chauffeur, who used also to act as valet when she and Prince Rainier were in Paris. "He absolutely worshipped the ground she walked on," said Phyllis Earl. "I know that if he had had to kill to protect her he would have."

Grace inspired the same feelings of protective love in the people who worked for her outside the principality, men like Monsieur Alexandre, the famous hairdresser, and Marc Bohan of Dior, men who were used to dealing with the world's great beauties, royalty, celebrities, aristocrats, or simply the very rich. Alexandre, French in appearance, dapper, with a small elegant moustache and expressive gestures, has coiffed the most famous women in the world, Jacqueline Kennedy, Sophia Loren and Elizabeth Taylor among them. Grace, he said, was not only "the queen" of his elegant salon in the Avenue Matignon in Paris, but became also a personal friend. "She was born a princess," he said, echoing Frank Sinatra. "She was a great lady in all her attitudes. She had respect for working people, she was always on time or, if she was going to be late, she would always have someone telephone to warn us."

Grace, he said, consulted him early in her reign in Monaco. Although she could do her hair well herself, she found the climate of Monaco difficult for her fine hair, and the problems of having it look soignée, morning, noon and night, considerable. Alexandre made six different hair-pieces for her which she kept in her bathroom in the palace, each in a numbered box, with Alexandre's corresponding drawing, also numbered, hanging on the walls so that she could easily identify them. The hair-pieces would journey back and forth between Monaco and Paris, and, when Grace cut her hair short in 1957, a decision which enraged her husband, she was unable to cope with it and she too followed the hair-pieces to Alexandre's salon. After that, says Alexandre, "She stuck to a classic half-length with a permanent."

When Grace first visited Alexandre's salon he put her in a private *cabine* for privacy, but after a while she said to him gently, "Can I ask you something? I would like to sit with everybody else." So she moved to a corner chair by the window overlooking the Avenue

Matignon, which became "her" seat. She used to embroider all the time, and once she asked Alexandre what were his favourite colours. Brown, black and white, he replied. That Christmas she sent him a big cushion she had embroidered herself in a modern design using brown, black and white. Every time she came back from a trip she would bring small, well-chosen presents for the people who looked after her in the salon - Caroline, Annie, Françoise and, her favourite, Gwendoline, who travelled with her on her trips abroad and did her hair, except for very grand occasions such as the wedding of the King of Greece, when Alexandre himself would be there.

Gwendoline could not contain her tears as she spoke of Grace, whom she had looked after for twenty years. "What I loved about her", she said, "was her simplicity - she spoke a lot about her children. She was a mother above all." She never forgot Gwendoline's daughter's birthday and would always bring a present for her - "In spite of all her obligations she was always considerate of people, always had a word for them." When Gwendoline travelled with the Princess she always sat beside her and Grace would introduce her not as "my hairdresser" but by her married name, Madame de Flandres.

Grace, Alexandre said, had created her own ambience in the salon, just as she had in Hollywood with the people who worked with her there. "She was a lady who liked to be able to trust people and to have a close rapport with them." It was she, he said, who initiated this rapport - she liked "human contact". In the twenty-five years he had known her a friendship had grown up between them. She attended the wedding of his son in St Tropez in 1970 as the guest of honour and invited him to be one of the judges of the *Floralies de Monaco*, an internationally famous flower-arranging competition. The Prince presented him with the Order of St Charles, and Princess Grace became patroness of Alexandre's unique museum of hairdressing in Paris, intended as a centre for young students of the art. The Princess, he said, understood very well that in the position she had she could do a great deal for fashion. Above all, he said, he loved her for her personal qualities. "Among all the many celebrities I have met", he said, "she is the one who entered into my life." The same, he said, went for his employees. "She knew we loved, respected and admired her, she could have asked us for the moon."

Marc Bohan of Dior had the same reaction, considering Grace and her daughter Caroline as personal friends, having dressed Grace since 1960. Grace herself admitted to an interviewer that she was "stingy" about clothes and that Prince Rainier used to urge her to buy things at the Paris collections, and, Marc Bohan said, "Sometimes I had to fight to get her to have clothes for special occasions." Partly this was a sense of economy inherited from her mother; partly Grace's reluctance to give people trouble by asking for something special. She was very professional and knew what she wanted, he said, and very conscious of the image which people would have of her, choosing light, radiant colours, apricot, pale yellow, blue, banning brown as "too sad-looking", wearing black, "in which she looked fabulous", only in private. She became attached to her clothes, as for instance the beautiful fuchsia ball dress made for her on the occasion of the party in Venice for Olympia Brandolini – "Oh, that dress, she wore it for years, I couldn't get her out of it," said Bohan. She kept all the clothes from her films and her favourite couture clothes; at the Red Cross Ball in Monaco in 1982 Stephanie wore the pale blue faille mid-calf strapless dress that M. Dior had made for her mother in 1956. Grace worried about her figure, being, as she was, fond of food, and hated it when it was suggested she should wear waistless dresses, pleading with him for shirt-waists. She and Caroline loved hats, but she would laughingly repel Bohan's criticisms of the unbecoming turbans which she was all too prone to slip on when her hair was not looking good – "But my dear, it's practical, one can't have M. Alexandre every day."

Like Alexandre, Marc Bohan was struck by her consideration for people, her patience and her avoidance of fuss and scenes – "She always made it simple ... she would say 'Oh, the fabric isn't here? Then we'll wait.'" She had absolute confidence in her *vendeuse*, Madame Agnès, and, he said, all the people who worked for her were devoted to her. "She was a marvellous person in her contacts with people, cared about people – all sorts of people, even the little girl from the work room! The way she smiled at people made them feel she was interested in them ... she was unique in the personality that she radiated and the way in which she talked to people. She was reserved, yet very funny, with a very good sense of humour without ever being bitchy or malicious."

Thus, as Grace reached maturity, she had established her own identity in Europe, not only for herself but in the eyes of other people. She had created her own circle round her in the Old World just as she had in the New.

12

Sun and Shadow

Grace was forty on 12 November 1969. Poised on the threshold between youth and middle age, still radiantly beautiful – perhaps even·more so, since her insecurities were now a thing of the past – she could look back on her first thirteen years as Princess with a sense of achievement. Or at least she might have done so had she been given to looking back. She rarely did. Grace always looked to the future, trying, through her interest in astrology, to perceive what the stars had to foretell for her and for her family. The children were growing up – Caroline was twelve, Albie eleven and Stephanie, the baby, still only four – but they would need her less and less and the focus and direction of her life must inevitably change. Astrologers would have told her that she had now emerged from a chrysalis and that she could look forward to a more balanced, creative life.

To celebrate her fortieth birthday Grace gave a Scorpio party, inviting her friends from all over the world. The invitation, printed in English and French, ran as follows:

SCORPIO
Your horoscope for November 15th and 16th 1969.

———————

Day for Travel ... Journey to Monte Carlo indicated ...
You are being invited by
H.S.H. PRINCESS GRACE OF MONACO, HIGH SCORPIA
to come to her Scorpio party in Monaco.
Miss this at your own risk!

LOVE
Venus enters your sign
Romance is favored and may become
highly inspirational by mid-November

SOCIAL ACTIVITIES
You may meet many interesting people who
might influence your career ...

Saturday November 15th – 9.00 p.m.
Dinner and Dancing
Hôtel Hermitage, Monte Carlo

Sunday November 16th – 12.30 p.m.
Brunch
Hôtel de Paris, Swimming-pool

HEALTH
If you survive these two events ...
You are a very healthy person and
can look forward to an untroubled old age.

ADVICE
Ladies ... Do not ignore the colours of your sign ...
Red, Black or White only ...

Hôtel de Paris wholly converted for Scorpian occupancy.
Your private nest awaits you ... Courtesy of the High Scorpia.
Other signs married to Scorpians tolerated ...

Many of Grace's closest friends were born under the sign of Scorpio:
Maree Rambo, Hjordis Niven, Rupert Allan, Sam Spiegel. Richard
Burton, also a Scorpio, was invited and so naturally was his wife,
Elizabeth Taylor, to whom he had just presented the fabulous Krupp
diamond. Grace's party was to be the first public appearance of the
stone round Elizabeth Taylor's neck, and immense security precautions had to be taken to bring the jewel and its owner to Monaco
– a squad of policemen, and two safes: one for the real diamond and
one for the copy which the Burtons always carried with them. The
party took place in the beautiful Belle Epoque dining-room of the
Hôtel Hermitage, where Grace cut an enormous birthday cake iced in
yellow, scarlet and gold. It was a sparkling beginning to a new decade
for Grace.

The pattern of Grace's life in Monaco was by now well established.

She played an enormously important part in the life of the principality, not only as a glamorous figure acting as a magnet to tourists and playing hostess to the international set along the Côte d'Azur, but in her responsibility for the welfare of her husband's subjects – the four thousand-odd Monégasques. Running Monaco was a partnership between the Prince and Grace; while he took care of the business and governmental side, she was responsible for the cultural and welfare aspects.

Grace was President of the Monaco Red Cross and very much in charge. The Red Cross was designed to supplement the state welfare system, providing material assistance and amenities for people who were in particular need. It looks after elderly people in the Résidence du Cap Fleuri, the Fondation Otto and, in the Princess Grace Hospital, provides first-aid services, particularly important at the time of the Monaco Grand Prix. It offers courses in home nursing and is also responsible for the Garderie Notre Dame de Fatima, a day-care centre designed to help working mothers, and a children's home, the Foyer Sainte-Dévote. Grace was always on the look-out for improvements which could be made and ideas from other countries which could be applied to Monaco. The Red Cross occupied a great deal of her time, as she attended meetings of the administrative council where, according to Madame Rosine Sanmori, her colleague, she took all the executive decisions and also visited the hospitals and homes administered by the Red Cross. She was particularly interested in mothers and children, always visiting the maternity wards on Mother's Day with bunches of flowers and layettes for the mothers and new babies. Grace, who always breast-fed her own children and was a passionate advocate of breast-feeding, was also honorary President of the Monaco branch of the international La Lèche League.

The Red Cross was financed by a yearly subvention from the Government and from the proceeds of the annual Red Cross Gala, the most spectacular event of the Monte Carlo season. Held in the new Summer Sporting Club, which has huge Moorish arches and an electrically operated roof opening to the sky, the Red Cross Gala is a show-business spectacular, with which Grace was intimately concerned. It was "her" gala, said André Levasseur, the famous designer responsible for all the shows put on by the SBM in Monte Carlo, and they worked closely together on it. He would propose for her selection two or three themes for the evening and she would also choose the stars for the cabaret. The greatest triumph of all was that of Josephine Baker, who did her last show there in 1974; she was sixty-eight and it was her fiftieth year on the stage. She died the following April. Grace was a great friend of Josephine Baker. After Josephine went bankrupt and lost the château in which she and her large adopted family had been living, Grace and the Prince had loaned her money and offered her a house. There were less happy moments, as when Sammy Davis Junior, offended at not having been asked, through an unfortunate oversight, to a palace cocktail party, walked out before the gala, refusing to perform. Years later he would make amends, appearing with Frank Sinatra at the gala held in the year following Grace's death.

Levasseur, a talented designer who left Dior in 1956 to devote his gifts to designing and directing musicals and show-business extravaganzas, praised her for her tact, her taste, her artistic sense and her professionalism. She understood show business, he said, and everything that was required to put on a *grand spectacle*. The evening before the show she would come down to the Sporting Club, where he would prepare a table setting for her to approve and together they would check on the lighting and effects.

For this gala and for the Bal de la Rose, held in the spring at the beginning of the Monte Carlo season, Grace would take enormous trouble to make the occasion as glamorous as possible. She would appear like a star, usually dressed by Dior or Madame Grès, her hair personally coiffed by Alexandre, either with flowers, jewels or hairpieces, sometimes with huge and fantastical head-dresses. On one occasion one of Alexandre's set-pieces was so tall that Grace could not get into her car and had to be driven to the ball in a van, looking, she said, "like Radio Monte Carlo", with golden antennae sticking out all over her head. The guests would be equally glamorous: the Burtons, Gina Lollobrigida, Frank Sinatra, the Begum Aga Khan, Dewi Soekarno, often royalty such as the Conde of Barcelona, father of the King of Spain. Grace regarded it all as an important part of her job and one which she enjoyed, an opportunity to exercise her great talents as hostess and, giving her a nostalgic whiff of show-business sawdust and tinsel, to play a starring role.

Grace saw her role principally as looking after the Monégasques, helping them, bringing them together and improving the quality of their lives through the organizations of which she was executive head. Grace's work-load as Princess had expanded so greatly by 1969 that she had a secretariat of her own, headed by M. Paul Choisit, a cheerful, dedicated Monégasque with a remarkable grasp of colloquial English; her private secretary was Madame Louisette Levy-Sousann, an attractive woman, very much a part of the palace "family", her father having been one of the maîtres d'hotel there and her mother one of the maids; and there were two other secretaries, one of whom was a translator.

The secretaries were clearly devoted to her. "It was very easy to work with the Princess, we had direct contact with her and when she gave you her confidence it was absolute – she never checked 'Did you do it?'" Paul Choisit said. They would telephone her each morning to review the business for the day: letters to be written, appointments to be made, and so on. She was so busy that often they would have to run after her in corridors for decisions. She received a huge amount of mail, some of it from fans of all ages, a proportion of it from Monégasques who would write asking if they could come to see her to talk over their problems. She would always see the Monégasques, her secretaries said, even though the problems would often be run-of-the-mill difficulties – "I need an apartment" or "I need a job". Women would come to her to talk over their marital problems. "Sometimes", the two secretaries said, "we had the feeling that people came to her as an adviser – even on very private matters. She had a lot of wisdom and *bon sens*."

Ordinary people, many of them young or very young, came to her from all over the world. One Indian girl of about twenty-two, having written to Grace for years, suddenly turned up in Monaco with a request for an interview. When the Princess came into the room, the girl, overcome with emotion, burst into tears. On another occasion she received two young American boys in battered clothes going on a round-the-world expedition with a mule named "We'll make it". Sadly, one of them did not – he was subsequently murdered in Afghanistan.

There was also the Princess Grace Foundation to occupy her time. It began in a small way in 1964, when Grace inherited some money and created the Foundation, which then comprised only a little boutique selling artisan work and crafts from Monaco and the neighbourhood. It was so successful that in 1970 she opened a second boutique, choosing everything for it herself, even the colour of the paint and how the window should be dressed.

The Foundation and Grace's ideas of its potentialities expanded as the years went by: its resources were fuelled by contributions from her rich friends and by earnings from her own creative activities – the public poetry readings which she began in 1976, her flower collages, which she sold, the royalties from her designs for linen for the American brand, Springmills. The money was invested, giving the Foundation the flexibility to help people who could find assistance nowhere else. "Hundreds of people would write," said Paul Choisit, who administered the Foundation in Monaco, "such as a group of old people who wanted to visit Monaco for the first time in their lives – and she would pay for them." Later she was to add the word "cultural" to the constitution of the Foundation in order to help the international ballet school begun by Marika Besabrasova, which, under the title Académie de Danse Classique Princesse Grace, nowadays established in the beautiful villa which had once belonged to the Singer family. The Académie was a part of Grace's plan for re-establishing Monte Carlo as a centre for superlative ballet, as it had been in the days of Diaghilev, Nijinsky and Serge Lifar.

Grace aimed to bring people in Monaco together and one of her most successful initiatives in this direction was the Garden Club. "The atmosphere of the Garden Club was very friendly, it was a means of getting to know each other," said Rosine Sanmori. "Before the Princess came everyone lived in little circles. Even Monégasques didn't necessarily see much of each other. She made links, joined us together. Now we each give parties for the Club, it contributes to the spreading of human contact in Monaco."

Grace conceived the idea of the Garden Club in 1967, and in 1968 it was officially founded, with a committee consisting of the wives of the members of the Government. The members' list quickly became full and included Monégasque women, wives of functionaries, and foreign residents. Grace insisted that it should not be merely a social club but should fulfil charity obligations and have the serious purpose of improving knowledge of flowers and of gardening. At various charity fêtes during the year the members of the Club would provide and sell their own bouquets of flowers and at Christmas they would voluntarily decorate the old people's homes. "The Princess", Madame Sanmori said, "knew how to surround herself with the right people, the useful people." She chose the director of the Jardin Exotique, M. Kroenlein, as Treasurer and M. Giovannini, who was in charge of all the public and palace gardens in Monaco, as General Secretary of the Club.

The Garden Club was not purely parochial: Grace initiated the *Concours de Bouquets*, which became a fixture on the international flower-arranging calendar, and took place in May. Grace asked Monsieur and Madame Arpad Plesch, former owners of a celebrated botanical library, for advice as to international judges and, through their friend the Duc de Noailles, Julia Clements (Lady Seton) and George Smith were chosen. There would be also what Madame Plesch describes as the "unserious group" of judges, including herself, Alexandre, Marc Bohan and the writer, Anthony Burgess. Grace chose the themes for the categories in the competitions and there was always one for men only, which Prince Rainier took very seriously and in which he was an annual competitor. Grace, who worked as hard at this as she did at everything else, became an international judge of flower-arranging competitions.

Flowers, plants and gardening were a new interest in Grace's life, another outlet for her creative spirit, and she approached this new subject, about which she knew very little, with the same passion, dedication and questioning intelligence which she put into everything she did. With the help of M. Marcel Kroenlein, she began to study plants, reading specialist books and learning the Latin names. With M. Kroenlein and the children she would go for seven-hour hikes on the mountainside above Monaco. Wearing shorts and equipped with a simple picnic – a *pan bagna* or *pissaladière*, or the Monégasque speciality, *gian barba*, a vegetable-filled roll – she would collect interesting specimens of wild flowers for the pressed-flower collection which she kept in telephone directories until she was ready to use them in her dried-flower pictures.

Grace was inspired to do flower collages by a fellow Philadelphian, Mrs Henry King, and it soon became her most absorbing hobby. "As the design begins to take shape, you get the same feeling of tranquility as doing needlework," she wrote in her Flower Book, published in 1980. "It is a kind of deep satisfaction to know that without any formal training it is possible for everyone to express themselves." Her family told her that when she was engrossed in making one of these pictures she would talk to herself in the same way that a cat purrs. She designed textiles too – a scarf for the 1966 Monaco Flower Show, linen for the Springmills Company, all signed with the initials "GPK"; the proceeds from these and from the exhibition of her collages held in Paris in 1980 were to go to the Princess Grace Foundation.

All these hobbies were a means of releasing the great store of pent-up energy that she had once been able to express through her acting. Had she been a man, life might have, paradoxically, been easier for her; of all the Kelly children she was the one who had inherited Jack Kelly's qualities as a leader of men, his understanding of people, his discipline and his determination. Grace, a friend said, had a great capacity for business, but in marrying the Prince of Monaco she had chosen to play the feminine role, to divert her dynamic energy into other channels. Only subconsciously did she try to break out; in her opinions and beliefs Grace remained a 1950s woman. Frank Sinatra said affectionately of her that she was the squarest person he knew, while the American writer, Eleanor Perry, snapped after an interview of mutual incomprehension that Grace was "a relic of the fifties preserved in amber".

Grace's published opinions were indeed a red rag to a woman's libber – "Women's natural role is to be a pillar of the family. It's their physiological job. They should make themselves interesting for their families. Women only work to get off the hook and avoid their responsibilities. Emancipation of women has made them lose their mystery." At the Convention of the La Lèche League in Chicago in 1971 she spoke passionately against what she dubbed "the bad taste" prevalent in stage and film productions, magazines and songs, "the outright pornography that is thrown at us every day". She believed in what are called the good old-fashioned virtues inculcated in her by her parents – self-discipline, decency, patriotism, the family. Ideologically she was on the right, a gut reaction rather than an intellectual one, since she was not interested in politics as such, only in so far as they affected people *en masse*. She appeared shy and gentle, detesting confrontation, but, said her friend, Lynn Wyatt of Houston – a forceful woman herself – "When it came to something she believed in – and she believed in many causes – she would talk and talk and by the time she'd finished, you were convinced."

For Grace her Catholic religion was a source of strength, underpinning her commitment to the life she had chosen. Grace gave up her sexual freedom when she married Prince Rainier, channelling those energies exclusively into her marriage. Unlike her father, she took her marriage vows seriously and never broke them. For someone of her temperament and attraction it required a considerable effort of self-discipline – not so much at the beginning of her marriage, but over twenty years later, when there were rumours that her husband's interest was wandering while she herself was still beautiful and attractive to men. Her religion helped her to justify her decision and she clung to it; it was also a deep bond between herself and her husband.

April 1976 was the twentieth anniversary of the wedding of Princess Grace and Prince Rainier, focussing even more than usual the attention of the world's press upon the state of their marriage. The decision that Grace should, from the autumn of 1975, spend the weekdays in Paris in order to provide a home there for Caroline and Stephanie was taken as evidence of a split. "Princess Grace's marriage on the rocks", the headlines screamed. The couple themselves, interviewed in Paris by writer Curtis Bill Pepper, made it clear that as parents of a family and devout Catholics there never had been nor ever would be any question of divorce for them. Both of them had gone into the marriage determined to make the necessary compromises, although the compromises do seem to have been more on Grace's side than on her husband's. Prince Rainier was unquestionably the dominant figure.

Grace's freedom of action was indeed far more restricted than her husband's. While he could, and did, go out more or less as he liked, she never went anywhere unaccompanied and she had to obtain his agreement to everything she did. There were great differences in character and temperament between them. Prince Rainier, Grace said, was a Gemini with a character that was light and dark – "I avoid the dark sides". While he exploded, Grace would bottle things up inside her, secretive, reserved, leaning on no one. Nor, as a friend said, did she rely on any of the usual palliatives – sex, drugs or alcohol – but on her inner strength.

Both of them were interested in music and the theatre, and enjoyed watching movies in their "play room" at the palace. Otherwise their interests diverged considerably – Prince Rainier adored fast cars, Grace was frightened of them; he loved the sea and deep-sea diving, Grace got seasick and the sun hurt her eyes and burnt her skin. Prince Rainier compromised by giving up diving because it worried her, but she had to put up with a succession of yachts – the *Deo Juvante*, the *Albercaro*, the *Carostefal* – and cruises in the Mediterranean to such places as Mallorca or Sardinia. Grace loved parties and staying up late, Prince Rainier liked neither social life nor public appearances, enduring both out of duty. He would frequently fall asleep after lunch or dinner and at parties would often sit and talk to just one man whose conversation interested him. She would always keep an eye on him to see if he was getting bored and it was therefore time to go. People noticed how much consideration she had for him, how she would see that every detail was as he would like it, and make everything as easy and as pleasant as possible for him.

One thing compensated for the sacrifices – their genuine love for each other, something which the rest of the world refused to believe in either at the time of their marriage or twenty years later until faced with the evidence of her husband's total, desolate grief at his wife's funeral.

Lee Grant, the actress who had preceded Grace in Gene Lyons' affections, interviewed Grace and the Prince in the twentieth year of their marriage for a documentary on Grace's life produced by Bill Allyn. Her impression then, she later said, was of "a woman madly in love with her husband". When they were together there was "a lot of fun between them, they were easy together and sparked off each other", while "at functions there would be a lot of eye glances between them".

Nonetheless, stresses were to appear in Grace's private life during the late 1970s as both her marriage and her children grew older. A new friend meeting her then found beneath the serene exterior "a very vulnerable, sensitive, hurt, lonely individual". She was lonely because, as a princess, she had to protect herself from people, particularly in Paris. She would be asked to functions or glamorous evenings but rarely to dinner as a friend. She could not walk through Paris by herself or take the Metro. "She would tell me", her friend said, "of her fantasy that later on in life she was going to have the luxury of being like everyone else and just become a 'bag lady', wandering through Paris collecting things people leave behind. She has this kind of fantasy about being just very normal. ..."

Paradoxically, however, "she was happy with what she had ... she wasn't a struggler. I think she knew it was an incredible privilege to be what she was and I think she was grateful, but at the same time she was human."

Some of the hurt of those years came through her children. Grace had given up her career to become a mother; it was a role on which she had staked so much and, because success as a mother was a central reason of her being, every setback in that area was a bitter blow. There was, too, an element of guilt. She felt that in some way her own enormous celebrity had helped deny her children a normal life, exposing them to the fierce glare of publicity as the objects of intense attention by the world's press. Grace had done her best to bring up her children according to her father's code. Asked by Curtis Bill Pepper what she hoped for them, her words might have been Jack Kelly's: "that they become responsible people, with character – strong, able to take it, yet also understanding of the weak. That they be good sports and play the game according to the rules. But life's also a game of broken rules – and to be prepared for that, too. It's what my mother and father hoped for me. .... I've tried to take what I believe to have been best in my childhood."

But, however hard she and Prince Rainier tried to give their children a "normal" upbringing, growing up in a palace with your father a ruling prince and your mother one of the world's most famous women is not a normal situation. The Grimaldi children may not, in Maureen King's words, have realized that "they were anything special" while they were very young, but as they developed and came into contact with the outside world they very soon realized that they were.

Of the three, Albert was apparently to cope best with the pressures created by his position. Tall and blond, resembling his grandfather, Prince Pierre, in looks and his mother in temperament, he was, like her, shy, intelligent and reserved, holding everything inside himself. He was the closest to her and the one who would cause his parents the least problems. He is fortunate, too, in inheriting the Kelly athleticism, being a good tennis player and a skilful footballer. But because he was the only son, who would be the future Prince, his parents were harder on him than they were on the girls, just as Jack Kelly had been with Kell, and it has not always been easy for him to assert himself with a dominant father, a loving, anxious mother and two sisters, one older than himself and very assertive, the younger adoring him and smothering him with hero-worship.

From the palace schoolroom Albert went to the school in Monaco named after his great-grandfather, Albert I, until at the age of sixteen, when he had completed the standard two-part examination course known in France as the *baccalauréat* or *"bachot"*, his parents decided he should have a change of scene and go to college in the United States. Albert loved America; it was part of Grace's plan that the children should remain aware of their American heritage, and they would spend part of every summer with their Kelly cousins at Ocean City – where the younger generation had built a modern house right on the dunes in front of Wesley Avenue – or at summer camp in the Pocono Mountains in Pennsylvania. Albert chose Amherst College and, after two terms reading English literature at Cambridge, England, at the beginning of 1977, went to Amherst in the autumn, graduating in the summer of 1981 with a major in political science and economics. He was then to spend nine months in the French Navy as an ensign on board the *Jeanne d'Arc*.

Grace worried about Albert, always in the limelight wherever he went, whether at school in Monaco, at Amherst or in the Navy, always being, as she put it, "pointed out and picked on". Even though he did not want preferential treatment other people would not let him behave as if he were just anybody. "More is expected of him," she explained, "and all eyes are on him, waiting for him to make a mistake. Some even try to lay traps to pull him down." Like Prince Charles of England, she said, Albert has had to learn to be on his guard. "Albert is a nice, unsuspecting guy with a sweet nature, it's a shame."

Grace's real problems were to begin as her daughters grew up. Both were striking-looking girls with strong personalities. In looks and temperament Caroline resembles her grandmother, Princess Charlotte; even when she was very young she had a decided personality of her own, knew what she wanted and was determined to get it. Despite her close relationship with both her parents, and with her father in particular, Caroline's imperious, independent spirit, questioning intelligence and boundless appetite for life were bound to be a recipe for teenage-adult conflict.

At first all went well; after several years attending daily at a convent in Monaco, the Dames de St Maur, Caroline aged fourteen went to St Mary's Convent, Ascot, England, in the autumn of 1971. Sister Bridget, IBVM, headmistress of the convent, remembers Caroline as "very happy, as good as gold and . . . highly intelligent". She worked hard, doing the first part of her French *baccalauréat* at the French Lycée in London and taking English, French and Spanish A-levels at St Mary's. Sister Bridget remembers the Grimaldis as a "very family family", and was amused by the practical, simple way in which Grace had brought them up – Caroline was not allowed to be extravagant, and once Sister Bridget found her teaching another sixth-form girl how to use a vacuum cleaner. Grace, she remembers, talked a great deal about America, her family and particularly her father. It amused her how, when Grace first visited the school, she had obviously tried to make herself look plain, with screwed-back hair and spectacles, severely dressed in grey and very serious in manner. Although she never stood on her dignity, she never quite forgot herself and could look, and behave, in a manner which even a nun could find "quite prim and proper". Yet, despite this matronly role-playing, Sister Bridget said, the total impression was of "shining good" and of "total sincerity and integrity".

Caroline was sixteen when she left St Mary's in July 1973 and returned to Paris to take the second part of her *baccalauréat* with the Dames de St Maur at their convent in the Bois de Boulogne. After a year she passed very well with a *"mention bien"*, and decided she wanted to go to university in Paris. Grace moved to Paris to be with her, taking nine-year-old Stephanie, too, and the three of them settled in the apartment in Avenue Foch. This decision, as we have seen, provoked much speculation about the state of Grace's marriage, giving rise to rumours that she and the Prince no longer spoke to each other and occupied separate beds in separate apartments, when in fact, both in Paris and Monaco, they always shared the same double beds. The simple reason for Grace's move was that she and the Prince felt that the girls needed her in Paris; so they would spend the week there, while Prince Rainier and Albert stayed in Monaco, and at weekends Grace and the girls might take the night train down to Monaco or the Prince and Albert would come up to Paris.

Having a Paris base was an advantage for all of them. Monaco, for those who live there, is essentially a small provincial town where the company is limited and everyone knows everyone else's business. For the princely family, sitting in the spotlight in their palace on the hill, it could become claustrophobic, however much they loved it. Although they were instantly recognizable everywhere they went, in a capital city people would be less obsessively interested in their movements, which was for them the advantage of Paris and, still more, of London, where Grace and the Prince might be seen, often hand-in-hand, shopping in Bond Street or Knightsbridge. When she travelled alone, without the Prince, Grace was careful to combat the rumour machine, always taking a female companion with her, a lady-in-waiting or a friend. In London she would stay with Phyllis Earl and in New York with Vera Maxwell, avoiding not only gossip but the loneliness and the expense – for she was careful about money

– of a grand hotel. It was the same system she had used with such success in her Hollywood career. Otherwise, when the Prince and the family were with her they would always stay in their favourite hotels, the Connaught in London and the Regency in New York.

In Paris they moved in 1976 to a house which Grace loved, 26 Square de l'Avenue Foch. Grace decorated the house herself, this time without the assistance of George Stacey; it was quietly, elegantly French with good eighteenth-century furniture and porcelain, unobtrusive colours, the drawing-room looking out on to a tiny garden. Its only disadvantage was an infestation of cats, who lived, fought and reproduced in an abandoned car nearby and were encouraged to do so by a cat-loving neighbour who brought them food. The other infestation, which was perhaps even more of a nuisance as the Princesses grew older, was of *paparazzi*, permanently stationed outside the gate, so much so that Stephanie, who detested being photographed, was forced to go to her gymnastics classes in the evening hidden in the boot or trunk of a car.

Caroline was a natural for the photographers – at eighteen she had a voluptuous figure, loved clothes and was always chic. Bored by her course at the School of Political Science (the "Sciences-Po") where she had enrolled to please her father, and pursued by all the attractive young men in Paris, she had discovered Parisian night life. 27 January 1975 was her eighteenth birthday. Photographed by Norman Parkinson, featured on the cover of *Time* magazine, coiffed by Alexandre and dressed by Dior, St Laurent, Lagerfeld and Givenchy, she was, with Caroline Kennedy, the most famous teenager of the year. She took up smoking and wore too much make-up, unremarkable in any ordinary girl of her age but unwise in a princess whose every step was dogged by photographers and gossip columnists. Worse still from the publicity point of view, her warm, outgoing nature and youthful desire to be liked led her into giving interviews to journalists which were then spread across the world's press. With her boyfriend, rich pop-singer Philippe Laville, she was photographed in a Paris night-club, L'Aventure, wearing a pink satin crêpe dress which, as *Time* magazine reported, "revealed a bit more of Caroline than caution".

"Rainiers clip daughter Caroline's wings, Now pals call her 'Princess Grim'", headlines ran. Caroline defended her parents and herself, denying that they were too strict or that she spent her time in night-clubs, but nobody believed her, or Grace, when they denied

199

rumours of furious quarrels over Caroline's way of life. When she failed to take the examinations at the Sciences-Po at the end of the first year everybody said she had "flunked" them, when in fact she and her parents had agreed she could change courses and take up philosophy and child psychology at the University of Paris. Grace was, however, bitterly hurt at the image of Caroline as a playgirl princess and of herself as an icy Victorian mother. "We have our differences over clothes and boy-friends. But all mothers and all adolescents are like that, aren't they?" she said. "Caroline wants to fly with her own wings, live for herself. It's natural and normal. In one sense she is more mature than I was at her age. . . . But in another sense she is more vulnerable."

There were tensions – Grace was firm and Caroline was wilful – but for Caroline's parents the hurt came from the publicity that surrounded everything she did and their fears for the future, that she might be kidnapped, or, celebrity that she was, get in with the wrong set of people.

Then, in the spring of 1976, what they had feared happened. Caroline fell in love with a man seventeen years older than herself – Philippe Junot. Philippe Junot was neither aristocratic nor very rich, but he came of a good upper-middle-class family – his father was a distinguished politician and the family had owned a charming country house, the Abbaye de Belhomart, for the past two hundred years. Philippe himself was clever, energetic and physically attractive. A dashing sportsman, he was captain of an amateur football team which included celebrities like Jean-Paul Belmondo, and had been an enthusiastic rally driver until a serious accident made him decide to give it up; he was also a good all-rounder at sport and an expert ski-er and tennis player. Brought up, like Caroline, on the Côte d'Azur, he had, like her, attended the Sciences-Po, and had gone on to learn about politics and business, including a period on the New York Stock Exchange and in banks in Brussels, London and New York. When he met Caroline he was consultant to an international investment bank and, with a partner, had offices in Paris and Montreal. He had many good qualities: he was decisive, generous, quick-witted and amusing, but, from Caroline's parents' point of view, he had one major defect – he was a paid-up and practising member of a vanishing species, the European playboy. He belonged, in short, to a group of people to whom having a good time, and having it in the right place with the right people, was a major object of existence. As such, he was hardly a solid matrimonial prospect in any parents' book.

At Christmas 1976 Philippe Junot asked Caroline to marry him, and Grace and Prince Rainier were presented with an agonizing dilemma. Caroline and Philippe were undoubtedly in love, but her youth and inexperience plus his experience and way of life did not seem to hold out the prospect of a lasting marriage. According to one friend, Grace wanted Prince Rainier to tell Caroline that if she married Junot she would be cut off as Princess of Monaco and member of the family, just as her own father had threatened her over Oleg Cassini. It had worked with her and it might well have worked with Caroline, who loved her family and liked the perquisites of being a princess. But neither of them – and particularly not the Prince – could bear the prospect of Caroline's misery, and so they consented. At Easter Philippe was invited to join the family circle at Roc Agel and in July he went on a long cruise to the Galapagos islands in the South Atlantic with the Prince, Albert, Caroline and two family friends. Away from the jet-set social carousel, Philippe's charm and manly qualities appeared reassuring, and on 25 August their engagement was announced, the marriage to take place the following summer when Caroline was due to finish her philosophy course at the Sorbonne.

The wedding took place on 29 June 1978, preceded by a ball for eight hundred guests, attended by a galaxy of European royalty and pretenders; ex-King Umberto of Italy, King Constantine of Greece, Prince Bertil of Sweden, the Comte de Paris, the Conde and Condesa of Barcelona, Fouad of Egypt, the Aga Khan, the Archduke Otto von Hapsburg, the Duque and Duquesa of Cadiz, Princess Maria Gabriella of Savoy – an illustrious guest list which indicated how much the Grimaldis had risen in status since the wedding of Grace and Prince Rainier just over twenty-two years earlier. Grace's faithful show-business friends were there too – Cary Grant, Frank Sinatra, Gregory Peck, Ava Gardner and the David Nivens.

The civil marriage took place in the Throne Room, just as Caroline's parents' had two decades before; Caroline, wearing an ice blue crêpe dress by Dior, was in tears, while her parents could barely contain theirs. The religious wedding was held in an improvised chapel under a trellis in the palace courtyard followed by a lunch for four hundred. Remembering the press hurly-burly of their own wedding, the Prince and Grace rigorously excluded photographers; only Grace's old friend and personal photographer, Howell Conant, was allowed into the palace, the common herd being contained behind barriers outside. One audacious photographer hired a hang glider and flew over the palace courtyard taking a colour film of the ceremony, only to find himself grabbed by police and his film confiscated on landing.

Caroline and Philippe were installed in Paris in a large, bright apartment on the Avenue de Breteuil near the Invalides in the seventh arrondissement. It was painted in pastel tones – white, pink and peach – with a dining-room lined with Indian cotton, a huge country-style kitchen with herbs in pots and a small study containing a magnificent Persian carpet, a wedding present from the Shah. With a maid, Félicie, who was both housekeeper and cook, there was not a great deal for Caroline to do but get up late, walk her Yorkie and lunch with Philippe at home, then go to a cinema or an exhibition and spend the evening out with friends.

The Junots' close friends were not quiet, home-loving folk, but people like his best man, Hubert Michel Pelissier, once linked with Christina Onassis, and Alix Chevassus, who married and then left Caroline's friend, Stavros Niarchos's daughter Maria; their lives revolved round Castel and Régine in Paris, and Studio 54, then Xenon, in New York. Philippe was always the life and soul of parties wherever they went, and at first it was all fun for Caroline, who adored the night life and the jetting round the world with him. It was very amusing to begin with, but in the end not enough to satisfy an intelligent girl. "After a while she got fed up and realized she didn't like night clubs," Junot's friends say. "Philippe was losing the upper hand with her and so he tried to keep it by charming other women." As a remedy for the increasing disillusionment of a beautiful and intelligent young wife it was dangerous and doomed to disaster. After an incident at a party near Monte Carlo in the week of the Grand Prix in May 1980, the storm broke. Caroline left, and in mid June came the terse announcement from the palace which signalled to the world that the marriage of Philippe and Caroline was over.

Caroline had set out with the best of intentions – "I'm grateful to my parents for having given me an education which respected some traditions that one doesn't find anymore," she declared. "I grew up in a family and, for me, to be married means living forever with the person you love."

Divorce proceedings began in September; by the first weeks of October, after a formal attempt at reconciliation had failed, Caroline was no longer Madame Philippe Junot in the eyes of the law. Both parties appeared sad and strained. Junot, admitting that he still loved Caroline, returned to his business and was welcomed back as a prodigal by his jet-set friends. Caroline returned to her family, a sad child, as though her marriage had never been. Apart from the pain, the sadness and the sense of failure which is the inevitable accompaniment of divorce, for Caroline, as a Catholic, there was a serious question-mark over her future. She petitioned the Pope for an annulment of her marriage to Junot for, without it, she would not be able, in the eyes of her Church, to marry again. But three years later, on 29 December 1983, Caroline did remarry, in a private civil ceremony at the palace. Her new husband was Stefano Casiraghi, a rich twenty-three-year-old Italian.

Caroline's marriage to Junot and its failure had been, said a friend, "heart-break" for Grace, a blow at her most vulnerable point. But with Caroline's increasing maturity, her relationship with her mother after her return home was, said Marc Bohan, "the best".

Over the next few years, however, Stephanie, in a different way, was to cause her mother as much *angst* as Caroline had. Stephanie had been spoiled by her parents. They were conscious of the age gap between her and her elder brother and sister, and over-protective as a result. Always treated as the baby of the family, she had developed into an immature teenager, refusing to grow into an adult. Open and affectionate to the people she knew well, and adored by the palace servants, she was violently possessive about her mother and would resent – and show her resentment of – Grace's American friends who presumed to share in her mother's affections. Not unnaturally, those friends found her spoiled and rude – "Ma Kelly could hardly keep her hands off that Stephanie," one of them said. Unlike Caroline, Stephanie did not enjoy being a princess, and suffered under and raged against the restrictions which her position imposed upon her. She hated publicity and, above all, photographers, hiding her face from them if she could or even sticking out her tongue at them. Utterly and childishly dependent upon her mother, she was equally childish in defying her, longing desperately to live a normal life, expending her Kelly energy in gymnastic classes at which she was expert, riding her motor scooter round Monte Carlo or dancing tirelessly at Jimmy'z at night.

She was gifted, with a real talent for drawing and designing, and promised to become a stunning beauty. Despite her dark hair and grey-green eyes, she was growing more and more like her mother in looks, the shape of her face with that Kelly jaw and her flawless complexion. She did not however, resemble her in temperament – a tomboy, headstrong and stubborn, she frequently argued violently with her mother. She was, unlike Caroline, unsophisticated, and after she met racing driver Paul Belmondo, son of the famous French star Jean-Paul, they became inseparable and would sit silently close together at parties, not talking to anyone else. Stephanie, in a word, did not want to be made to do anything she did not feel like doing – including being expected to behave like a princess.

Grace worried desperately about Stephanie, was hurt by the arguments they had and was distressed by her daughter's suffering in the limelight. She felt guilty, too, at leaving Stephanie behind on her now frequent visits to America since Stephanie, after the sensational abduction of the wealthy Belgian Baron Empain, whom they knew personally, had a deep terror of being kidnapped. She worried more about her children, perhaps, than most mothers might because she was aware of the abnormal pressures upon them and their harassment by the press. She worried, too, because she felt partly responsible for their predicament. She could bear it for herself, but not for them.

To compensate for these personal disappointments, Grace's horizons were expanding. She found satisfying new outlets for her energies, returning often to the United States, where she could feel free, see her friends, go to the theatre and eat her favourite hamburgers in small neighbourhood restaurants. Her love of acting, so long suppressed, was once again coming to the fore.

"I don't think Grace ever gave up the idea of wanting to act and to perform and to express herself," Bill Allyn said. She had never been able to bring herself to throw away her old Academy make-up box, and in the mid-seventies Grace discovered a way of satisfying her actor's need for self-expression and, above all, for communication with an audience. The idea for public poetry readings came from Gwen Robyns, with whom she collaborated on *My Book of Flowers*. Peter Diamand, then director of the Edinburgh Festival, asked producer-director John Carroll to arrange a celebration of the American Bicentennial in poetry, to be read by an American star. Carroll mentioned his request to Gwen Robyns, who came up with the suggestion of using Grace. For Grace, who loved poetry and performing, the combination was ideal: in September 1976 she made her first appearance at Edinburgh, with the American actor Richard Kiley and the English actor Richard Pasco, in a programme devised by John Carroll entitled "An American Heritage". Her rendering of a poem by Elinor Wylie on the American South, "Wild Peaches", which she read in a soft Southern drawl, was to be chosen on BBC Radio 4 *Pick of the Year* as the best poetry reading of 1976.

Edinburgh was the beginning. It was followed by a series of poetry readings right up to the time of her death, the programmes devised by John Carroll and read by Grace, usually with Richard Pasco or another English actor, John Westbrook. In 1977 she performed "A Remembrance for Shakespeare" in the church at Stratford-on-Avon, bringing a rose – "I've brought this for William" – to lay upon the tomb of the poet who had meant so much to her and to her Uncle George. The following year she took part with Peter Pears and Mstislav Rostropovitch in "Theme and Variations" at Aldeburgh, and undertook an ambitious tour of American universities reading "Birds, Beasts and Flowers" for the World Wildlife Fund, beginning in Pittsburgh at the invitation of the International Poetry Forum. In November she read a shortened version of the same programme at a charity evening in St James's Palace, and again in the following year in Dublin. In 1980 it was the turn of Vienna for a programme entitled "Evocations" – there Grace delighted the audience by reading a specially devised epilogue of poetic extracts in German – and then to America again. March 1981 was a special occasion, when Grace performed from "Theme and Variations" at the Goldsmiths' Hall, London, at a gala in aid of the Royal Opera House, Covent Garden, of which Prince Charles is patron. His engagement to Lady Diana Spencer had been announced only two weeks before and this was to be the first public appearance of the future Princess of Wales. Grace already counted the Prince's great-uncle and mentor, Earl Mountbatten, as one of her admirers and had been hostess to Prince Charles in Monte Carlo; now she, who had learnt so successfully how to be a princess, was a great comfort to Lady Diana, shy and uncomfortable in the famous strapless black dress. "Diana was very nervous and shy that night," said one of the guests, "but Grace was marvellous with her, so kind and sweet, she put her at her ease."

A year later, Grace made her last appearance in England, at Chichester in March 1982; another performance, of a special programme for the Windsor Festival, was scheduled for St George's Chapel on 26 September of that year. John Carroll sent her the script and received his last letter from her, dated 31 August, saying how happy she was with his choice of poems and music. "I have been struggling with bronchitis," she wrote, "but I will be in form by end of September." Like everyone who worked with Grace, John Carroll found her a great professional; once he had her confidence she trusted him absolutely with the choice of poetry and music, stage-management and where she should perform. "I always stage-managed her entrance," Carroll said, "because one of the things I used to adore wherever she made her entrance – Vienna, Dublin, anywhere – there were always gasps. . . . She was endowed by the good God with great beauty but she had this tremendous presence . . . she used to float on."

Grace's reappearance on stage prompted the inevitable rumours that she was planning a return to films, but ever since the *Marnie* episode she had been well aware of the limitations on her freedom of action. As Princess of Monaco, appearing in a CBS-TV travelogue, *A Look at Monaco*, was acceptable; a full-length feature film was not. Scripts arrived on her desk, she read them all, and turned them down – even her friend Sam Spiegel's *Nicholas and Alexandra* and, with more regret, the ballet film *Turning Point*, sent her by Jay Kanter. She could, however, still keep in touch with the world of which she had once been queen. She sent in her ballot every year for the Academy Awards and in 1968 she narrated the sequence on films of the fifties for a taped show for the fortieth Awards ceremony. In 1974 she attended Lincoln Center for the tribute to her old friend and mentor, Alfred Hitchcock, and recalled the feebly risqué quip he made when she appeared in the famous strapless gold lamé ball gown in *To Catch a Thief*: 'There's hills in them thar gold, Grace. . . .'

Two years later, at the suggestion of her old friend and former agent, Jay Kanter, then a Vice-President of Twentieth Century-Fox, she joined the company as the only woman director on the ten-member board. Publicly she declared that she wanted to help change the face of modern movies – "There is too much crude sex and violence in movies and television today. I want to help change all that. I want to bring love and peace back to the screen." Privately she told Rupert Allan happily that one of the reasons she wanted to join Fox was "so she could get to read all the scripts. She *loved* reading scripts." Grace, said Kanter, was an ideal board member. "She didn't hesitate to put her point of view across and if she didn't understand something she wouldn't just rubber stamp it, she would stop and ask a question until somebody gave her a satisfactory answer." Sadly, Grace was to discover that despite the awed treatment she received from the board she had absolutely no power, and that corporations like Fox were far more interested in investing their assets in other money-making areas than in sponsoring new talent. And though it was fun and a new experience to begin with, disillusionment set in and, after the company was taken over by oil millionaire Marvin Davis, she left in 1981.

Sitting on the board of Fox surrounded by bankers and financial experts discussing investments and balance sheets was remote from the experience of film-making which she had loved. Increasingly, though in a small way, she was becoming involved again – first through the documentary biography of her life, *Once Upon a Time is Now*, produced in 1976 by Bill and Sandy Allyn and directed by an Englishman, Kevin Billington. He was surprised to find that Grace, in front of the cameras again, had a most un-actressy lack of vanity, showing very little concern about how she would look on film and never asking anxiously about the lighting as other actresses would. She had, he said, an amazingly vivid recall of her acting life, of every scene she had played and, unusually for an actor, of everything other actors had done in that scene – even down to the opening of a door. With Bill and Sandy Allyn she was happy and relaxed; Billington, expecting an ice princess, was surprised at "how giggly she was ... laughing and joking with Bill Allyn and loving it". Lee Grant acted as "interlocutor" for the film, but one figure from Grace's past did not feature in the Allyn production, that of Gene Lyons, whom both Grace and Lee had loved. Gene had died just over a year before. Grace's conclusion to this film was a fair one: "I've had an interesting and wonderful life, and I like to think I have made it so. If I've had unhappy moments, I've probably made them so. We do it to ourselves ..."

More new film projects were coming Grace's way, of the kind in which she would feel able to participate. One, *The Children of Theatre Street*, was to lead her into a favourite area, ballet. When she was asked to do the narration for the film, a documentary on the Kirov

Ballet School in Leningrad, she jumped at the proposal. She was becoming again as fascinated by ballet as she had been when as a child in Philadelphia she had been overwhelmed by a performance of the Ballets Russes. Narrating the film, which had been shot in Leningrad in 1976, gave her the chance to work with an old friend, Jean Dalrymple, who had once auditioned her for the part of Roxane for the City Center, and to make new ones – Oleg Briansky, the artistic director, and Robert Dornhelm, the director.

Briansky, who had been a well-known dancer himself, was artistic director of the Saratoga-Briansky ballet school, and a Scorpio, the same age as Grace and born only three days apart. "My twin brother" was how she introduced him to her friends, and together they planned to realize a long-held dream of Grace's: to have a ballet company in Monte Carlo and, indeed, to revive Monte Carlo's former status as a centre of ballet. There were to be thirty or thirty-five dancers in the company and George Balanchine was to be artistic director. Grace hoped to set up a Foundation in America which might help to finance the company and to increase the funding of her Foundation in Monaco, but by the time she died the project was very far from being realized. The ballet company, Briansky said, was her greatest desire. "She wanted to bring a more cultural atmosphere to Monte Carlo, to raise the standards, to give the people something of quality, of elegance of life, of culture. They have a very good orchestra there and they have the opera company and the flower show, and she wanted a permanent ballet company because that would have given a certain international prestige."

Grace did not get her ballet company but, with Prince Rainier's support and encouragement, she did get a theatre, restoring and redecorating an old building which had been a theatre fifty years before, overlooking the sea below the Hôtel de Paris. Renamed the Théâtre Princesse Grace, it was very much "her" theatre. She discussed all the details of its design and decoration with the architect, choosing all the materials to be used, the paint colours and carpets, and even designing dew-drop glass chandeliers to be made in Murano. Instead of the traditional red and gold she wanted her auditorium to have light blue seats and carpet, and pale oak pillars. The two bars, designed on the lines of an ocean liner, were to be comfortable enough for people to sit in and use for receptions, unlike the squalid crush bars of older theatres. She took a special interest in the actors' dressing-rooms, insisting on details for their comfort such as sofas long enough to rest on and electric kettles (almost unknown in France) specially ordered from London; and she gave orders that there should always be teabags, instant coffee and chocolate available so that the actors could help themselves when they wanted. "When I was an actress I always used to have tea," she told the administrator, M. Patrick Hourdequin. As an actress she supported the artistic director, M. Raymond Gerôme, when he complained that ceiling spotlights in the auditorium were no good for actors, in opposition to the architect, M. Baudouin, who argued against side spotlights on aesthetic grounds. "He must have his lights," Grace said. "She always worried about the actors," Hourdequin said: "Were they all right? Were they well lodged? What criticisms did they have?" She insisted, too, that the public should not have to pay for the programme or the cloakroom, only for the theatre tickets, because "they should feel at home". When the administrator argued that they could not afford to give away programmes free, she replied shrewdly that she could always recoup the money through luxury advertising in the programmes.

The opening show of the theatre was held, at Grace's wish, in the three languages of Monte Carlo, French, English and Italian. Grace, said Dirk Bogarde, who was invited to be the theatre's English "godfather"*, was determined to make the theatre work and pay. They discussed the auditorium, agreeing that at prevailing rates it was too small to make a profit. "I'll raise the prices," she said. "They'll have to be very good shows." "They will be," she said tartly. "I have excellent contacts." "And of course, she had," Bogarde said. "She named a few. ...."

The supper party after the opening show, of which Dirk Bogarde, Edwige Feuillère and Valentina Cortese were the patrons and stars, was held in Grace's favourite hotel, the Hermitage, which she herself had saved from the developers. Perhaps the prettiest Edwardian hotel in the world, it had been restored under her supervision as part of her greater plan to preserve and restore what remained of the elegance of Monte Carlo. Grace had insisted that only the company should be invited to the party, the audience - which, as Bogarde said, had paid a small fortune for their seats - being excluded. There were three tables, each separately presided over by Prince Rainier,

---

* It is customary in France to have "godparents" for the opening of new theatres, hairdressing salons, etc.

Grace and the children, and everyone concerned with the new theatre was invited, from the stars down to the youngest solo dancer. It was a happy, easy, informal evening and went on late. Bogarde noticed that at all times during the evening she was very aware of her husband's table – "I hope to goodness he's not being bored to death" – and by three o'clock in the morning, when the Prince showed signs of restlessness, she said instantly, "Off we go. ..." Under all the glitter and pomp that surrounded her, Bogarde said, she was still an actress. "And she played her part quite brilliantly. She appeared to enjoy it too, although confessing that it could be quite boring sometimes, and she admitted that she 'adored staying up late'." "A gracious, proud, determined 'Royal' and an amusing woman," was how he described her. "Monte Carlo", he said, "will always be 'Grace's Place' and she is, and will be always, deeply missed: because she really did care."

"She was not just a film star but a woman of considerable intelligence," said Anthony Burgess, the celebrated novelist and resident of Monaco, who collaborated with Grace in her cultural plans for Monaco. He watched with admiration her transformation from "celluloid goddess to real-life goddess", the skill with which she played her role as Princess – "she compounded her natural demeanour with her screen persona" – and the sensitivity with which she adapted herself to her background, becoming almost a Monégasque. "She knew all the old ladies in Monaco *ville*, kissed them on the cheek and was affectionate with them. ... She was actually dealing with people." He recognized how Grace's pursuit of her Irish roots helped her to feel a part of Europe. "As a European she was an Irish European," he said. Grace's collection of Irish music was unique, and she prized her library of five hundred Irish books, including a second edition of *Ulysses*. She and Burgess collaborated on the Monte Carlo James Joyce Festival in April 1982 and, after the success of four lectures given by Burgess on modern literature, Grace had the idea of starting an "open university" there. The last letter she wrote to him concerned a series of courses in Shakespeare which he had suggested. At her last St Patrick's Night dinner, an event which Grace always attended, Burgess played Irish songs on the piano with Grace leaning on it talking with immense vivacity about Irish music and upbraiding the orchestra of the Hôtel de Paris because they did not know any Irish tunes.

Through the director of *The Children of Theatre Street*, Robert

Dornhelm, a young Romanian now an Austrian citizen, Grace had become involved in further film projects. She and Caroline planned a film with Dornhelm on world child protégés for the Year of the Child, to be produced by Sam Spiegel, but nothing came of it. There was to be an ambitious film about Raoul Wallenberg, the Swedish Red Cross representative who mysteriously disappeared in Russia and is rumoured to be still alive in a Russian prison camp. Grace was to be casting director on the film and she hoped that Albert, too, could be involved, while just before she died she and Dornhelm were discussing another film plan, *The Dangerous Gift*, based on a Gore Vidal story to be scripted by Richard O'Brien.

Only one of their mutual projects was actually realized, a film entitled *Rearranged*, a lightweight tale of mistaken identity woven round the Monaco Flower Festival, directed by Dornhelm, scripted by the French novelist Jacqueline de Monsigny, with Grace acting herself and de Monsigny's husband, the American actor Edward Meeks, co-starring. The idea had all the elements which interested Grace; acting, film-making, promoting Monaco and, as it was to benefit the Garden Club, advancing a cherished cause. Nonetheless she approached the project gingerly – after the *Marnie* affair, film-making was a potentially explosive subject. For this film she was to be the producer and, since she was financing it, had control, while her partners in the project were people she had chosen herself, whom she knew she could trust.

The resulting film, shot round the Monaco Flower Festival in May 1980, is a pretty, innocently banal affair with a strong flavour of the fifties, a romantic travelogue of Monaco given poignancy and interest by the radiant presence of Grace in her last appearance as an actress on the screen. The magnetism is still there, and so is the camera's love affair with the planes of that beautiful face, fuller now, as is the matronly figure beneath the garden smock. The voice is as cool and alluring as it was in *To Catch a Thief*, and the light touch of a talented comedienne is still there. Only the *persona* which Grace projects is different; the fragile "Fair Miss Frigidaire" of Grace Kelly's last film, *High Society*, has been replaced by the serene beauty, charm and warmth of Grace in her maturity. The message, that human beings can find joy and self-expression through flowers, sounds trite but is nonetheless deeply felt; in many ways Grace was closer to the "flower children" of the 1960s than to the hard world of the eighties.

13
The Wheel of Fortune

"I'm out of school," Grace wrote happily to a friend at the end of June 1982 after hearing that Stephanie had passed her *"bachot"*. After more than twenty-five years devoted to bringing up the children, she felt that she was free. True, Stephanie remained difficult, but she was now seventeen, her childhood and her schooldays were over and Grace could look forward to a new era. A month later, in a televised interview with Pierre Salinger, she explained, "My youngest child has now just graduated from high school. And so this is another kind of turning-point in our lives."

Poignantly, for what was to be the last year of her life, 1982 had been a year of nostalgia, of renewing old friendships and reliving former experiences, culminating in a tribute to her past achievements by her native city. First, the "Night of One Hundred Stars" at Radio City Music Hall, New York, organized to benefit the Actors' Fund of America in its centenary year, brought together no less than two hundred and six stars for an evening's spectacular. Almost everybody who was anybody in American show business – apart from the President of the United States, Ronald Reagan – was there and, as a fellow-participant put it, the evening was "one enormous love-in" for Grace, a joyous reunion with fellow actors, old friends, past colleagues, all the people with whom she felt most at home.

Grace was lodged for the occasion in a VIP suite at the Helmsley Palace Hotel, with fellow superstar and ex-MGM colleague Elizabeth Taylor in its equivalent on the same floor. Stunned and amused by the magnificence of her three-storey apartment with its private elevator, two dining-rooms, three sitting-rooms and two terraces, she called her friend, super-rich Texas beauty Mrs Lynn Wyatt: "You've got to come over and have lunch with me.... I want you to see this three-storey apartment I have because it's fantastic!" Despite nearly thirty years as a princess, Grace remained a little Germantown girl at heart in her reaction to wealth and opulence, revelling wide-eyed

in the luxury of the Wyatts' properties at Houston and La Maur-
esque, Somerset Maugham's former villa at Cap Ferrat in the South
of France, where she and Prince Rainier enjoyed Texas steaks flown
in by the Wyatts' private jet. While the Helmsley Palace pastry chef,
who used to work in Monaco, paid his homage by sending up no less
than seven different desserts, Madame Nella Rubinstein, Grace's
friend and former neighbour from Paris, widow of the great pianist,
occupied her time in sending her maid out to buy chicken carcasses
to make plain chicken soup.

At the end of March Grace flew to Philadelphia for what *Variety*
described as a "nostalgiathon", the city's "Tribute to Grace Kelly"
in the Annenberg Center, with a gala evening on 31 March to usher
in a four-day showing of Grace's films. It drizzled and the marching
band which was supposed to open the proceedings failed to turn up,
but nonetheless it was a triumphant evening for Grace, radiant,
despite a heavy cold, in a primrose yellow ruffled silk gown by Dior.
Three of her former leading men were there to pay tribute to her –
James Stewart, Frank Sinatra and Stewart Granger – while old
friends like Brian Aherne and Rita Gam reminisced about her life.
Frank Sinatra was so moved by his feelings for "Gracie" that he
ended his eulogy with the words "Gracie, I love you dearly," and
walked off stage, apparently forgetting to introduce Walter Annenberg, "the landlord", as Bob Hope, who filled the gap, quipped.

Curiously, in view of what was to happen, Grace recalled that
evening that her driving in *To Catch a Thief* had caused Cary Grant
to turn "dead white under his tan". "I am overwhelmed," she said,
"and so filled with love I would just like to hug every one of you."
"The supper afterwards was a crush," she wrote to Marie Magee,
"and it was impossible to move, so about thirty or forty of us ended
up in my suite for an impromptu party that lasted until 4 am!"

It was a triumphant return to Philadelphia for Grace, but the
story of the other Kellys, meanwhile, had not been so happy. In 1975
Margaret Kelly suffered a stroke which left her alive but without her
memory or reasoning power. When Grace died Lizanne gently told
her mother the news but Margaret Kelly did not seem to comprehend
what had happened and still does not realize that her daughter Grace
is dead. It was a sad fate for a beautiful, charming and dynamic
woman.

Her stroke had been preceded in 1975 by her last public exertion
of parental authority over her son Kell, then forty-eight years old, a

City Councilman and in the running for the Democratic Policy Committee's endorsement as candidate in the mayoral race against Frank Rizzo. Kell was the favourite; he would undoubtedly have won the Committee's endorsement and he might very well have become Mayor of Philadelphia, since Rizzo eventually won by only a very small margin against what a local newspaperman described as a "colourless" candidate. But at the last minute, as the Kelly family biographer, Arthur Lewis, put it, "Ma Kelly surfaced". With two telephone calls she ensured that the Democratic Committee did not endorse her son. For Kell, Jack's loyal son, who had also seen this as a chance to make up for his father's defeat in the mayoral campaign of 1935, it was a shattering public humiliation.

Ma Kelly had her reasons, born of bitter past experience: when she heard that the opposition were planning a smear poster campaign directed at Kell's private life, memories of political dirty tricks came flooding back and she stepped in to save the Kelly name being dragged through the mud. The opposition poster, she was told, was to pose the question, "Will the First Lady be Harlow?", a reference to a beautiful trans-sexual, Rachel Harlow, formerly night-club owner Richard Finocchio, with whom Kell had been seen in various Philadelphia nightspots. The cause of *l'affaire* Harlow, which friends claim to have been quite platonic, was, they say, Kell's weakness for publicity. He not only liked taking out what a local reporter described as an assortment of blondes, brunettes and redheads, but liked to be seen to be doing so, boosting an ego which had long ago been kept deflated at the hands of his father, John B. Sr.

"The old man pushed the hell out of me," was Kell's explanation for the highly visible bachelor-about-town life he had led since, at the age of forty, he walked out on his wife Mary and their six children, including John B. Kelly Jr. Kell had always been under his father's thumb, training relentlessly to achieve his rowing triumphs, never touching alcohol until he was well into his twenties, marrying a Catholic girl, Mary Freeman, who was also an athlete and a champion swimmer, with, of course, his father as best man. When Kell lost his first try for the Diamond Sculls, a friend recalled, "They had to peel Kell's hands off the oars and carry him out of the scull. He could not deal with the fact that he had disappointed his father." Even as an adult he walked in his father's shadow, and although his rowing career was more successful than Jack's, men would still come up to him in front of other people and say, patting him on the back, "He's great, but his father was greater. His father was the *greatest*."

John B. Kelly Jr has his father's superb physique, his blue eyes, strong jaw and finely chiselled mouth. Like his father, he keeps himself in good physical shape, so that at over fifty he looks ten years younger. He is chairman of John B. Kelly, Inc., the brickwork and masonry firm founded by his father in 1923. Since his second marriage in May 1981 he has given up his bachelor ways and once more cherishes political ambitions. Grace, though very fond of her brother, did not hesitate to tell him in the strongest possible terms if she disagreed with him. On one occasion, at an intimate gathering of her old Philadelphia friends, she was heard to do so in loud and most un-Princessy tones.

Jack Kelly's heritage has been hard for his children; of the four Grace is the one who has had the strength to withstand it and to live up to his high standards of behaviour and achievement. While Lizanne remains married to her first love, Donald LeVine, now a racehorse trainer in Phoenix, Arizona, and has two children by him, Grace and Christopher, Peggy, Jack Kelly's adored "Baba", with two broken marriages behind her, lives the life of a recluse. She has two children by her first husband, Margaret "Meg" and Mary Lee, Grace's favourite niece, whom Grace cherished and helped through the difficulties of a teenage elopement and the bearing of twins. Perhaps, too, Grace's own brilliant successes have posed problems for her siblings, who as children far outshone her. The Philadelphia Kellys are exceptionally good-looking and thoroughly nice people, but, lacking their sister's star quality, they live in a different world from the Grimaldis, and even Grace did not succeed in cementing the two families together.

One wonders what Grace thought of herself in middle age as she attended that Philadelphia "nostalgiathon", seeing images of her flawless, exquisitely slender, twenty-five-year-old self flit across the screen. Unlike most actresses and famous beauties in middle age she seemed unworried by the process of ageing and took no drastic steps to arrest it. "I'm past all that, I'm just not interested," she told one interviewer, and when she attended a party at the chic New York night-club Xenon for a charity showing of *The Children of Theatre Street*, a society woman, surveying the crowd of taut jawlines and wide-open eyes, remarked, "She's the only fifty-year-old woman here who hasn't had a face-lift." Having never thought of herself as a great beauty, Grace worried less about her looks. "People kept telling her she was beautiful," Rupert Allan said. "But she didn't, inside herself, believe it. She never saw herself as other people saw her ... she didn't feel she was beautiful."

Grace's bone structure and the quality of her skin ensured that her face remained beautiful, both in photographs and in the flesh. Even in unposed snapshots taken on the beach without make-up her features retained that lovely calf-like quality which Cecil Beaton had noticed over a quarter of a century earlier. The sylph-like figure of the twenty-five-year-old Grace was, however, no longer there. As she approached fifty she began to put on a great deal of weight, no longer really caring that she did so. As a film star she had rigorously watched her weight, keeping herself down to 115 pounds even though her height was 5 ft 7 in. In earlier years in Monaco she had been disciplined about it, putting weight on during her pregnancies, when she ate happily, taking it off when she stopped breast-feeding the children, and dieting and using an exercise bicycle at the end of every summer to counteract the effects of dinner and lunch parties during the Monte Carlo season.

But Grace – and her husband – enjoyed their food. "They were always eating and always desperate about their weight," said one ex-palace observer. At Dior Marc Bohan would counsel dresses which would not emphasize the waist, while Grace pleaded with him like a guilty little girl for her beloved shirt-waists – "People won't like it," she would say of the waistless models. But at fifty she became more relaxed about it. "I'm fifty-two and the mother of three children – why should I care?" she told a friend. When she and Fleur Cowles Meyer went to Dallas for the Flower Festival there in 1971, they decided to go to the famous "fat farm", the Greenhouse, before Prince Rainier arrived. "We'll appear in Dallas looking beautiful," Grace said. They both lost several inches round the waist, but quickly expanded again. "What's the point of it, Fleur?" asked Grace.

Her heaviness, and the puffiness which sometimes, due to her sinus trouble, affected her under her eyes, led to rumours that she drank, which her friends strenuously deny. She liked champagne at parties and American beer with a hamburger but otherwise, "She didn't drink and she didn't smoke, and she didn't take pills," Maree Rambo said. "She was so pure." Grace liked food, but she also liked exercise and was never sedentary. Whenever she could she went for long walks, preferably in the country in the rain, or in Monaco collecting plants on the mountainside, while in Paris she would take dance classes. And when she really felt she was looking too large, she did take steps to remedy the situation. In February 1982 she appeared, looking lovely but waistless, in New York at the "Night of One Hundred Stars", but by late July, when she was filmed for television, she was many pounds slimmer and dressed in a favourite green and white flowered shirt-waist.

The Philadelphia tribute was not the only nostalgic experience for Grace in 1982. "So far", Grace wrote to a friend on 2 May, "it has been an emotional year for me.... Rainier and I are now just back from three weeks in the Far East. We went to Taiwan to christen the *Constitution*, which was bought by a Chinese!"

Throughout the summer of 1982 Grace looked tired. She lost weight, but not the cold that had dogged her at the Philadelphia tribute. Still as an adult, just as she had when she was a little girl, she suffered terribly from colds; photographs taken of her that summer show a puffiness beneath the eyes contrasting with the slimmer figure and a new, becoming, softer and shorter hair style. To some of her friends she complained of headaches and tiredness. "She was actively overworked," said Fleur Meyer. "She was tired," said her hairdresser, Gwendoline. Virginia Gallico, Grace's friend and lady-in-waiting, agreed:

> In my opinion she was doing too much, she was in aeroplanes too much – juggling with her life and her health. When she arrived back in the palace there were so many pressures on her – secretaries asking her things – everything had to be fitted in. Sometimes she would have a moment to rest and sat in her chair knitting. Then there would be an official lunch, then it was off to the office – she would breakfast at eight in order to get through the day.

Grace was a professional – physical weakness or tiredness was not something which you complained of, or showed, in public. When Pierre Salinger of ABC News arrived in Monaco in the third week of July to interview her for American television, he found her "in very good form, absolutely beautiful and very relaxed". It was the first in-depth television interview which Grace had ever consented to do, and she agreed to do it, characteristically, out of loyalty to an old friend, Ann Levy Siegel of Philadelphia. Grace had specified that she wanted Salinger to do the interview – she had met him before when she visited the Kennedy White House and again when he was President of the Jury for the Monte Carlo Television Festival. The night before the interview, on 22 July, there was a concert and supper at the palace at which Grace and Salinger argued fiercely about the press – "She was incensed about the way they covered the children," Salinger said – but on the following day Grace, who hitherto had frequently turned to a block of ice for interviewers, was relaxed, warm and smiling as she sat talking to Salinger in the palace garden.

Naturally the talk ranged back to her life as an actress – how much she had loved acting, working in the theatre and in pictures. Perhaps a little wistfully, she said, "I don't feel as though I achieved enough in my career to be remembered, to stand out more than other people. . . . I was very lucky in my career and I loved it . . . but I don't think I was accomplished enough as an actress to be remembered for that particularly." She spoke of having so many plans and projects for the future, of how she saw this period as a crossroads in her life, and, for the first time, when asked if her poetry readings were "a kind of advanced step to going back to acting", she did not deny it outright. She didn't know, she said; acting was a very time-consuming profession and "it would mean a complete reorganization of my life . . . it would be a very difficult decision to make".

"In other words," Salinger said, "you're not saying that if somebody came along with that offer that you couldn't refuse, that you wouldn't say yes."

"I have always tried to avoid saying never or always."

Then – "I know that it's much too early in your life to answer this question," Salinger said, "but how are you going to want to be remembered?"

"I would like to be remembered as trying to do my job well," Grace answered, ". . . of being understanding and kind. . . . I'd like to be remembered as a decent human being and a caring one." She had spoken her own epitaph.

In August Grace and Prince Rainier went on a cruise to Scandinavia on the SS *Mermoz*. It was a family expedition; although Stephanie, not wanting to be parted from Paul Belmondo, had stayed behind, Caroline and Albert were on board with Prince Louis de Polignac, Prince Rainier's cousin. Grace enjoyed the cruise and organized exercise sessions, sightseeing trips, games and parties – one of the last photographs of the family together shows them dressed as pirates. Then it was back to Monaco, where Rosine Sanmori remembers the last meeting of the Garden Club, when the members gathered by the pool in the palace garden to lay out the tapestry squares based on botanical drawings which they had all been making for a large wall tapestry which was to be displayed in the Club building and for which Grace had, typically, done the most tedious part, the deep green border.

Monaco was hot and sultry, the palace closed for the holidays, the staff dispersed. Grace and her family retreated to the cool of their "ranch" high on the slopes of Mont Agel among the wild flowers which she loved – valerian, sweet pea, honeysuckle, canterbury bells, wild lavender. It was to be a last family vacation: the summer was ending and for Albert, Stephanie and Grace the autumn would be a new beginning. Albert was to start a course in finance and banking in New York, and Stephanie to enrol in the school for budding fashion designers in Paris run by the Chambre Syndicale de la Haute Couture, for a course which was to open on 15 September. Grace would accompany her to Paris, where she planned to discuss with Robert Dornhelm the question of adapting and lengthening *Rearranged* for American television, along with their other film plans, then to fly to London for the Windsor recital. After that she was to fly to the States in aid of actor-director Sam Wanamaker's project for the reconstruction of the Globe Theatre on its original site in London as a centre for classical theatre studies and training. Grace had become the first international patron of the project in 1974 and was involved in fund-raising for it. On 8 October she was due in Houston, Texas, to be guest of honour at a dinner for fifty people given by Lynn and Oscar Wyatt, at which she planned to perform selections from Shakespeare.

Grace had been depressed at the beginning of September – she was fighting bronchitis and there had been further rows with Stephanie – but as the time approached for her to leave Roc Agel she was optimistic. "It's going to be a happy year," she wrote to a friend.

Monday 13 September dawned bright and hot. At Roc Agel there was a pile of suitcases, bags and clothes to be loaded into the waiting brown Rover 3500, an 8-cylinder automatic which, with the old London taxi she also owned, was Grace's favourite car and which she had had for ten years. She was in a hurry – she had an appointment with her couturier in Monaco, Daniel Roland, for last-minute alterations to a dress – and when her secretary, Paul Choisit, telephoned her at about 9.30 asking to see her, she said, "Well, as soon as you stop talking to me, I'm on my way." Outside the door Christian Silvestri, Grace's preferred chauffeur, stood ready in his uniform beside the car to take the two Princesses down to Monaco. The car was piled with luggage; Grace's dresses for the couturier appointment were laid out across the back seat; there was only room for two in front.

"No, Christian," Grace told him, "that won't be necessary." When he protested, she joked, "But if you insist you can run behind us...".

According to Christian Silvestri, Grace was at the wheel as the car disappeared down the drive, turning left along the narrow winding road past the Mont Agel golf course and down the tortuous road with its hairpin bends, the hillside below dotted with wild olive trees, pines and twisted fig-trees, to the pretty little hill town of La Turbie, its rose-coloured tiled roofs dominated by the white ruins of the Tour Auguste, the Roman tower built for the greater glory of the Emperor Augustus. Below La Turbie, the road becomes tortuous again, a series of sharp hairpin bends with the mountain dropping precipitously away on the outside; it is always crowded with traffic, cars, buses, trucks. A sign warns "3 *lacets*" (sharp bends).

Truck driver Yves Raimondo followed the Rover as it negotiated the first right-hand curve, so sharp that you almost have to stop to get round it, then round the left-hand bend past the Monaco Aeroclub. Suddenly, some two hundred yards from the last corner, concealed by a projecting bluff of the mountainside, Raimondo saw the Rover zigzag, almost scraping the side – "One would have said", he explained, "a lack of attention." He sounded his horn and the car straightened up for the last eighty yards down to the sharpest curve of all, a right-hand bend with a crash barrier on the outside, beside which a dirt track led off to the left at right angles to the main road. "I don't know what happened", Raimondo reported. "The corner came up ... I did not see it [the car] slow down ... the brake lights didn't come on ... she did not even try to turn and I had the impression that she was going faster and faster ... it disappeared over the edge. ...."

The Rover glanced off the inner end of the crash barrier at the opening of the dirt road and somersaulted down a forty-metre drop, tearing the bark of a maritime pine, bending bushes and saplings, and landing on its side with its left-hand wheels in the air on a small plateau of market gardens beside a red-painted house. What happened then is confused, providing the basis for the rumours, widely believed, that Stephanie, not Grace, was at the wheel. According to another truck driver, also called Raimundo, who stopped his truck and ran down the slope, he found two men pulling a young girl out of the car by the front left-hand, driver's door. "In the back among the clothes there was a woman. She lay on her back across the seats, her head against the back side window. I asked her if she was all right. She didn't answer. Someone told me then that I must leave her and not touch anything."

Stephanie, shocked and groggy, wearing denim jeans and a blouson, walked by herself to the house, where she sat on the threshold repeating in French, "*Maman* is dead ... you must help *Maman*," then to the wife of the owner of the house, "You must warn papa." "Who is your papa?" "He's the Prince. I'm his daughter, Stephanie, and *maman* is in the car." A man rang the *gendarmerie*. It was 10 am.

The gendarmes arrived at 10.10 with two ambulances, into the first of which they put Stephanie. They found the car with the windows broken, the seats overturned, the seat-belts unfastened and the clothes strewn about the interior. The hand-brake was pulled up three notches and the automatic gear handle was in D (drive) position. The telephone hung outside the car and the dashboard clock had stopped at the moment of impact: 9.54 am. They broke the back window and dragged Grace out onto a stretcher, and as they did so, an onlooker noticed that her right leg was out of place. She had a deep wound on her forehead on the hairline and her eyes were open. When Paul Choisit arrived from the palace after a nightmare drive up through heavy traffic, Grace had already been placed in the second ambulance. Desperately he banged on the door shouting, "I speak English, I can help you," thinking that in the shock of the accident Grace might not be able to speak French. He was struck by the sadness of seeing Grace's belongings, "those bags I knew so well, scattered over the hill – her sewing bag ...". The Prince and Albert were on their way down from Roc Agel.

Professor Charles Louis Chatelin, head of surgery at the Princess Grace Hospital in Monaco, was warned of the accident at about 10.15 am and set off for the spot, but met the ambulance already coming down. Grace was carried into the emergency room – "The Princess was barely conscious, she reacted to pain but not if you spoke to her," said Professor Chatelin. She was immediately put on a life-support system as the doctor examined her injuries. He found that she had a cranial trauma with a large exterior wound to the forehead, a fracture of the right femur, a trauma to the thorax with fractures to the ribs, and a pneumothorax (collapsed lung). There was both air and blood in the thorax – injuries which were presumably caused by the steering-wheel – and numerous cuts and bruises.

Chatelin administered an analgesic, a narcotic known as Gamma H, anaesthetic being out of the question because of the suspected brain injury, and proceeded to deal with the most immediate injuries – the head wound, the fractured right leg and the thorax, which he opened in order to remove the air and blood and allow the lung to breathe – and he executed an abdominal laparotomy on the stomach to treat internal bleeding. Grace went into a coma, her brain activity being continuously monitored on an electro-encephalogram. After a four-hour operation on the external injuries it was clear that her condition was worsening. Dr Chatelin treated Grace in conjunction with the head of neurosurgery at Nice Hospital, Professor Jean Duplay, and, in view of the evidence of the encephalogram, they decided to take a brain scan.

Because of reconstruction work at the hospital, the scanner was temporarily located in the office of a local doctor, Dr Mouroux, on the Boulevard des Moulins in the centre of Monte Carlo. Unconscious, Grace was taken there at nine o'clock in the evening in an ambulance escorted by two motorcycle police. The lift was too small for the stretcher and so she was carried up two floors to the scanner room. The scanner pictures showed a very extensive area of bleeding in the brain – a cerebral contusion in the frontal lobe and parietal lobe, which was inoperable, and a small and restricted haemorrhage in the white matter of the posterior part of the right temporal lobe. According to Professor Chatelin this latter small haemorrhage would have made her dizzy or might have resulted in a black-out, causing her to lose control of the car while the large area of bleeding was a direct result of the accident and the wound to her forehead. In other words, she had had a slight stroke, which, had she not been driving, would certainly not have killed her.

Professor François Lhermitte, head of the department of neurology at the University of Paris, who arrived two days after the accident to examine Stephanie, was shown the scan picture and concurred with the two other doctors in their diagnosis. The first slight "accident" in the brain, he said, is of a type which many people can suffer without knowing it, something which might cause a person to feel dizzy or perhaps fall from their chair if they were sitting down, while the second area of bleeding caused by the accident would eventually have cleared, although it might have led to troubles with the memory and certain changes of mood, but these too would have disappeared within weeks. The coma in which Grace had arrived at the hospital would have been caused by a blow to the head during the accident; the fact that her condition steadily worsened was due to the cumulative effect of the number and gravity of her injuries. From the moment that the car left the road, tossing her against the steering-wheel and the roof, Grace was, in fact, doomed.

And so, during the night of 13 September, Grace, lying in the resuscitation room on the fourth floor of the hospital named after her, plunged into an ever deeper coma. By the following afternoon, 14 September, the encephalogram went flat; all brain activity had ceased. As a human being Grace was dead. Four hours later, at 10.30 pm, Prince Rainier, with Albert and Caroline at his side, gave the doctors permission to turn off the life-support system.

As Grace had lain unconscious and dying on the fourth floor of the hospital during Monday and Tuesday, confusion had reigned in Monaco. As far as the outside world was concerned, Grace had had a slight accident, breaking her leg. The first official press release, issued on the evening of the accident, simply (and inaccurately) stated that she had had an accident after a brake failure and that her "condition is satisfactory".

Nadia Lacoste, Monaco's chief press officer, was abroad on holiday in Germany, as were half the senior staff of the palace. Princess Caroline was in England, while Stephanie lay in a state of shock, suffering only from a hairline fracture of a vertebra in her neck. When Professor Lhermitte saw her on the 15th she was unaware of her mother's death and chatted to him, telling him how she had tried to stop the car by pulling on the handbrake. No one seems to have realized how serious Grace's condition actually was; on Monday Prince Rainier told his sister Princess Antoinette, who telephoned from Scotland, where she was on holiday, that "there was no need to hurry back", and the palace seems to have been chiefly concerned to keep press interest at a minimum, refusing to let the doctors issue bulletins. Prince Rainier, with Albert and his niece, Elisabeth de Massy, were in constant attendance at the hospital and hardly in any condition to handle the world's press. Christine Plaistow, in Paris at the time of the accident, arrived back on Tuesday to find that everyone at the palace seemed "spellbound, not daring to speak about the accident". "The feeling everybody had after the accident", said Paul Choisit, "was that this woman could not die." "It was only on Tuesday they told us it was serious," Elisabeth de Massy said. Caroline arrived back at lunchtime on Tuesday, just a few hours before her mother died, to comfort her father and take charge of her mother's body, which was taken straight up to the palace after she died to lie in state in the palace chapel. The palace staff came flocking back to help their Prince in his grief – "Everyone turned up out of loyalty to Grace," said Virginia Gallico, her lady-in-waiting, who flew back from England. The gardeners were up all night collecting and arranging flowers for the chapel and the courtyard. "She was never left alone," Virginia Gallico said simply.

Nadia Lacoste arrived back from Germany on the Wednesday to find Monaco in a state of shock, telephones ringing incessantly and journalists from all over the world besieging the principality. Immediately the rumours started – there had been a cover-up by the palace; Rainier had had the Rover removed from the scene of the accident before the French police could examine it; the terrible truth that they were trying to conceal was that Stephanie, under the legal driving age, had been at the wheel. There were rumours, which even intelligent people believed, that she had been killed by the Nice Mafia for trying to keep them out of Monte Carlo, and that her car had been tampered with. American newspapers alleged that the medical treatment she had been given was inadequate and that she could have been saved. In fact Grace could not have survived her terrible injuries. Prince Rainier had indeed had the Rover removed, but it was examined and reported upon by the French police; and as for the rumour that Stephanie had been driving at the time of the accident, Paul Choisit said indignantly, "The Princess was a woman of such integrity, she would never have allowed her daughter to drive – if I'd seen it with my own eyes I wouldn't have believed it." John J. Louis II, the then US ambassador in London, who with his wife had been staying at Roc Agel and left the house just after Grace and Stephanie, saw Grace at the wheel as he overtook her car on the way down to Monte Carlo. Stephanie herself would only say, weeks after the accident, "Mommy panicked and lost control," and it seems likely that, as she told Professor Lhermitte, she was the one to seize the handbrake and pull it up those three notches as the car hurtled towards the corner.

No one could believe that Grace was dead. "Imagine us having to organize a huge state funeral," Elisabeth de Massy said. "We kept waiting for her to come in and take over. My mother [Princess Antoinette] kept saying, 'Well, you must ask your Aunt Grace.'"

As Grace's body lay in state in the palace chapel, where mass was said every day and the doors were kept open for Monégasques to pay their respects, dignitaries from all over the world flooded in to pay their homage. On Wednesday evening the King and Queen of Belgium arrived and on the next day the Queen of Spain. Mrs Reagan arrived on Friday, the day before the funeral, and the Kelly family flew in in a US Army jet provided by the President and arranged by Grace's cousin, Secretary of the Navy John Lehman, who accompanied them.

On Saturday, the morning of the official funeral, royalty and celebrities from all over the world flew in to Nice airport to be transported by helicopter to Monaco. Diana, Princess of Wales, ex-Queen Anne-Marie of Greece, Prince Bertil of Sweden, Princess Benedikte of Denmark, Grand Duchess Josephine-Charlotte of Luxembourg, Prince Philip of Liechtenstein, the Duca d'Aosta representing the Italian royal family, Princess Paola of Liège, the ex-Empress Farah of Iran, the Aga Khan and the Begum Salima, Madame Danielle Mitterrand, wife of the President of France, Madame Claude Pompidou, wife of the late French President, and from Hollywood, Mr and Mrs Cary Grant. Frank Sinatra, tied up by concerts in the States, was unable to come, as was Grace's equally loved friend, David Niven, ill in his villa at Cap Ferrat. Grace's bridesmaids, Maree Rambo, Rita Gam, Bettina Gray and Judy Quine, were also there, unable to believe that they had come to bury their friend, twenty-six years after they had followed her to the altar in that same Cathedral on a sunny April day.

The morning of Grace's funeral, Saturday 18 September, blazed with the heat of late summer. Monaco seemed as if stunned by the death of its Princess; the grieving and respectful silence impressed the Prince, even in his state of shock. "The day of the funeral, there was no sound in all the principality," he later told a friend. At 10.15 am the silence was broken by a brief fanfare of trumpets as Grace's ebony coffin, covered with a white pall bearing the arms of

Monaco and four bouquets of pink roses, her favourite flower, was carried from the palace for the last time by black-robed penitents. Behind walked Prince Rainier, a man clearly shattered by grief, flanked and indeed supported by a black-veiled Caroline, her eyes swollen with tears, and Albert, as calm, strong and dignified as his mother would have been.

Within the Cathedral where the Prince and Grace had been married and their children baptized, the family sat beside her coffin, a desolate, tragic trio. The simple requiem began with the moving words of Archbishop Brandt: "We weep for our Princess Grace. The brutal suddenness of her death accentuates our pain." During the service Caroline cast looks of anguished concern at her father as he sat hunched with bowed head beside her; once she reached to squeeze his hand. In the cruel gaze of the television cameras trained upon him, the Prince looked a man destroyed by grief, occasionally wiping away a tear. "May our Princess, so helpful towards us in life, receive now the help of our prayers," the Archbishop concluded. The service over, the family returned to the palace gardens to receive the condolences of the dignitaries; and that afternoon at five they had to undergo a second ordeal at a requiem mass attended by Monégasques and local residents. For three days the coffin, banked by flowers, lay in a side-chapel of the Cathedral, until, on Tuesday 21 September, Grace was laid to rest in the Grimaldi family vault beneath the high altar. The inscription on the white marble slab of her tomb was a simple one: "Grace Patricia, wife of Prince Rainier III, died the year of our Lord, 1982."

Epilogue

The manner of Grace's death was as sensational as her life had been. In dying as she did, suddenly and dramatically, without growing old, she had conformed to the public image of her, completing the transformation from Hollywood celluloid goddess to real-life heroine. In the eyes of the world she would remain golden, beautiful and, finally, good – in her own words, "a decent human being and a caring one".

Few people have, as she had, the capacity to act out a private fantasy in real life. The little girl in 3901 Henry Avenue who dreamed of being a princess actually became one, not only once, but twice, as a top Hollywood star and then as Princess of Monaco. The transition from Hollywood to Monaco was not as difficult for Grace as it might have been for any other American girl; both were in a sense fantasy places – living in a palace as royalty is as far removed from ordinary experience as is life as a Hollywood star, and Grace, having, even as a little girl, invented her own idea of a princess, simply went on playing and perfecting the same role.

Myth and fantasy played a large part in her make-up – "She was a real dreamer," a friend said of her – and her dreams were also a release, an escape from the pressures and restrictions of everyday life. As the unconsidered middle child in the suburban Philadelphia house had dreamed of being treated like royalty, so the Princess in her palace had fantasies of freedom, of going as a "bag-lady" poor and unnoticed through the streets of Paris. Like most actors she had a strong sense of the drama in life and, staying in a Scottish castle, surrounded by aristocrats, she would emphasize, not her suburban upbringing but her humble Irish roots, as a more telling contrast to her present station in life.

Paradoxically, alongside that romantic streak was the other Grace, the executive Princess, competent and conscientious about her job as actress, wife, mother to her children and to the Monégasques, going beyond mere competence in the love and care which she devoted to

227

all the things she did. Then there was the loved and loving friend, the woman who liked parties and jokes and staying up late. These were all sides of the same Grace, who remained unchanged by all the success, adulation and glamour.

Perhaps, like other gods and goddesses, she was the victim of her own fame; perhaps the strain of living up to the image which the public, and indeed she herself, had of "Princess Grace" contributed to her death. Living up to the standards which she had set herself and which she knew were expected of her required extreme self-discipline, even sacrifice. "She was a very normal human being", a close friend said, "with basic healthy instincts, and it was a very abnormal way she had to live." Whatever pressures she felt, she faced without palliatives and within herself. Everybody depended upon her; she had to depend on her own inner strength. The enormous expenditure of emotional, physical and moral resources by someone who was, as she was, always in the public eye, produced beneath that serene surface a stress which perhaps, indirectly, caused her death.

Grace had led a charmed life, but at the end her luck deserted her. That small, insignificant haemorrhage in her brain struck at the one moment which could make it fatal. That Grace, who hated driving and had a terrible fear of dying in a car, should have been at the wheel on a particularly dangerous road when it happened was indeed a strange twist of fate.

Grace succeeded in most things she did, apparently effortlessly. Like all true champions she made it seem easy, concealing the effort, the hard work, the self-discipline which she put into being an actress, wife, mother, princess and friend. Although she never achieved the success she longed for on stage, she reached the top in Hollywood, married a prince and created a family in the real sense. Even though she was an American and therefore a foreigner, she made herself not only adored by the Monégasques but accepted as "a part of us", and she made Monte Carlo, in Bogarde's words, "Grace's place". When she died she was mourned not only by her friends across the world but by people who had never known her. "She touched all our lives," a friend said simply. Even Jack Kelly would, at the end, have been proud of her.

Brief Filmography

In order of release

Fourteen Hours (*20th Century-Fox*) 1951
Produced by Sol C. Siegel, directed by Henry Hathaway, screenplay by
John Paxton from the book *The Man on the Ledge* by Joel Sayre, camera
Joe Macdonald.
  With: Paul Douglas, Richard Basehart, Barbara Bel Geddes, Debra
Paget, Agnes Moorehead, Robert Keith, Howard da Silva, Jeffrey Hunter.

High Noon (*United Artists*) 1952
Produced by Stanley Kramer, directed by Fred Zinneman, screenplay by
Carl Foreman based on the story "The Tin Star" by John W.
Cunningham, camera Floyd Crosby.
  With: Gary Cooper, Thomas Mitchell, Lloyd Bridges, Katy Jurado,
Otto Kruger, Lon Chaney Jr, Henry Morgan.

Mogambo (*MGM*) 1953
Produced by Sam Zimbalist, directed by John Ford, screenplay by John
Lee Mahin based on a play by Wilson Collison, camera Robert Surtees,
costumes Edith Rose.
  With: Clark Gable, Ava Gardner, Donald Sinden, Philip Stainton, Eric
Pohlmann, Laurence Naismith.
  Grace was nominated as Best Supporting Actress for her role as Linda
Nordley.

Dial M For Murder (*Warner Bros*) 1954
Produced and directed by Alfred Hitchcock, script by Frederick Knott
from his play, camera Robert Burks, costumes Moss Mabry.
  With: Ray Milland, Robert Cummings, John Williams, Anthony
Dawson, Leo Britt, Patrick Allen.

Rear Window (*Paramount*) 1954
Produced and directed by Alfred Hitchcock, screenplay by John Michael

Hayes based on a story by Cornell Woolrich, camera Robert Burks, costumes Edith Head.

With: James Stewart, Wendell Corey, Thelma Ritter, Raymond Burr, Judith Evelyn, Ross Bagdasarian, Georgine Darcy, Sara Berner.

The Country Girl (Paramount) 1954
Produced by William Perlberg and George Seaton, directed by Seaton, based on the play by Clifford Odets, camera John F. Warren, costumes Edith Head.

With: Bing Crosby, William Holden, Anthony Ross, Gene Reynolds, Jacqueline Fontaine, Eddie Ryder, Robert Kent, John W. Reynolds.

Grace won the Academy Award as Best Actress for the role of Georgie Elgin.

Green Fire (MGM) 1955
Produced by Armand Deutsch, directed by Andrew Marton, screenplay by Ivan Goff and Ben Roberts, camera Paul Vogel.

With: Stewart Granger, Paul Douglas, John Ericson, Murvyn Vye, Joe Dominguez.

The Bridges at Toko-Ri (Paramount) 1955
Produced by William Perlberg and George Seaton, directed by Mark Robson, screenplay by Valentine Davies from the novel by James A. Michener, camera Loyal Griggs, costumes Edith Head.

With: William Holden, Fredric March, Mickey Rooney, Robert Strauss, Charles McGraw, Keiko Awaji, Earl Holliman, Richard Shannon.

To Catch a Thief (Paramount) 1955
Produced and directed by Alfred Hitchcock, screenplay by John Michael Hayes from the book by David Dodge, camera Robert Burks, costumes Edith Head.

With: Cary Grant, Jessie Royce Landis, John Williams, Charles Vanel, Brigitte Auber, Jean Martinelli.

The Swan (MGM) 1956
Produced by Dore Schary, directed by Charles Vidor, screenplay by John Dighton based on the play by Ferenc Molnar, camera Joseph Ruttenberg, Robert Surtees, costumes Helen Rose.

With: Alec Guinness, Louis Jourdan, Agnes Moorehead, Jessie Royce Landis, Brian Aherne, Leo G. Carroll, Estelle Winwood.

High Society (MGM) 1956
Produced by Sol C. Siegel, directed by Charles Walters, screenplay by

John Patrick based on the play *The Philadelphia Story* by Philip Barry, songs by Cole Porter, music director Johnny Green, orchestrators Nelson Riddle and Conrad Salinger, camera Paul C. Vogel, costumes Helen Rose.

With: Bing Crosby, Frank Sinatra, Celeste Holm, John Lund, Louis Calhern, Sidney Blackmer, Margalo Gillmore, Louis Armstrong.

Screen Appearances by Grace Kelly as Princess Grace after her marriage

The Wedding In Monaco (*Citel Monaco & Compagnie Française de Films*) 1956

A Look at Monaco (*CBS TV*) 1963

The Children of Theatre Street (*Peppercorn-Wormser*) 1977
Produced by Earle Mack, associate producer Jean Dalrymple, directed by Robert Dornhelm, artistic director Oleg Briansky, screenplay Beth Gutcheon, camera Karl Kofler.

One of the five nominees for Best Documentary Feature for 1977.

The Story of Princess Grace ... Once Upon a Time is Now (*NBC TV*) 1977
Produced by William and Sandra Allyn, directed by Kevin Billington, with Lee Grant as interlocutor.

Rearranged (as yet not on commercial release)
Produced by Princess Grace, directed by Robert Dornhelm, screenplay by Jacqueline de Monsigny, with Edward Meeks playing opposite Princess Grace as herself.

Select Bibliography

Arce, Hector, *Gary Cooper, an Intimate Biography*, 1979

Aumont, Jean-Pierre, *Sun and Shadow*, trans. Bruce Benderson, 1977

Baltzell, Digby E., *Philadelphia Gentlemen*, University of Pennsylvania Press, 1979
    Puritan Boston and Quaker Philadelphia, 1979

Beaton, Cecil, *It Gives Me Great Pleasure*, 1955
    The Face of the World, 1957

Bernardy, Françoise de, *Princes of Monaco*, trans. Len Ortzen, 1961

Bowers, Ronald, *Grace Kelly*, in *Films in Review*, vol. xxix, no 9, Nov. 1978

Brooks, Tim, and Marsh, Earle, *The Complete Directory to Prime Time Network TV Shows, 1946–Present*, rev. ed., 1981

Cameron, Roderick, *The Golden Riviera*, 1975

Carey, Gary, *All the Stars in Heaven: The Story of Louis B. Mayer and MGM*, 1981

Champlin, Charles, *The Movies Grow Up*, 1981

Clark, Dennis, *The Irish in Philadelphia*, Temple University Press, 1979

Crowther, Bosley, *The Lion's Share: The Story of an Entertainment Empire*, 1957

Fielding, Xan, *The Money Spinner: Monte Carlo Casino*, 1977

Ford, Dan, *The Unquiet Man: The Life of John Ford*, 1982

Frischauer, Willi, *Onassis*, 1968

Gaither, Gant, *Princess of Monaco: The Story of Grace Kelly*, 1957

Gianakos, Larry James, *Television Drama Series Programming: A Comprehensive Chronicle, 1947–59*, Scarecrow Press, Metuchen, New Jersey and London, 1980

Granger, Stewart, *Sparks Fly Upward*, 1981

Graves, Charles, *Royal Riviera*, 1957

Guinther, John, *Philadelphia: A Dream for the Keeping*, Continental Heritage Press, Tulsa, Oklahoma, 1982

Hawkins, Peter, *Prince Rainier of Monaco*, 1966

Head, Edith, and Calistro, Paddy, *Edith Head's Hollywood*, 1983

Higham, Charles, *Ava: A Life Story*, 1975

Howlett, John, *Frank Sinatra*, 1980

Kaminsky, Stuart, *Coop*, 1980

Lewis, Arthur H., *Those Philadelphia Kellys*, 1977

Massey, Raymond, *A Hundred Different Lives*, Boston and Toronto, 1957

Maxwell, Elsa, *The Celebrity Circus*, 1964

Milland, Ray, *Wide-Eyed in Babylon*, 1974

New York Times Film Reviews, 1913-1968, 1970

Parrish, J.R., *The Hollywood Beauties*, 1978

Princess Grace of Monaco with Gwen Robyns, *My Book of Flowers*, 1980

Robyns, Gwen, *Princess Grace*, 1982

Rose, Helen, *"Just Make Them Beautiful ..."*, Santa Monica, California, 1976

Samuels, Charles, *The King of Hollywood: The Story of Clark Gable*, 1962

Sinden, Donald, *A Touch of the Memoirs*, 1982

Spoto, Donald, *The Art of Alfred Hitchcock* (with a foreword by Princess Grace), 1977

    The Dark Side of Genius: The Life of Alfred Hitchcock, 1983

Swindell, Larry, *The Last Hero: A Biography of Gary Cooper*, 1980

Thomas, Bob, *Golden Boy: The Untold Story of William Holden*, 1983

Thompson, Charles, *Bing*, 1975

Sources

I should like to acknowledge the kindness of the following for granting me permission to quote from works in their copyright:

MGM/UA Entertainment Co. for permission to quote from the MGM files.

McCalls Publishing Company permission to quote from an article by Curtis Bill Pepper in *McCalls*, December 1974.

Little, Brown & Co. and William Collins Publishers for permission to quote from a transcript of an interview given by Princess Grace to Donald Spoto and passages from *The Dark Side of Genius: The Life of Alfred Hitchcock*, including a section from the script of *To Catch a Thief*.

Pierre Salinger, Bureau Chief of ABC News, Paris, for permission to quote from the transcript of his interview with Princess Grace.

E. P. Dutton, Inc. for permission to quote passages from *Edith Head's Hollywood*.

Index